Entrepreneurship, Innovation and Business Clusters

To my father
Professor Georgios Pan. Piperopoulos

Entrepreneurship, Innovation and Business Clusters

PANOS G. PIPEROPOULOS
Newcastle University Business School, UK

Routledge
Taylor & Francis Group

LONDON AND NEW YORK

First published 2012 by Gower Publishing

2 Park Square, Milton Park, Abingdon, Oxon OX14 4RN
711 Third Avenue, New York, NY 10017, USA

Routledge is an imprint of the Taylor & Francis Group, an informa business

First issued in paperback 2016

Gower Applied Business Research
Our programme provides leaders, practitioners, scholars and researchers with thought provoking, cutting edge books that combine conceptual insights, interdisciplinary rigour and practical relevance in key areas of business and management.

British Library Cataloguing in Publication Data
Piperopoulos, Panos G.
  Entrepreneurship, innovation and business clusters.
  1. Entrepreneurship. 2. Small business. 3. Creative ability
  in business. 4. Strategic alliances (Business) 5. Business
  networks. 6. Industrial clusters. 7. Intellectual capital.
  I. Title
  338'.04-dc23

ISBN 978-1-4094-3442-9 (hbk)
ISBN 978-1-138-27034-3 (pbk)

Library of Congress Cataloging-in-Publication Data
Piperopoulos, Panos G.
  Entrepreneurship, innovation and business clusters / by Panos G.
  Piperopoulos.
    p. cm.
  Includes bibliographical references and index.
  ISBN 978-1-4094-3442-9 (hbk)
  1. Diffusion of innovations. 2. Technological innovations--Economic aspects. 3.
  Entrepreneurship. 4. Industrial clusters. I. Title.
  HC79.T4P56 2011
  338'.064--dc23

                                                                    2011034696

Contents

List of Figures

List of Tables

Preface

The book deals with the current issues in entrepreneurship, innovation, small and medium-sized enterprises (SMEs) and business clusters and, linking these concepts in a creatively fresh approach, comes to cover these areas where, despite the works already in print, there appears to be a need for a different perspective.

The book's 11 chapters are divided into three functional parts: in Part 1 we introduce the reader to the concepts of entrepreneurship, innovation and systems of innovation. Building on this introduction, we delve more substantially into the how, when and why innovation springs forth and what are the crucial socio-economic factors influencing entrepreneurial and innovative activities in the individual company or at a corporate level as well as on local, regional and national geographic areas.

In Part 2 the reader will be able to learn what a typical SME is and what are its main characteristics, and simultaneously will be able to grasp the fact that SMEs constitute the backbone of most of the developed and developing economies around the globe. The catalytic role played by the entrepreneurs/managers/owners of SMEs in their survival and growth is examined and so are the fascinating characters of ethnic and female entrepreneurship. In this part we also present the concept of evolution of competition, and analyze the significance of strategic alliances between SMEs and the resulting effect of knowledge transfer and diffusion, which act as springboards in enhancing SMEs' competitiveness and innovative capabilities. We also bring forth the concept of open innovation which, in the last few years, has been proposed as a new paradigm for the management of innovation. In the closing section of the second part of the book we present a hypothetical model for enhancing the competitiveness and performance of the SME by properly utilizing employees' creative potential, emotional intelligence, tacit knowledge and innovative ideas.

In Part 3 the ways, means and methods through which SMEs' competitiveness and innovation can be enhanced within business clusters are examined. Here we present a historical perspective of the appearance of industrial districts which acted as forerunners to the contemporary business clusters (the Prato region of Northern Italy and the Silicon Valley of California). The partners of a contemporary business cluster (such as universities, research centres, governments, competitors, institutions and other agents) are presented and their role towards the desired end of entrepreneurial spirit and innovative capabilities is examined, discussed and evaluated in depth. The book closes with the presentation of an original, two-dimensional model of innovation and business clustering, differentiating and presenting in this context, for the first time, four characteristic types of SMEs and their potential performance and growth.

The book is intended to provide its readers (a student, graduate, management practitioner, aspiring or established entrepreneur, business mentor, policy maker or government official) with an opportunity to develop a critical awareness of the current theories concerning the origins and roles of entrepreneurship, innovation, business clustering and small and medium-sized enterprises in the economy and in society. It aims to enable its readers to identify, analyze, discuss and debate the broad range of perspectives and practical issues concerning the nature of these concepts, as well as encourage them to critically evaluate the determinants of competitiveness of SMEs, regions and nations within the business world.

Acknowledgments

My deep appreciation is hereby expressed to Dr. Richard Scase, Emeritus Professor of Organisational Change at the University of Kent, for his continuous support and guidance throughout the years of my doctoral studies at the Kent Business School. He has been a role model for me not only as an academic but also as an entrepreneur. Additionally, I wish to express my deep gratitude to Professor Ian Clarke and Professor John Leopold, Director and Deputy Director, respectively, at the Newcastle University Business School, for offering me my first employment base in British academia. Furthermore, I address my sincere gratitude to all of my esteemed colleagues at the Innovation and Enterprise subject group of the Newcastle University Business School, who have made me feel at home ever since September 2010 when I joined them as a new member of staff. Finally, I would like to thank Martin West, Commissioning Editor at Gower Applied Research, Gower Publishing, for responding favourably to my initial proposal for this book and encouraging me to bring it to its conclusion.

Chapter by Chapter Synopsis

Part 1

In Chapter 1 we present the theoretical concepts of entrepreneurship and innovation. We investigate and discuss the major schools of thought on innovation, how entrepreneurship is linked to innovation and we present the various definitions that appear in the relevant literature when one consults it in regards to the concept of entrepreneurship.

In Chapter 2 we evaluate and examine innovation as a strategy and a competitive advantage. We delve into the now classic work of Drucker (1985), presenting the principles and practices of innovation as well as the more influential works of Porter (1985, 1990), who brought forth the competitive advantage that innovations bring to the company and to a nation, and how they should be mastered.

Chapter 3 focuses on the concept of the systems of innovation based on the rationale that innovation and entrepreneurship are closely interrelated. The concept of innovation systems conveys the idea that innovations do not originate as isolated, discrete phenomena within a firm, but are generated by means of interaction of a number of entities, actors and agents. Such factors as organizations, institutions and other agents that are all co-developed and co-evolved dynamically in line with the economic, political and social development of a country and/or region have to be taken into account.

Part 2

In Chapter 4 we define what constitutes an SME (from the Bolton Committee to the unified definition of an SME by the European Commission) and identify its most prominent characteristics with particular emphasis to the organizational structures and management of SMEs. We examine how SMEs can play a key role in triggering and sustaining economic growth in developed and developing countries.

In Chapter 5 we bring forth the central and important role played by entrepreneurs/owners/managers in the survival and growth of the SME. The entrepreneurial competencies and how they are linked to the competitiveness of the SME are explored, as well as the external barriers (finance, lack of skilled labour, etc.) and the personal characteristics and managerial deficiencies of the entrepreneur/owner/manager.

Chapter 6 concentrates on the areas of ethnic groups and female entrepreneurship. Focusing on the entrepreneurial behaviour of such ethnic groups as blacks, whites, ethnic minorities, Chinese and other Asians and females, we examine the challenges faced in the course of seeking resources, venture capital, labour and access to markets, as well as the motivating push and pull factors related to entrepreneurship and self-employment. Cultural and social barriers and constrictions faced by women in various parts of the world in their efforts to develop entrepreneurial activity are examined in depth.

In Chapter 7 we describe the concept of the evolution of competition and how it affects SMEs and the business world in general. Furthermore, we discuss the importance of co-operative/strategic alliances and networks between firms which seem to strengthen SMEs' competitiveness because the sharing of knowledge and resources can also enhance innovative capabilities.

The main argument of Chapter 8 is that what is missing in entrepreneurship research, literature and management practice is the role emotional intelligence can dramatize in affecting employees' creativity, innovation and tacit knowledge, as well as the manager's/entrepreneur's personality in leading his employees and the SME towards increased performance and competitiveness, and thus augmenting a firm's value. Attempting a creative synthesis of the above, a conceptual model is developed in this chapter based on eight propositions; linking and organizing entrepreneurial characteristics, emotional intelligence, tacit knowledge and innovation, creativity and firms' performance/competitiveness.

Part 3

Chapter 9 deals with the concepts of industrial districts, networks and business clusters and explores how business clusters affect innovation and competitiveness in SMEs. In this chapter we look at the paradox of localization and its emerging importance in the era of globalization. We define the concept of clustering and its life cycle and also explore and present the important role of institutions, agents and governments in promoting business clusters, networks and university-business relations.

Adding to the theoretical framework that was established in the previous chapters, in Chapter 10 we examine how and why clusters can affect SMEs' innovative capabilities and competitiveness, as well as the importance and central role of entrepreneurship and innovation. Furthermore, we attempt to answer how important is the role of institutions, agents, authorities and the government in promoting and supporting business clusters and university-business relations. The Silicon Valley and the 'Third Italy' Prato model are described to enhance the readers' understanding of how a cluster works, and what factors affect its competitiveness and success.

In Chapter 11 we set up, describe and analyze a theoretical, two-dimensional model of SMEs that links the concepts and relations of innovation and business clustering, and we provide four typical cases that describe the characteristics and dynamics of SMEs. Each case represents a different type of SME based on the relations between the concepts of innovation and business clustering and the relative position of each company in the ensuing scheme. The aim of this descriptive, two-dimensional model is to link the concepts of and relations between innovation and clusters/networks in an attempt to explain how the relations between these concepts affect the performance, growth and ultimately the competitiveness of SMEs.

PART 1

The Concepts of Innovation, Entrepreneurship and Systems of Innovation

Prolegomena of Part 1

In the last few decades it has become universally accepted that innovations of any kind are important sources of productivity growth. They are considered as major means through which not only organizations, but also countries can gain and sustain competitive advantages in globally competitive marketplaces: at the beginning of the twenty-first century, for example, the European Council called for a challenging programme for building knowledge infrastructures, enhancing innovation and economic reform and for modernizing social welfare and education systems (European Communities 2000). The strategy to achieve this was mapped out at Lisbon in the March 2000 conference. An *open method of co-ordination* was already formulated with the economic convergence of the member states. Based on this foundation the European Council highlighted the importance of two key messages; namely *research* and *innovation* where the member states had to combine their efforts and devise policies for creating new skills and capacities.

The importance of innovation for an organization of any kind and for a country as a whole is undisputed in the management literature and the business world of the twenty-first century (Cefis and Marsili 2006, da Silveira 2001, Cullen 2000). And yet, despite the general consensus for the necessity to invest in innovative practices and processes that will assist companies and countries to be more competitive, innovation, however it is defined, turns out to be a very complex process (McDonough III et al. 2006, Muller and Zenker 2001). Innovation is dealt with in the literature from a variety of perspectives making it often very unclear for someone to grasp its fundamental nature and gain a clear understanding of what this concept entails.

When management practitioners turn to the literature for advice on how to be innovative in their organizations or when they try to understand the meaning of being innovative and pursue a strategy to promote innovation, they find a variety of sometimes contrasting or very vague prescriptions that are often too difficult to implement in reality. As Wolfe (1994) remarks in his work, 'the most consistent theme found in the organizational innovation literature is that its research results have been inconsistent.' The levels at which innovation is analyzed in the literature and in different research studies conducted all over the world cover the range of national and social systems, international and national economies, industries, organizations, groups and individuals. Authors like Lundvall (1995) and Nelson (1993), for example, deal with innovation as a national and social system affecting the whole economic and social structure of a country. Porter (1990), on the other hand, sees innovation as a determinant of industrial structures, a barrier to entrance and a competitive advantage. Drucker (1985) talks about innovation as a specific function of entrepreneurship at an individual level, while Rosenfeld and Servo (1991) look upon the issue of innovation at an organizational level.

It thus should be obvious that different writers and researchers look at the subject of innovation from a variety of perspectives. The aim of this part of the book is to investigate and present the major schools of thought on innovation, how entrepreneurship is linked to innovation and the differing definitions that can be encountered, while scanning the pertinent innovation literature and the concept of entrepreneurship. Furthermore, the aim of this section (Chapters 1 to 3) is to provide a picture, as clear as possible, of the major approaches to the concept of innovation systems.

Some authors are already characterizing the twenty-first century as the *innovation century*:

> Thinkers like MIT's Lester Thurow (1999) and Harvard's David Moss (1996) claim we are now in a Third Industrial Revolution, characterised by rapid advances in robotics, computers, software, biotechnology, new materials and microelectronics ... in the Third Revolution markets are

global, rather than national. Nations grow wealthy by successfully competing in world markets … take for example Singapore. This small nation of only 3.3 million inhabitants, with a land area of a few hundred square miles, has soared from $1,060 per capita GNP in 1970 to $32,810 in 1997 – five doublings of living standards in a single generation (World Bank, 1999) … in the Third Industrial Revolution, small innovative countries flexible enough to reinvent their core activities in line with world demand can grow rich very quickly. In 1980, Singapore made no disk drives. In 1982, it was the world's leading producer of them … Grupp and Maital (2001) argue that just as countries grow rich by innovation, so do companies. In the third industrial revolution, companies that excel in innovation have become phenomenal engines for generating wealth, income and jobs and bring examples of companies like Microsoft, Cisco Systems and General Electric … the authors go on to suggest that it is widely known that on average, fully one-quarter of all corporate profits come from only 10 per cent of companies' products – the innovative 10 per cent. (Grupp and Maital, 2001: xiv–xv)

Drucker (1985), in his work *Innovation and Entrepreneurship*, argues that these two concepts, taken together, are the driving forces of revitalization in any entrepreneurial society. In his perspective (as well as those of other influential scholars) innovation is understood as a process of continuity and transformation development at the same time. As the author quotes in his work, Tomas Jefferson (1985) believes that, 'every generation needs a new revolution'. For Drucker, innovation and entrepreneurship tend to be incremental (one product, one policy, one process and one step at a time). They focus upon an opportunity or a need that is temporary and will vanish if it is not realized on time or if it does not succeed. In other words, they are pragmatic and as such can maintain every society, economy, industry, public organization or private enterprise is flexible and self-revitalizing. They are the new notion of a *revolution*, which does not end in catastrophe since it is under control and has a positive target and direction.

1

The Concept of Innovation and Entrepreneurship

Definitions and Types of Innovations

In the decades following the Second World War, a lot of attention was given (in economic and management literature) to the reasons for the presence and intensity of innovation and creative activities in various enterprises, both in the manufacturing and service sectors. In the following pages we investigate and discuss the major schools of thought on innovation and look at how entrepreneurship is linked to innovation and we present the various definitions that appear in the relevant literature when one consults it in regards to the concepts of innovation and entrepreneurship.

A number of authors have suggested that creative competition renders innovation indispensable for every enterprise wishing to survive and grow. Nonaka and Kenney (1991) note that:

> Increasingly, corporate competitive success is hinging upon the effective management of innovation ... For us, innovation is a process by which new information emerges and is concretised in a product that meets human needs. The healthy firm is a negative-entropy system, which constantly creates new order and structure in its struggle to survive and grow ... To remain competitive any firm must constantly be creating new strategies, new products, new ways of manufacturing, distributing, and selling.

Some argue that competition will not automatically lead to greater innovation potential or greater innovative orientation. Thus, the need arises for investigation of the broader framework that includes organizational and psychological factors within enterprises that will enable any company to innovate. As observed by Tom Peters (1994):

> *Microsoft's only factory asset is the human imagination, observed the* New York Times Magazine *writer Fred Moody ... After exposing an audience to the Microsoft quote, I ask a telling question: "Does anyone here know what it means to 'manage' the human imagination?" So far, not a single hand has gone up, including mine. I don't know what it means to manage the human imagination either, but I do know that imagination is the main source of value in the new economy. And I know we better figure out the answer to my question-quick.*

According to Robinson and Stern (1997: 11), 'A company is creative when its employees do something new and potentially useful without being directly shown or taught ... The tangible results of corporate creativity, so vital for long term survival and success, are *improvements* (changes to what is already done) and *innovations* (entirely new activities for the company).'

Strategists and managers want to be creative but often fail to understand creativity's constituent ingredients. Creativity involves skills that can be learned and developed, which depend as much on the systematic application of formal tools as on the expenditure of management inspiration. Passive information systems rarely facilitate creativity. It is when organizations invest in active, self-organizing systems which establish asymmetric patterns that challenge orthodox thinking and responses that creativity begins to surface.

Knowledge diffusion and innovation constitute the process through which an innovation, in the course of time, is dispersed through certain channels to the members of a social system (Rogers 1995). According to the author innovation is an idea, a practice or an object, which is considered new by the subject or some other evaluating agent. It matters minimally in consideration to human behaviour if the idea is new from its conception. The way in which a person perceives the novelty of the idea determines their reaction to it. If the idea seems new to the person then it constitutes an innovation.

Innovation can be divided into two distinct activities in terms of when and where the innovation occurs. One type of innovation occurs in the development of a new product or process, and the second type occurs in improvements on the shop floor of a product or process. Long run competitiveness of a leading-edge company depends on its product line, while short run competitiveness depends on price and reliability. Both long run and short run innovation processes are critical to company performance, but their relative importance to the firm depends upon the company's technology strategy.

The complexities involved with the concept of innovation and the ways in which it evolves from the various enterprises does not permit a singular view or the use of only one definition. The Oslo Manual (2005) presents a multitude of definitions for innovation emerging from research activities in OECD (Organization for Economic Co-operation) countries, commencing in 1990 and continuing to date, so that the processes of innovation may be better understood and the formation of policies by governments and other agents may be better aided.

According to the Oslo Manual (2005: 46), 'an *innovation* is the implementation of a new or significantly improved product (good or service), or process, a new marketing method, or a new organizational method in business practices, workplace organization or external relations.' The innovation must be at least new or significantly improved for the firm. *Innovation activities* are all scientific, technological, organizational, financial and commercial steps which actually, or are intended to, lead to the implementation of innovations. Innovation activities also include R&D (research and development) that is not directly related to the development of a specific innovation (Oslo Manual 2005: 47).

The Oslo Manual distinguishes between four types of innovation: product innovations, process innovations, marketing innovations and organizational innovations:

> *A product innovation is the introduction of a good or service that is new or significantly improved with respect to its characteristics or intended uses. This includes significant improvements in technical specifications, components and materials, incorporated software, user friendliness or other functional characteristics. Product innovations can utilize new knowledge or technologies, or can be based on new uses or combinations of existing knowledge or technologies ... A process innovation is the implementation of a new or significantly improved production or delivery method. This includes significant changes in techniques, equipment and/or software. Process innovations can be intended to decrease unit costs of production or delivery, to increase quality, or to produce or deliver new or significantly improved products ... A marketing innovation is the implementation of a new marketing*

method involving significant changes in product design or packaging, product placement, product promotion or pricing. Marketing innovations are aimed at better addressing customer needs, opening up new markets, or newly positioning a firm's product on the market, with the objective of increasing the firm's sales ... An organizational innovation is the implementation of a new organizational method in the firm's business practices, workplace organization or external relations. Organizational innovations can be intended to increase a firm's performance by reducing administrative costs or transaction costs, improving workplace satisfaction (and thus labour productivity), gaining access to non-tradable assets (such as non-codified external knowledge) or reducing costs of supplies. (Oslo Manual 2005: 48–51)

On the other hand, *the following changes do not constitute innovations*: 'ceasing to use a process, a marketing method or an organization method, or to market a product; simple capital replacement or extension; changes resulting purely from changes in factor prices; customization; regular seasonal and other cyclical changes; and trading of new or significantly improved products' (Oslo Manual 2005: 56–57).

Entrepreneurship and Innovation

CLASSICAL AND NEOCLASSICAL ECONOMIC THEORY

Classical economic theory or, as otherwise stated, classical growth theory deals with the functioning of the market as a resource allocation mechanism in which the demand functions interact with the supply functions in order to determine prices that balance and sustain the market equilibrium. Adam Smith, Thomas Robert Malthus and David Ricardo, the leading economists of the late eighteenth century and early nineteenth century, postulated this theory. The classical economic theory does not deal with the dynamics of growth; the economy is understood to function according to deterministic laws in which the future is a predictable repetition of the past. It proceeds in a regular manner according to the economic laws of supply and demand, the equivalent of natural laws. *Hence, innovation is dealt as nothing more than an unexplained and unexpected shift in the supply function.*

Within this system, people are conceived to be *rational individuals* in that they are thought to calculate and predict the economic consequences of every action, choosing those actions that will maximize their individual utilities: driven by profit and utility maximization, the market functions efficiently to optimize resource allocation. The classical economists of the eighteenth and nineteenth centuries believed that technological change and capital accumulation were the engines of growth. However, they also believed that no matter how successful people were in inventing technologies that were more productive and investing in new capital, they were destined to live at the subsistence level. These classical economists based their conclusion on a belief that productivity growth caused population growth, which in turn caused productivity to fall. They believed that whenever economic growth raised incomes above the subsistence level, the population would increase. In addition, they went on to reason that the resultant increase in population would bring diminishing returns that would lower productivity. As a result, incomes must always fall back to subsistence level. Only when incomes are at the subsistence level is population growth held in check. *In such a system the notion of novelty, entrepreneurship and innovation are incompatible* (Parkin et al. 1997).

The neoclassical development of the economic theory continues, according to Fonseca (2002), with the framework that innovation is a variable in the supply/production function of the market equilibrium. Neoclassical growth theory is a theory of economic growth that explains how saving, investment and economic growth respond to population growth and technological change. Robert Solow of MIT suggested this theory during the 1950s, for which he received the Nobel Prize for Economic Science.

In neoclassical theory, the rate of technological change influences the rate of economic growth, but economic growth does not influence the pace of technological change. Rather, technological change is determined by chance. When we are lucky, we have rapid technological change, and when bad luck strikes, the pace of technological advance slows down. Nevertheless, there is nothing we can do to influence its pace. According to Fonseca (2002), innovation is caused by independent variables (exogenous variables) and mechanisms and so rational calculating managers can control it, to a certain extent, but cannot influence its pace. Innovation caused most frequently by technological, and less by organizational, changes disturbs the market equilibrium, usually by changing the position and shape of the production function and replacing the labour factor of production with the capital factor. Consequently, market forces will react to produce a new equilibrium state. *However, technological and organizational innovations are not, according to Fonseca, explained in the neoclassical economic theory, but are merely taken as causes embodied in capital assets or knowledge that are necessary to manage capital and labour resources.*

This way of thinking led neoclassical economists to search for the specific variables and circumstances that trigger innovation to occur and thus help managers to control it. At the level of industry though, innovations are understood as a choice made by organizations on rational grounds in order for them to secure temporary monopoly positions that would maximize their profits. This was based on the thought that since innovations disturbed market equilibrium it could take some time before market mechanisms could react and re-establish the balance between supply and demand. Innovation thus becomes a source of, temporarily at least, monopolist power and more than normal profit. No matter how important innovation came to be in the neoclassical economic theory, it could not, yet, be adequately explained (Fonseca 2002).

Schumpeter's Evolutionary Economic Theory

The analysis of innovation in a free enterprise system was long framed by the work of Joseph Schumpeter (Casson 2005, Martin and Scott 2000, McDaniel 2000). Evolutionary economics, the work attributed to Schumpeter (1942), is one of the first and most influential economic theories to explain innovation and entrepreneurship and to link the two concepts together. The central analytic scheme that pervades all of Schumpeter's work is the evolution of economic systems, or '*processes of economic development*', as he labelled it. These processes are inherently dynamic, as opposed to the static structures of the theory of equilibrium which, explicitly or implicitly, always has been and still is the centre of traditional theory (Schumpeter 1934). *This does not mean that Schumpeter rejects the theory of equilibrium, but on the contrary, it serves as the underlying base for his dynamic model.* This occurs because capitalism is, according to Schumpeter, by nature a form or method of economic change that is never stationary (Schumpeter 1942).

The fundamental impulse that sets and keeps the capitalist engine in motion comes from the introduction of so-called '*new combinations*' (new consumers' goods, new methods of production or transportation, new markets, new forms of industrial organization) that capitalist enterprise creates (Schumpeter 1942). Schumpeter argues that the disruptive processes of 'creative destruction', which results in new combinations, account for the greater part of economic growth.

Schumpeter's model of economic development is not a substitute for the theory of equilibrium but rather a necessary complement. Without it, it is impossible to understand the functioning of an economic system. But the static description of an economic system – economic life from the standpoint of a circular flow – is an essential building block for the dynamic model, and Schumpeter spends the entire first chapter of his work, *The Theory of Economic Development* (1934) on it. The essential difference between Schumpeter's evolutionary perspective and that of neoclassical economists, as we described them above, is that Schumpeter treats uncertainty as a key explanation for the patterns of economic development, whereas in the economic theories presented above, the notion of uncertainty is wholly absent. Schumpeter is interested in explaining why economic growth occurs, rather than simply ascribing it to unexplained variables. *He thus places innovation inside the economic system for the first time rather than considering it as an exogenous shock to which economic systems react.* Schumpeter is rightly recognized as the founding father of evolutionary economics.

THE CONCEPT OF INNOVATION AND THE ENTREPRENEUR

Schumpeter does not deny the existence of autonomous growth in economic systems, for instance, due to a quasi-automatic increase in population and capital. But the fundamental impulse that sets and keeps the capitalist engine in motion comes from new consumers' goods, new methods of production, new markets and new forms of industrial organization that capitalist enterprises create:

> *The slow and continuous increase in time of the national supply of productive means and of savings is obviously an important factor in explaining the course of economic history through centuries, but it is completely overshadowed by the fact that development consists primarily in employing existing resources in a different way in doing new things with them irrespective of whether those resources increase or not. (Schumpeter 1942: 64–65)*

While consumers' wants are the fundamental force in a theory of circular flow, for a theory of economic change the producers take the leading role:

> *Innovations in the economic system do not as a rule take place in such a way that first new wants arise spontaneously in consumers and then the productive apparatus swings around through their pressure. We do*

not deny the presence of this nexus. It is, however, the producer who as a rule initiates economic change, and consumers are educated by him if necessary; they are, as it were, taught to want new things, or things which differ in some respect from those they have been in the habit of using. (Schumpeter 1942: 65)

Schumpeter already seems to anticipate the importance of the management of niches for the successful introduction of new products and practices. The focus is on the producer and it is here that the *entrepreneur* enters the stage. Schumpeter (1942: 65) defines production as, 'the combinations or materials and forces that are within our reach'. The producer is not an inventor (Schumpeter 1947). All components that the producer needs for the product or service, whether physical or immaterial, already exist and are in most cases readily available. The basic driving force behind structural economic growth is the introduction of new combinations of materials and forces, not the creation of new possibilities:

The new combinations are always present, abundantly accumulated by all sorts of people. Often, they are also generally known and being discussed by scientific or literary writers. In other cases, there is nothing to discover about them, because they are quite obvious ... It is this 'doing the thing', without which possibilities are dead, of which leader's function consists ... It is, therefore, more by will than by intellect that the leaders fulfil their function, more by 'authority', 'personal weight', and so forth than by original ideas. Economic leadership in particular must hence be distinguished from 'invention'. As long as they are not carried into practise, inventions are economically irrelevant. And to carry any improvement into effect is a task entirely different from the invention of it, and a task, moreover, requiring entirely different kinds of aptitudes ... it is, therefore, not advisable, and it may be downright misleading, to stress the element of invention as much as many writers do. (Schumpeter 1942: 88–89)

Innovation in the Schumpeterian sense is then defined by the carrying out of new combinations. This concept covers the following five cases (Schumpeter 1942: 66):

1.   The *introduction of a new good* – that is one with which consumers are not familiar yet – or a new quality of a good.

2.   The *introduction of a new method of production* – that is one not yet
        tested by experience in the branch of manufacture concerned, which
        need, by no means, to be founded upon a discovery scientifically
        new, and can also exist in a new way of handling a commodity
        commercially.

3.   The *opening of a new market* – that is a market into which the country
        in question has not previously entered, whether or not this market
        has existed before.

4.   The conquest of a *new source of supply of raw materials or half-
        manufactured goods* – again irrespective of whether this source
        already exists or whether it has first to be created.

5.   The *carrying out of the new organization* – that is of any industry,
        like the creation of a monopoly position (for example, through
        trustification) or the breaking up of a monopoly position.

ENTREPRENEURS AND VENTURE CAPITALISTS

Schumpeter is realistic enough to see that the carrying out of new combinations
involves more than *an act of will*; command over means of production is
necessary. In most of the cases the entrepreneur must resort to credit, especially
since most new venture starts do not have returns from previous production.
Consequently, if someone wants to become an entrepreneur at all, they must
succeed in raising funds; that is in convincing someone to sponsor their ideas.

The provision of credit comes from a second hero in the play of economic
change; the 'capitalist'. Schumpeter anticipates the rise of the *venture capitalists*,
'because most of the money that circulates flows in definite established
channels, by far the greater part of the funds of the capitalist consists of funds,
which are themselves the result of successful innovation and "entrepreneurial
profit"'. (Schumpeter 1942:72)

According to Schumpeter (1942), these venture capitalists are entrepreneurs
in their own right. First, it is they who bear the financial risk (the entrepreneur
only risks his reputation). Secondly, because capital is nothing but the diversion
of the factors of – established – production to new uses, the venture capitalist
needs to be a bold and outspoken person too. They need to dictate a new
direction to production.

The basic structure in Schumpeter's model of economic development has two distinctive spheres in a 'neutral' surrounding environment. On the one hand, it is the semi-closed system of the circular flow, which is either in equilibrium or striving for it. On the other hand, it is the symbiotic pairing of the entrepreneur and the sponsor who are always looking for ways to induce change in the peaceful, yet boring routine life of the circular flow. Both spheres function within an endless reservoir of new combinations (e.g., scientific knowledge and technological inventions), but it is only the entrepreneur – backed by the capitalist – who is able to introduce new combinations and new routines in the circular flow. Moreover, Schumpeter uses a definition that strictly separates the two spheres, 'everyone is an entrepreneur only when he actually carries out new combinations, and loses that character as soon as he has built up his business, when he settles down to running it as other people run their business.' (Schumpeter 1942: 78)

A core element of entrepreneurship is the ability to deal with uncertainty. This should be further specified in relation to the dynamic linkage between the two spheres. Once a new introduction gets a foothold in the circular flow, the hitherto stable data of the system are altered and the equilibrium is upset. Schumpeter (1934) argues that this makes accurate calculation in general impossible, but especially for the planning of new enterprises. Thus, successful entrepreneurs cannot deal very well with uncertainty in the circular flow. What they are relatively good at is in foreseeing what kind of improvement a certain new (but existing and known) combination will bring to the established structure of the circular flow, and in actually realizing these improvements.

Schumpeter is not so much interested in the individuality of entrepreneurs and in the concrete factors of change, but in the method by which these work with the mechanism of change. He sees the entrepreneur merely as the bearer of the mechanism of change (Schumpeter 1934: 61). These changes, that is, the appearance of new markets and/or new scientific findings, are generated by the evolution of the socio-economic system and would have occurred anyway, but they have to be effectuated by an acting individual: *the entrepreneur*. Schumpeter's theories are a major contribution to the study of technological change, innovation and entrepreneurship. Furthermore, Schumpeter suggests a strong link of entrepreneurship to innovation as we described it above. It is an abiding perception that when current economic analysis attempts to explain the rationale for developing and/or implementing innovation and the concept of the entrepreneur, the analysis ultimately relies more or less on the original criteria developed by Schumpeter.

A Sociological Approach

THE WORK OF MAX WEBER

The central role that entrepreneurship has on innovation and vice versa, according to Schumpeter's writings, stimulates us to explore the sociological and cultural factors that affect entrepreneurship, by focusing on the historical routes of entrepreneurship and the works of Max Weber, *The Protestant Ethic and the Spirit of Capitalism* (1930) and, *Theories of Economic and Social Organisation* (1947). It should be understood that the depth and scope of Weber's works and of the research and literature around them are overwhelming to be dealt with, even in a summary form, in this chapter.

In the Middle Ages Europe's population growth and natural resource endowments, coupled with improved techniques of production, facilitated both the expansion of production and the extension of markets. Thus, by the fourteenth century the extension of the market was the primary force leading to the decline of the medieval handicraft system just as the expansion of trade was a primary force in destroying the manorial system two centuries earlier. By the end of the fifteenth century only the last vestiges of rural feudalistic economy remained. Many islands of capitalism flourished in both northern and southern Europe and were on the verge of expanding over European economic life as a whole. Only one essential prerequisite of capitalism was absent: an ethical standard that was compatible with accumulation of capital.

AN ETHIC FAVOURABLE TO THE ACCUMULATION OF CAPITAL

According to Lehmann and Roth (1993), the prevailing ethical standard was negative towards activities aiming for the pursuit and accumulation of wealth. If capitalistic production was to continue its growth, an entirely new ideology was required to give moral sanction to acquisitive behaviour. As the authors argue, the sanction came with the framework of a wholly new intellectual climate which was to stimulate the birth not only of modern philosophy and the *Protestant Reformation*, but also of modern science. The authors suggest that while Luther's interpretation of Christian teachings was not particularly sympathetic to industry and trade, the reform movements of John Calvin, John Knox and the Puritans in the same century (sixteenth) were much more so. Indeed, they adopted such strongly favourable attitudes towards acquisition by useful labour and the judicious and prudent use of wealth, that their views have been described as the *Protestant Ethic* which launched and encouraged the development of capitalism in northern Europe. Max Weber, the German sociologist and economist, in *The Protestant Ethic and the Spirit of Capitalism* (1930), advanced this thesis in the nineteenth century:

> *Weber began his essay on* The Protestant Ethic and the Spirit of Capitalism *with the assurance that it was the conventional opinion of his contemporaries that there was a close connection between religion and society. He especially believed that the differences between Protestants and Catholics had a strong impact on social structure and social status; in a society composed of mixed religions, the higher strata, the more advanced and more modern elements, were definitely more Protestant than Catholic: scholars, business leaders, white-collar employees, even skilled workers. The burden of proof was not with those who held this assumption but with those who would deny it. (Lehmann and Roth 1993: 73)*

According to Max Weber, Protestantism was congenial to the development of personal attributes, which encouraged business activity. In this sense, the Reformation contributed towards capitalist development and economic thought. Protestantism considers capital acquisition a virtue rather than a sin, and instead of merchants being considered as unchristian because of their activities for profit, they came to be regarded as pillars of the church and the community. Their pursuit of gain, unrelated to material needs and the virtue of frugality, became as integral a part of the Protestant ethic as the autonomy of the individual. Joined with the notion of the dignity and moral worth of work, Protestant emphasis on frugality served the capitalistic system well, for it stimulated thrift and capital accumulation (Lehmann and Roth 1993).

Furthermore, according to Swedberg (1998), Weber, in his work of economic sociology, compares and contrasts two types of economies: *those that are static and aim at rent and wealth* and *those which are dynamic and aim at profit and capital*. In the latter economy, as the author argues, the concept of *opportunity* is decisive since the profit-making action is in principle a type of action that is oriented towards the exploitation of opportunities in the market. Swedberg notes that Weber presented a very useful typology for different kinds of capitalism: *rational capitalism, political capitalism* and *traditional commercial capitalism,* in which he defines what he conceives as the entrepreneur:

The last of these three categories represents a kind of capitalism that has existed very far back in history and which consists of fairly systematic forms of trade and money change. Political capitalism essentially means profit making through political contact or under direct political protection, and it can be found in antiquity as well as in modern world. Rational capitalism is what we today sometimes call free market capitalism. The main actor here is not the typical merchant (as in traditional commercial capitalism) or the political-economic operator (as in political capitalism), but the modern enterprise led by an entrepreneur (the moving spirit), and oriented to the exploitation of market opportunities. (Swedberg 1998: 13)

At this point, we note that Weber recognizes the *entrepreneur as a main actor of capitalism and defines him as a moving spirit oriented towards market opportunities.* This is in line with Schumpeter's arguments that the entrepreneur is a dynamic person or organization seeking new combinations and market opportunities where others fail to see them.

Furthermore, the collapse of feudal society gave birth to the liberation of the workforce, permitting the individual labourer to seek employment where wages are higher and simultaneously permitting the individual entrepreneur to abdicate the classical feudal lord's responsibility toward his workers. The employee can move freely and the entrepreneur can hire and fire according to the needs of the factory. Thus, industrial capitalism grew, in addition to the religious spirit, because other changes of sociological nature such as the factory become the unit of production, application of science and technology to production and distribution methods and the development of free markets and world trade operating on competitive practices (Henderson and Parsons 1965).

Definitions of Entrepreneurship

At this junction, it behoves us to get a clearer picture of what is entrepreneurship and how it is linked to innovation. As mentioned already, Schumpeter's and Weber's writings define the entrepreneur while the former also links entrepreneurship to innovation. It appears that there are as many definitions of entrepreneurship as there are writers on the subject. The critical researcher and reader will trace that the dominant themes in entrepreneurship rely to a lesser or greater extent on the description and criteria that Joseph A. Schumpeter set in his work, back in the 1930s and 1940s, and at the personality characteristics associated with the entrepreneur in David McClelland's *Need for Achievement* theory in the 1960s. Table 1.1 provides a selection of definitions of entrepreneurs, from the most influential writers and scholars in the subject of entrepreneurship, in an attempt to shed some light on the meaning of 'entrepreneurship'.

Table 1.1   Definitions of entrepreneurship

Source	Definition
Richard Cantillon (1755)*	A person, 'undertaker', who bears the risk of fixed costs of production (consciously making decisions about resource allocations) and of uncertain selling prices.
Jean Baptiste Say (1803)	A person, 'a contractor', who coordinates, organizes and supervises (possess managerial skills) an enterprise with exceptional moral qualities, perseverance and knowledge of the world's and society's needs.
Frank Knight (1921)	A person, 'competitor', using critical judgment to decide whether to engage in business activity or not (make profit), in conditions of uncertainty and risk.
Joseph A. Schumpeter (1934)	A person who carries out new combinations (innovations) – new goods (products/services), new methods of productions, opening of a new market, new sources of supply of raw materials, carrying out of new organization.
Arthur H. Cole (1949)	An individual, or group of individuals, who purposefully initiates, maintains or grows (aggrandize) a profit-oriented business.
David C. McClelland (1961)	People with a high need for achievement (nACH), strong self-confidence, independent problem-solving skills who prefer situations characterized by moderate risk.
Mark C. Casson (1982)	A person who specializes in making judgmental decisions about the co-ordination of scarce resources.
Peter F. Drucker (1985)	Someone (a person or an enterprise) who creates something new, something different, in conditions of risk and uncertainty.
William B. Gartner (1988)	'Who is an entrepreneur is the wrong question?' ... more relevant ... entrepreneurship is the creation of new organizations.
Stevenson, Roberts & Grousbeck (1989)	Individuals who pursue opportunities regardless of the resources they currently control.

* Note: The definition of an entrepreneur by Richard Cantillon was obtained from the book of Antoin, M. (1986) *Richard Cantillon: Entrepreneur and Economist,* Oxford: Clarendon.

According to Dollinger (1999: 4), 'entrepreneurship is the creation of innovative economic organization (or network of organizations) for the purpose of gain or growth under conditions of risk and uncertainty'. As Dollinger argues, the term 'economic organization' refers to an organization whose purpose is to allocate scarce resources: this can be a new venture/firm, a business unit within a firm, a network of independent organizations or not-for-profit organizations. The term creation encompasses, according to Dollinger, the categories of new combinations that Schumpeter suggested as given in the table above: new product, new service, new sources of raw materials and so on. Finally, entrepreneurship exists under conditions of risk and uncertainty. Risk refers to the variability of outcomes and/or returns while uncertainty refers to the fact that the environment around the entrepreneur, society, economy and organizations cannot be perfectly known. Hence, entrepreneurs rely on their understanding of the causes and effects in their environment and have confidence in their estimates on how the world works. Moreover, according to Dollinger (1999: 6), two conditions must exist in order for entrepreneurship to flourish: 'first, there must be freedom: freedom to establish an economic venture, and freedom to be creative and innovative with that enterprise. Second, there must be prosperity: favourable economic conditions that give entrepreneurial organization the opportunity to gain and grow.'

Again entrepreneurship is linked to innovation, but as Weber stated in his work on the Protestant ethic, the surrounding environment of businesses, namely the social and economic conditions of a particular region or country, will affect both entrepreneurship and innovation. These relations are explored later in this part of the book and specifically in Chapter 3, which presents and analyzes the concept of the systems of innovation. It is important to add here the note that Schumpeter (in his 1949 work *Economic History and the Entrepreneurial History*) explicitly recognizes the rise of what he sees as collective entrepreneurship, adding to another dimension of entrepreneurship as an act not of one individual but of a group of people:

> *The entrepreneurial function needs not to be embodied in ... a single physical person. Every social environment has its own ways of filing the entrepreneurial function ... it may be and often is filled cooperatively. With the development of the large-scale corporations this has evidently become of major importance: aptitudes that no single individual combines can, thus, be built into a corporate personality; on the other hand, the constituent physical personalities must inevitably to some extent, and very often to a serious extent, interfere with each other. (Schumpeter 1949: 260–261)*

Schumpeter, and many of the writers and researchers presented in Table 1.1, argues that entrepreneurs are the creators of new combinations. The definitions of entrepreneurship, as we have presented above, explicitly or implicitly encompass the notion of innovation. Despite the link we are tracing between entrepreneurship and innovation, readers should not assume that all innovations result only from entrepreneurs.

2

Innovation as a Strategy and a Competitive Advantage

Principles and Practices of Innovation

The link between entrepreneurship and innovation emerges from the influential writings of Drucker (1985). He argues that innovation is the specific function of entrepreneurship. It is the means by which the entrepreneur either creates new wealth-producing resources or endows existing resources with enhanced potential for creating new wealth. Drucker argues that innovation can be presented as a methodology, it can be taught and it can be applied. The entrepreneur must purposefully and systematically search the sources of innovation, the changes and the indications that create opportunities for a successful innovation. For Drucker, the entrepreneur must know and apply the 'principles' of successful innovation. What all the successful entrepreneurs have in common is not a certain kind of personality, rather a commitment to the systematic practice of innovation (Drucker 1985).

In his work, *Innovation and Entrepreneurship*, Drucker attempts to explain how he understands the concept of entrepreneurship since he believes that there is great confusion around the proper definition of the term. He argues that some researchers use the term to describe either small businesses or new businesses. In practice, however, a great number of well-established, large companies engage in successful entrepreneurship and he gives examples such as the McDonalds Company and the General Electric Corporation, amongst others.

For Drucker, companies that engage in successful entrepreneurship share some common characteristics, far from only being small or new. The term of entrepreneurship, then, refers not to the age or size of an enterprise, but to a certain kind of activity. Entrepreneurship is a special characteristic of an individual or organization. *Innovation is at the heart of entrepreneurship; the effort to create purposeful, focused change in an enterprise's economic or social potential* (Drucker, 1985). As we have seen in Chapter 1 of this book, Schumpeter, in his 1949 work, anticipated and identified the rise of collective entrepreneurship.

Drucker argues that entrepreneurs innovate and that innovation is the specific function of entrepreneurship. The activity endows existing or new resources with the potential for creating new wealth: innovation creates new wealth. All the resources in nature remain potential creators of new wealth until someone has the ability to endow to the resources the potential to create new wealth. Whatever changes the nature of the existing resources in order to gain financial advantages from it is an innovation. Drucker argues that we are not in a position to develop a comprehensive and adequate theory on innovation, but rather to understand the practice of innovation. We have the knowledge to identify when, where and how we should systematically search for innovative opportunities and how we should estimate their potential success or failure. At this point, and in addition to explaining the notion of innovation and entrepreneurship, we present Drucker's views and suggestions of where innovative opportunities exist and what are the principles of innovation. So, from an abstract and theoretical analysis of entrepreneurship and innovation, we move to a closer examination of how innovation is dealt in the business world.

SOURCES OF INNOVATIVE OPPORTUNITIES

Most innovations result from a conscious, purposeful search for innovation opportunities. More specifically, Drucker (1985) identifies *seven sources of innovation opportunities*. The first four are areas of opportunities existing within a company or an industry and as such should become visible mainly to the people that work in the specific company or industry in general. Three additional sources of opportunities exist outside a company in its social and intellectual environment:

1.   *Unexpected occurrences.* It is the easiest and simplest form of innovation opportunity. He argues that unexpected successes, unexpected failures or unexpected events are productive sources of innovation opportunities (Drucker 1985: 53).

2.   *Incongruities.* An incongruity within the logic or rhythm of a process is a possibility out of which innovation opportunities may

arise. Another source is incongruity between economic realities. An incongruity between expectations and results can also open up possibilities for innovation (Drucker 1985: 75).

3. *Process needs.* In contrast to the innovation based on unexpected occurrences or incongruities, process needs is very specific and starts with exploiting a need: for example, around 1909 a statistician at AT&T projected that with the telephone traffic, in about 15 years every single female in the USA would have to work as a switchboard operator. The process need was obvious and within two years the company developed and installed the automatic switchboard (Drucker 1985: 88–90).

4. *Industry and market changes.* Managers and businessmen often tend to believe that industry and market structures are stable, but they can – and often do – change overnight. Such changes create tremendous opportunity for innovation. (Drucker 1985: 96–97).

5. *Demographic changes.* Demographic events have known lead times, but yet policy makers often neglect them. The changes in the numbers of people, age distribution, education, occupations and geographic location may open up innovative opportunities which are highly rewarding and yet the least risky among a variety of entrepreneurial pursuits (Drucker 1985: 110).

6. *Changes in perception.* The glass is half-full and the glass is half-empty are descriptions of the same picture of reality, but have vastly different meanings. Changing a manager's perception of a glass from half-empty to half-full may open up tremendous innovation opportunities (Drucker 1985: 122).

7. *New knowledge.* Among history making innovations, those based on new knowledge, whether scientific, technological or social rank high. They are the superstars of entrepreneurship; they get the publicity, the money and the fame. They are what people usually mean when they talk about innovation. Knowledge-based innovations differ from all other innovations in their basic characteristics: lead times are longer, failure rates are higher, they are difficult to predict and pose greater challenges to entrepreneurs (Drucker 1985: 131).

PRINCIPLES OF INNOVATION

Drucker identifies certain principles of innovation. He argues that purposeful innovation begins with the analysis of the sources of new opportunities, as presented and analyzed above. He also suggests that innovation has to be simple and focused. The innovation has to do only one thing in order to work properly and efficiently: the more complex the innovation, the greater the number of problems and unexpected failures that will have to be dealt with. According to Drucker (1985), the best award any innovation can get is to make other people say, *'this is so obvious, why haven't I ever thought of that?'*. Even in the case that an innovation introduces a new product/service or opens up a new market, it has to be focused on one specific market segment and address one specific need.

Moreover, according to the author, effective innovations start small. They are not grandiose. They try to do one specific thing. A simple innovation in the Swedish (lighting) match industry gave them virtually a global monopoly for over half a century: filling the same number of lighting matches in every matchbox became an innovation that allowed the automation of the production line. Drucker (1985) suggests that the ostentatious ideas that aim to create a revolution in an industrial segment will most likely fail. It is better, according to the author, for an innovation to start as a small-scale project, involving few R&D personnel, a modest budget and to aim for a niche market. The company can alter in this way, during the course of time, any of the ingredients for the innovation to succeed and most importantly to avoid a failure that would have cost dearly to the organization in human and capital investment.

Furthermore, an innovation should aim at becoming the 'standard setter', stay ahead of the pack. As Drucker (1985) argues, an innovation should not target to evolve into a big business. Nobody really knows or can predict whether an innovation will result in a large enterprise or a mediocre business. What is important for the entrepreneur is to aim to become the standard setter, either by dominating gradually a whole industry, as Intel Corporation did in the IT market, or by dominating a privilege niche market, as Ferrari has done in sports cars.

Above all, innovation is work rather than genius. It requires knowledge, hard, focused and purposeful work. As the author explains, most of the time innovators focus on one specific segment. Thomas Edison, for example, was indisputably an innovator and a great scientist who focused all his efforts and talents in the field of electricity. As with any job, entrepreneurship and innovation require, for Drucker, talent and creativity, but most importantly they require hard and focused efforts, diligence, persistence and commitment to the work.

Drucker's analysis is used in this chapter as the foundation in understanding innovation and entrepreneurship in the real business world, with examples of where to search for innovative opportunities and how to establish a strategy for innovation. *Above all, entrepreneurs, whether individuals starting their own businesses or entrepreneurial organizations that want to continue to thrive, see or at least they should see innovation as a strategy, an ongoing process that will bring profits and a competitive advantage to the company.*

Innovation as a Competitive Advantage

We will now concentrate on the works of Michael Porter (1985, 1990), who is one of the first scholars to recognize the competitive advantage that innovations bring to the company and to a nation, and how they should be mastered. This section of Chapter 2 aims to strengthen our understanding of the concept of innovation by presenting a list of the most typical causes of innovations. In his work, *The Competitive Advantage of Nations*, Porter develops a theory about why nations succeed in particular industries and he analyzes the implications of his theory for firms and national economies. His ideas and concepts are also applicable to political or geographical units smaller than a nation. He is interested in explaining how a firm's proximate environment shapes its competitive success over time and why some organizations prosper while others fail. Porter (1990) argues that firms will not ultimately succeed unless they base their strategies on improvement and innovation, an eagerness to compete and a thorough understanding of their national environment and ways to improve it. In his work, *Competitive Advantage, Creating and Sustaining Superior Performance*, Porter has defined what he understands as competitive advantage:

> *Competitive advantage is about how a firm actually puts the generic strategies into practice. How does a firm gain a sustainable cost advantage? How can it differentiate itself from competitors? How does a firm choose a segment so that competitive advantage can grow out of a focus strategy? When and how can a firm gain competitive advantage from competing with a coordinated strategy in related industries? How*

is uncertainty introduced into the pursuit of competitive advantage?
How can a firm defend its competitive position? (Porter 1985: xvi)

For Porter (1990), firms create and sustain a competitive advantage by perceiving or discovering new and better ways to compete in an industry and bringing them to market, which is ultimately an act of innovation. Porter sees innovation in very broad terms and as inherent to the firm's strategic and competitive context:

> *Innovation includes not only new technologies but also new methods or ways of doing things that sometimes appear quite mundane. Innovation can be manifested in a new product design, a new production process, a new approach to marketing or a new way of training and organising. It can involve virtually any activity in the value chain. (Porter 1990: 579)*

For Porter, much of innovation is not radical but rather cumulative and incremental, consisting of small insights and advances rather than on radical technological or other kinds of breakthrough. He argues that innovation is as much a result of organizational learning as it is of formal research and development activities. It also requires investment in developing skills and knowledge. Porter explains the importance of innovation in creating a competitive advantage for the firm. Innovative opportunities usually grow out of some discontinuity or change in industry structure that could ultimately give a competitive advantage in the company that can see and grasp the opportunity. According to Porter (1990: 45–47), the five most typical causes of innovations that shift competitive advantage are the following:

1. *New technologies.* Technological change creates new products, new possibilities for the design of an existing product, new ways of marketing, delivering and the supplementary services provided, even new industries. For the author, it is the most common originator of strategic innovation.

2. *New or shifting buyer needs.* When people change priorities or develop new needs, an innovative opportunity is created that could lead to a competitive advantage for the company that can respond to these changes.

3. *The emergence of a new industry segment.* Another opportunity to create a competitive advantage is when a new segment in an

industry emerges or when several existing segments are regrouped. This could lead to new customers, new ways of marketing and reaching particular customers and new ways of producing particular products.

4. *Shifting input costs or availability.* Competitive advantages often are the results of changes in the costs of inputs such as labour, raw materials, energy, transportation, machinery and so on. Such changes can shift the competitive advantage to companies that are able to optimize their organizing and managing processes according to the new conditions.

5. *Changes in government regulations.* Other stimuli to innovation, which ultimately can result in a competitive advantage, are the changes in government regulations in areas such as product standards, environmental rules, barriers to entry and restrictions on trade and so on. Small or early mover companies that are quick to adjust to such changes can gain an advantage against established industrial companies that have built their businesses around certain regulatory regimes.

Porter (1990) also presents the significant role of information in the innovation process. Sometimes it can be the result of sheer R&D investment or market research, but quite often it is just unconventional wisdom, simply looking in the right place at the right time. Innovation for Porter is, with few exceptions, the result of unusual effort. Companies that innovate are frequently not large or established companies, but rather new, early movers or small companies. In his research he discovers that where the innovators are large firms, they are often new entrants to the industry from an established position in another industry. The innovative firm is the one that pursues doggedly innovation in its strategy. *For Porter, innovation is a means for the company of gaining and sustaining a competitive advantage.* It should be inherent to a company's strategy and competitive context.

Individual and Organizational Innovation

INNOVATION AT AN INDIVIDUAL LEVEL

In order to assess innovation at the individual employee level, personality-based research has dominated, specifically in mainstream literature.. This has lead to attempts to isolate personality traits, for example, those related to creative problem solving or identification and to measure these creative traits within individual personalities. One of the most famous attempts to define innovation in trait terms was that of Kirton's (1976) 'adaption–innovation' dimension. In his work he claims that, 'adaption-innovation is a basic dimension of personality relevant to the analysis of organizational change, in that some people characteristically adapt while some characteristically innovate.' (West 1990: 17)

Kirton's work has been questioned by several researchers, Torrance and Horng (1980) being among them, and has the inherent problem of completely disregarding the social and organizational factors that influence creativity.

An extensive body of studies has focused on the individual level of innovation, investigating variables of a more situational nature. The focus is on the work setting, directly relevant to innovation.

According to Farris (1973), Pelz and Andrews (1976), *moderate freedom of choice* refers to how one employee's expenditure of their time combined with supportive consultation from the supervisor will be a positive precursor to innovative performance.

Isen et al. (1987) examined the effects of *positive affect* on creative problem solving by conducting a series of experiments. These investigators found that people to whom they induced positive feelings (e.g., a small gift) performed better in creative problem solving and innovative thinking.

Many studies have focused on the effects of *leadership* style on people's ability to innovate. Most of the writers have suggested a participatory and collaborative leadership style (Peters and Waterman 1982) as a means to promote self-direction, which leads to innovation.

One of the most important factors in the individual level of innovation is the *feedback* and *recognition* employees receive for their accomplishments. Lack of appreciation and feedback for results and performance demotivates the individual and acts as an obstacle to innovation.

The last implication on the situational influences on innovation is the very nature of the organizational structure and the company's hierarchy. Kanter (1983) claims that the old bureaucratic model will act as an obstacle to innovation and diffusion of knowledge, while in support of that notion, Lovelace (1986) claims that a more decentralized, organizational structure, a matrix organization, provides the individual with sufficient freedom and opportunities to be creative, innovative and exchange valuable knowledge and information.

INNOVATION AT AN ORGANIZATIONAL LEVEL

A substantial volume of work has concentrated on the wide range of organizational characteristics that have been studied as possible contributors to innovation and knowledge diffusion. Emphasis has been placed on structure, knowledge of innovations, age, climate and culture, resources and strategy.

Kimberly and Evanisko (1981) concluded in line with Schumpeter's theory that *organizational size* does appear to have a positive influence on the speed of adoption of innovations. One of the major problems associated with this characteristic is the very definition of organizational size since it does not become clear as to the reference of size at financial levels or of the number of employees the firm employs.

The structural variables that have received most of the attention in regards to innovation at organizational level deal with the organizational structure. Zaltman et al. (1973) identify three structural variables, namely *centralization*, *formalization* and *complexity* that have divergent effects at the instigation and operation of the innovation process. They found that high *centralization* restrains the instigation of innovation by restricting available information and knowledge at the higher level of command, and thus it acts as an obstacle at the commencement of innovation. Decentralization should result in the bringing together of people and a greater divergence of ideas. Increasing employees' commitment to participate in the working of the organization through an open style management should enhance the implementation and foundation of innovation.

They furthermore identify *formalization* as another inhibitor of organizational innovation at the instigation stage, defining it as the degree to which emphasis is placed upon the rules and procedures that govern the operations of the organization. The more formal and rigid these rules and procedures, the less decision makers are able to see and adopt new ideas in the workplace.

There is clear empirical evidence for Zaltman et al.'s proposition that organizational *complexity* has a positive relation to innovation instigation and a negative relation as far as implementation is concerned. Organizational diversity at the initiation stage will bring a variety of views and ideas to the forefront, resulting in increased knowledge and awareness of innovations, but on the other hand a problem may arise as the greater the knowledge, the more difficult it is to reach an agreement and actually implement one or more of the innovative ideas.

The next variable refers to the *organizational knowledge of innovations* or, to phrase it differently, the ability of an entity to identify innovations in the workplace and outside it (Rogers 1995, Kimberly and Evanisko 1981). This is determined by the combination of the characteristics of personnel in key positions that are able to recognize potential innovative individuals and creative ideas, and the extent to which the enterprise engages itself and has the procedures to encourage innovation and creativity.

Aiken and Alford (1970) suggest a negative relationship between *organizational age* and innovativeness, emphasizing that the older the organization, the more its bureaucratic form will inhibit new policies and efforts to innovate. On the contrary, Kimberly and Evanisko (1981) found a positive correlation between age and innovation in particular for administrative innovations due to their need to ensure and enhance their status in their community.

A number of studies have been carried out in relation to organization *strategy* and innovation in the workplace. Brooks-Rooney et al. (1987), extending the work of Meyer (1982) in American hospitals, concluded that strategy was an important determinant of the level and type of innovation. Organization *culture* and *climate* were also identified by numerous studies as important variables to organizational innovation. There is an increasing emphasis in the literature for an organizational climate supportive of innovation. According to Bower (1965), such a climate will allow participation, relevant freedom of choice and expression, but also set out performance standards, rules and procedures. More recently, there has been a move away from corporate climate to corporate culture. Handy (1985) puts forward a corporate cultural model which is flexible, open, adaptable to changes and based on team-working, one that enhances innovation and knowledge diffusion.

3

The Concept and the Characteristics of 'Systems of Innovation'

The Concept of 'Systems of Innovation'

The concept of the 'systems of innovation' is a relatively new approach to the study of innovation that has emerged during the past couple of decades, starting mainly with the influential writings of Lundvall (1992) and Nelson (1993). In this period the development of national innovations systems has become the objective of many countries trying to strengthen their industrial and economic performance. The approach of innovation as a system is based on the idea that innovation processes occur over time and are influenced by many factors. *The concept of innovation systems conveys the idea that innovations do not originate as isolated, discrete phenomena within a firm, but are generated by means of interaction of a number of entities, actors and agents.*

The approach seems to be very attractive to policy makers of national economies and international organizations, like the Commission of the European Communities, as we briefly mentioned in Part 1 of the book. According to Edquist (1997), the systems of innovation approach is considered to be a useful and promising analytical tool for better understanding the innovation process, as well as the production and diffusion of knowledge in the economy. He argues that it is also highly useful and relevant from an innovation policy making point of view.

Hence, while the first two chapters of this part of the book explored the concept of innovation and entrepreneurship and the link between the two concepts, Chapter 3 investigates the concept of the systems of innovation. As we will see, innovation systems can be national, regional or local. They are shaped by the specific and characteristic economic and social conditions and factors of a country. In understanding the competitiveness of a country and the competitive advantages of businesses and business sectors of a country, we need to explore the concept of a system of innovation. Important factors such as institutions, authorities and governments at local, regional and national levels may affect the businesses' performance and innovative capabilities. The aim of this chapter is to investigate the concept and the characteristics of the systems of innovation commencing with exploring the historical roots of innovation systems, as put forward by Karl Marx and Max Weber.

Historical Roots of Innovation Systems

Although the terminology *innovation systems* or *national innovation systems* is only a couple of decades old, if we were to delve into the theoretical positions and writings of such seminal, classical economists-sociologists as Karl Marx and Max Weber, we could rather readily trace the historic roots of these concepts of innovation systems to their thoughts. Under careful scholarly scrutiny, it emerges that these scholars were pioneers in explaining the dynamics of the correlating nature between sociological and economic phenomena, and in providing a heuristic, sociological prism in investigating the evolution of modern economies through a historic perspective.

In the middle of the nineteenth century Karl Marx formulated a *Theory of History* which subsequently became an important influence on the work of other social theorists, and, according to some writers, a central force behind the rise of the social sciences themselves. His theory put forth the principles on which the relations between different forms of social, economic, political and cultural activities are based. More importantly, Marx proclaimed to have located the motive force lying behind social transformations of central importance in world history. *Marx defines economics as the science which studies how historically specific systems of economic relations originate, operate and change.* He does not make a sharp distinction between sociology and economics and in fact is the first scholar to exhibit social qualities in theoretical economics. According to Karl Marx:

> *Neither legal relations nor political forms could be comprehended whether by themselves or on the basis of a so-called development of the human mind, but on the contrary they originate in the material*

conditions of life, the totality of which Hegel embraces within the term 'civil society'; that the anatomy of this civil society, however, has to be sought in political economy. In the social production of their existence, men inevitably enter into definite relations, who are independent of their will, namely relations of production appropriate to a given stage in the development of their material forces of production. The totality of these relations of production constitutes the economic structure of society, the real foundation, on which arises a legal and political superstructure and to which correspond definite forms of social consciousness. The mode of production of material life conditions the general process of social, political and intellectual life. It is not the consciousness of men that determines their existence, but their social existence that determines their consciousness. At a certain stage of development, the material productive forces of society come into conflict with the existing relations of production or with the property relations within the framework of which they have operated hitherto. From forms of development of the productive forces these relations turn into their fetters. Then begins an era of social revolution. The changes in the economic foundation lead sooner or later to the transformation of the whole immense superstructure. In studying such transformations, it is always necessary to distinguish between the material transformation of economic conditions of production, which can be determined with the precision of natural science, and the legal, political, religious, artistic or philosophic – in short, ideological forms in which men become conscious of this conflict and fight it out ... no social order is ever destroyed before all the productive forces for which it is sufficient have been developed, and new superior relations of production never replace older ones before the material conditions for their existence have matured within the framework of the old society. In broad outline, the Asiatic, ancient, feudal and modern bourgeois modes of production may be designated as epochs marking progress in the economic development of society. The bourgeois mode of production is the last antagonistic form of the social process of production ... but the productive forces developing within bourgeois society create also material conditions for a solution of this antagonism. (Marx 1971: 20–22)

According to Howard and King (1985), Marx's *A Contribution to the Critique of Political Economy* stresses the pre-eminence of the economic structure in explaining all other aspects of a society, including the prevailing forms of social consciousness. The authors argue that Marx's explanations of all economic phenomena (i.e., methods of resource allocation, the distribution of income, labour division, dynamic laws of economic development) are based upon the historically specific social relations of the relevant mode of production, and are what they are because of the nature of the relations between economic agents: 'when these relations change so do the economic laws to which they give rise.' (Howard and King 1985: 42)

MAX WEBER'S SOCIAL ECONOMICS

Some decades later, in the beginning of the twentieth century, Max Weber was one of the German economist-historians and sociologists who attempted to trace the distinctive features of the capitalist social and economic order. The basic idea behind Weber's concept of social economics is that not one, but several of the social sciences are needed in order to effectively analyze economic phenomena. According to Weber, in the economic theory, material interests exclusively drive the actor but his behaviour is not necessarily oriented to the behaviour of other actors; traditions and emotions play no role either. The only types of actions that are analyzed in economic theory are consequently those that are purely economic; the relationships of the economy with politics, law and religion and so on, are ignored. We can summarize Weber's position in the following words: economic sociology, as opposed to economic theory, considers the social structure and looks at the impact of traditions and emotions on economic actions. Furthermore it looks at both economically relevant phenomena *and* economically conditioned phenomena, not just at economic phenomena alone. According to Weber's work, *The Theory of Social and Economic Organisation* (1947):

> Weber begins the chapter by stating emphatically that what he is about to present is not in any sense 'economic theory' ... what he presents is rather an account of the social, or perhaps better the institutional, structure of systems of economic activity and above all the ranges of variation to which this structure is subject ... two deep underlying convictions dominate his work ... the first is the conviction of the fundamental variability of social institutions. To him, the institutional system of the modern Western World is not a 'natural order' ... but only one of several possible lines of social development. Other radically different structures, such as those found in the great oriental civilisations, are not 'arrested stages' in a development leading in the same direction, but are simply different ... the second closely related conviction is that of inherent instability of social structures. For Weber, human society and underlying that, the situation of human action and

*the character of humanly possible responses to that situation, are shot
through with deep-seated tensions which make the maintenance of any
given state of affairs precarious. (Henderson and Parsons 1965: 31–32)*

As should be understood by the brief look at Marx and Weber's thoughts
presented above, innovation processes are influenced by many factors; they
occur in interactions between institutional and organizational elements, which
together may be called '*systems of innovation*'. Thus, if we want to describe,
understand, explain and even perhaps influence processes of innovation,
we must take all important factors shaping and influencing innovations into
account. As we will see in the following pages, in the process of innovation
firms interact with other organizations, such as other firms but also universities,
research institutes, investment banks, schools, government ministries and so on.
Furthermore, social patterns and social institutions, not necessarily economic
in their nature, may operate positively or negatively, giving rise to constraints
and/or incentives for innovation; these can be laws, health regulations, cultural
norms, social rules and technical standards which also shape the behaviour of
firms (George and Prabhu 2003). Interaction and relations between the various
agents, institutions and actors shape the systems of innovation.

Current Approaches to Innovation Systems

At the core of modern thinking about innovation processes, scholars attempt
to describe, explain, understand and potentially influence the structure and
dynamics of the systems of innovation. It is the new approach for the study of
innovation in the economy, as mentioned earlier, which argues that innovation
processes are influenced by many factors as well as the interactions between
those factors.

BENGT-ÅKE LUNDVALL

According to Lundvall (1992), one of the first and very broad definitions of what
constitutes a system is given by Boulding (1985): 'anything that is not chaos'.
Lundvall suggests that a number of elements and the relationships between
these elements compose a system. In his theory, the starting point is that
innovation is a ubiquitous phenomenon in the modern economy. Whichever
part of an economy we look at, we will always find an ongoing process of
learning, searching and exploring that ultimately results in new markets,

products and forms of organizing, as well as new techniques (Lundvall 1992). Hence:

> *A system of innovation is constituted by elements and relationships which interact in the production, diffusion and use of new, and economically useful, knowledge and that a national system encompasses elements and relationships, either located within or rooted inside the border of a nation state ... it is a social system where learning is the central activity and also a social activity ... it is also a dynamic system characterised both by feedback and reproduction. (Lundvall 1995: 2)*

He then proceeds to a more detailed definition by making a distinction between the narrow sense and the broad sense of a system of innovation:

> *The narrow definition would include organisations and institutions involved in searching and exploring – such as R&D departments, technological institutes and universities. The broad definition ... includes all parts and aspects of the economic structure and the institutional set-up affecting learning as well as searching and exploring – the production system, the marketing system and the system of finance present themselves as sub-systems in which learning takes place ... determining in detail which sub-systems and social institutions should be included, or excluded in the analysis of the system is a task involving historical analysis as well as theoretical considerations ... a definition of the system of innovation must, to a certain degree, be kept open and flexible regarding which sub-systems should be included and which processes should be studied. (Lundvall 1995: 12–13)*

It becomes clear that in order to study innovation within a business, clusters of businesses, regions, nations or other geographic or economic units, we need to look at several different aspects of the economic and social environment that affect, directly or indirectly, entrepreneurship and innovation. How knowledge is diffused in the economic system, how local institutions, agents and governments shape and affect the environment of the business has a deterministic effect to the competitive advantage of the businesses and their potential.

NELSON RICHARD AND ROSENBERG NATHAN

In the introductory chapter by Nelson and Rosenberg (1993) in Nelson's book, *National Innovation Systems, a Comparative Analysis*, the authors produce no explicit definition of a system of innovation. Nelson's seminal book is a comparative study examining 15 countries on the similarities and differences of their institutions, mechanisms and general factors that support and shape technical innovation. Nelson and Rosenberg explore the national system of innovation by discussing individually and in detail the three terms, innovation, national and system, which comprise the concept.

As far as innovation is concerned, Nelson and Rosenberg treat the term rather broadly. For them, innovation as a concept covers the processes by which firms master and get into practice product designs and manufacturing processes that are new to them, if not to the universe or even to the nation (Nelson and Rosenberg 1993: 4). For Nelson and Rosenberg the system is neither created nor developed. In their own words:

> The concept is of a set of institutions whose interactions determine the innovative performance ... of national firms. There is no presumption that the system was, in some sense, consciously designed, or even that the set of institutions involved works together smoothly and coherently. Rather, the 'systems' concept is that of a set of institutional actors that, together, play the major role in influencing innovative performance. The broad concept of innovation that we have adopted has forced us to consider much broader than simply the actors doing research and development. Indeed, a problem with the broader definition of innovation is that it provides no sharp guide to just what should be included in the innovation system, and what can be left out. (Nelson and Rosenberg 1993: 4–5)

For the authors, the system of innovation is not consciously designed and the term innovation is broadly defined. The final component in the national systems of innovation concept for Nelson and Rosenberg is the notion of national. The authors implicitly argue more for a sectoral approach on the concept of systems of innovation rather than a national approach:

> On the one hand, the concept may be too broad. The system of institutions supporting technical innovation in one field, say pharmaceuticals, may have very little overlap with the system of institutions supporting

innovations in another field, say aircraft. On the other hand, in many fields of technology, including both pharmaceuticals and aircraft, a number of the institutions are or act transnational. Indeed, for many of the participants in this study, one of the key interests was in exploring whether, and if so, in what ways the concept of 'national' systems made any sense today. National governments act as if it did. However, that presumption, and the reality, may not be aligned. (Nelson and Rosenberg 1993: 5)

CHARLES EDQUIST

Another approach to the concept of systems of innovation is proposed by Edquist (1997), who argues in his work that innovations are the most important source of productivity growth and increased material welfare, as well as a major cause for the destruction of old jobs and the creation of new employment. For Edquist, innovation processes occur over time and are influenced by a variety of interdependent and interactive factors. Firms rarely innovate in isolation; rather, in their pursuit of innovativeness, they interact with other organizations to exchange, develop and gain knowledge, information and other resources. Organizations can be other firms such as suppliers, customers, competitors, universities, research laboratories, financial institutions and banks or government institutions and so on. Largely, institutions also shape the behaviour of firms. According to the author, institutions constitute laws, technical standards and incentives for innovation, health regulations, cultural norms and constraints. The various actors and organizations that operate under certain institutional contexts are the elements of the system that create and use knowledge for economic purposes, while innovation emerges in such a system (Edquist 1997).

Attempting to define the national innovation system in his work, *Systems of Innovation, Technologies, Institutions and Organisations*, Edquist follows the path of Nelson and Rosenberg, defining separately the three terms that comprise the concept; namely, national, innovation and system.

Starting with the term innovation, Edquist (1997) argues that different authors who adopt the system of innovation mean different things by the term innovation. For him, there is neither a bad nor good, a useful or not useful definition of innovation. He argues that when one is interested in examining the systems of innovation, they must be clear at the outset if they are interested in technological process innovations, organizational innovations, product innovations, institutional and organizational change, a combination of some of them or in all of them. Accordingly, the conceptual tools that will be used for the approach to systems of innovation will be influenced by the relative decision.

The notion of a national system of innovation for Edquist should be discussed in conjunction with regional and sectoral. Edquist seems to reject the term national, in line with the writings of Nelson and Rosenberg. Systems of innovation other than national can and should be identified and studied:

> *An innovation system can be 'supranational' in several senses; it can be truly global, or it can include only a part of the world (e.g., an integrated Europe). It can also be 'regional' within a country, an example being the Silicon Valley area in California ... an innovation system can also be supranational and regional within a country at the same time, as are part of Germany, France, and the UK ... we can distinguish between a supranational system at the European Union level, the national level, and the regional/local level ... leaving the geographical dimension, we can talk about the 'sectoral' systems of innovation (i.e., systems that include only a part of a regional, a national, or an international system) ... 'sectoral' is determined by generic technologies, which can be, but are not necessarily restricted to one industrial branch ... (Edquist 1997: 11)*

The system of innovation, according to Edquist (1997), can be supranational, national, regional and local and at the same time sectoral within any of the previous geographic demarcations. The author identifies several potential combinations and argues once more that the final choice of definition relies on the object of the particular study. He goes on to suggest that the approaches given complement rather than exclude each other. Having provided definitions of the terms national and innovation, Edquist considers increasingly important the provision of a definition for the third concept, that of the system. He argues that the approaches of Lundvall (1995) and Nelson and Rosenberg (1993) are vague in specifying the boundaries of the system, and thus proposes the following definition:

> *One way of specifying the 'system' is to include in it all important economic, social, political, organisational, institutional, and other factors that influence the development, diffusion and use of innovations ... provided that the innovation concept has been specified, the crucial*

issue then becomes one of identifying all those important factors ...
admittedly, this is not as easy in practice as in principle. We simply
do not know in detail what all the determinants of innovation are
particularly not for all types of innovations ... in spite of that fact ... for
the time being ... we will specify the 'system' as including all-important
determinants of innovation. An advantage of this definition is that it is
open in the sense that it does not a priori exclude any determinants. A
disadvantage is that it is unspecific ... (Edquist 1997: 14–15)

Characteristics of the Systems of Innovation

Having defined the systems of innovation concept, the next step is to identify
the factors (elsewhere stated as determinants or elements) that constitute the
systems of innovation approaches. It should be noted that different scholars
assign greater or lesser importance to the various characteristic elements of the
systems. In the following pages an attempt is made to list and explore in some
detail the characteristics that the various systems of innovation approaches
have in common.

THE CONCEPT OF LEARNING

Despite the somewhat different interpretations of innovation given by the
various scholars, they all appear to place innovation at the very centre of their
focus. They see innovation as a matter of producing new knowledge or combining
existing knowledge in new forms and then transforming it into products or
processes that have some economic significance. According to Lundvall (1995),
learning is the central activity in the system and it is fundamental to the process
of innovation. A feature of modern economies is that they seem to develop their
mechanisms and capabilities to learn. Basic and applied research is increasingly
institutionalized and wedded to science through R&D departments, public
and private research laboratories, institutes and universities (Johnson 1995).
Furthermore, Johnson argues that economic activities are explicitly aiming at
increased knowledge in order to stimulate innovation and he sees the economy
as a process of communication and cumulative causation where learning can
be conceptualized as the source of innovation.

For Lundvall (1995: 9), many different actors and agents are involved in the
learning processes and the everyday experiences in the activities of engineers,
sales representatives and other employees: 'such activities involve learning-
by-doing, increasing the efficiency of production operations (Arrows 1962),

learning-by-using, increasing the efficiency of the use of complex systems (Rosenberg 1982), and learning-by-interacting, involving users and producers in an interaction resulting in product innovations' (Lundvall 1988).

Edquist (1997) argues that we are experiencing the knowledge-based economy and the learning economy. For him, it is of vital importance to analyze the knowledge and learning aspects of the system of innovation, including the formal R&D systems, the education and the training systems, as well as other processes of learning that are inherent in routine economic activities.

TRANSFER OF KNOWLEDGE AND INFORMATION

Most of the research on innovation has identified a variety of factors (e.g., human, social and cultural) that are decisive for the innovation process at an organizational level and which are largely based around the concept of *learning* (Oslo Manual 1997). Transfer and diffusion of knowledge and information between the innovative enterprise and the other actors in the innovation system (e.g., governments, universities, institutions, R&D laboratories, customers, suppliers and competitors) are amongst the most crucial factors that foster innovative activities. Most of the characteristics of the systems of innovation that are examined in the following pages of this chapter relate and depend upon the ease and effective communication, channels of knowledge, information and skills transmission between and within organizations and the other actors in the innovation system.

According to the Oslo Manual (1997), some kinds of information and knowledge can only be effectively and efficiently transferred between individuals that have the experience and expertise to fully understand it, while other kinds require the physical transfer of the individuals that are carriers of the knowledge and information.

Communication constitutes the process through which members, participating in a collective effort, create and share amongst themselves information in order to reach a common understanding (Piperopoulos 2007). Diffusion is a specific kind of communication through which new knowledge is exchanged and transferred: 'Diffusion is the spread of innovations, through market or non-market channels, from first implementation anywhere in the world to other countries and regions and to other markets and firms.' (Oslo Manual 2005: 78)

A key point in the transfer and diffusion of knowledge and particularly technological knowledge is that most of this knowledge is tacit. Thus, for the growth of innovative capabilities an enterprise must transform itself into a learning enterprise. According to the Oslo Manual (1997: 21–22) the most important factors for the transfer of knowledge and information, are the following:

Formal and informal linkages between firms, including networks of small firms, relationships between users and suppliers, relationships between firms, regulatory agencies and research institutions, and stimuli within clusters of competitors, can all produce information flows conducive to innovation or lead firms to be more receptive to it.

The presence of expert technological gatekeepers or receptors, individuals who, through many means, keep abreast of new developments (including new technology and codified knowledge in patents, the specialised press and scientific journals), and maintain personal networks, which facilitate flows of information – can be crucial to innovation within a firm.

International links are a key component of the networks through which information is channelled – networks (invisible colleges) of international experts are a key means of transmitting up-to-date scientific understanding and leading edge technological developments.

The degree of mobility of expert technologists or scientists will affect the speed at which new developments can spread.

The ease of industry access to public R&D capabilities.

Spin-off company formation, usually involving the transfer of particular skilled individuals – is often a valuable means of achieving commercialisation of new developments arising out of public sector research.

Ethics, community value-systems, trust and openness that influence the extent to which networks, linkages and other channels of communication can be effective, by affecting the informal dealings between individuals which underpin many business arrangements, and setting the parameters and accepted rules of behaviour within which communication and exchanges of information occur.

Codified knowledge in patents, the specialised press and scientific journals.

HOLISTIC SYSTEM

Furthermore, the systems of innovation can be characterized as holistic in the sense that contrary to the theories of innovation that we examined, in the first two chapters of this part of the book, this approach tries to encompass a wide variety, if not all, of the determinants that are important to the process of innovation. Moreover, this approach investigates innovation in an international, national, regional, local or sectoral context.

According to Edquist (1997), for example, the traditional OECD approach to measure innovation was to measure technical change and innovation based on the kind of data collected on R&D and technical change. The approach used a very narrow insight by focusing mainly on resource inputs such as money and personnel in the R&D system. As the author argues, one reason why the systems of innovation approach goes beyond this limited scope is that innovation processes are also developed outside the formal R&D department through, for example, learning-by-doing, learning-by-using, knowledge diffusion, and so on. Furthermore, as we saw in the previous two chapters, sociological factors, as well as a variety of other factors, affect the process of innovation and these can all be included in a system of innovation approach.

INTERDISCIPLINARY APPROACH

As Edquist (1997) suggests, the systems of innovation is an interdisciplinary approach and could be best labelled a *political-economic* approach; for, not only are economic factors that affect innovation encompassed in the systems approach, but also included are organizational, institutional, social and political factors. In his own words:

> *The system of innovation should be looked upon as a whole because many of its elements are – more or less closely – related to each other. Otherwise, there would be no system. But is also sometimes necessary to deal only with parts of the system – one at a time or a few in relation to each other. (Edquist 1997: 18)*

The systems of innovation develop over time and so do institutions and organizations within a nation. Nelson (1993), in his work, *National Innovation Systems, a Comparative Analysis* as mentioned above, tries to describe, analyze, compare and understand the similarities and differences across 15 countries in their innovation systems. He begins each case study by a close examination of the historical background of each country. The economic history of each country is carefully delineated from the industrial revolution to the period between the two World Wars and the post-Second World War era. Nelson (1993) argues that the historical dimension should be stressed in a national innovation system since it is highly influential in determining and understanding the direction and processes of innovation.

Edquist and Lundvall (1993: 265), in their comparative study of the Danish and Swedish systems of innovation, argue that, 'the Danish and the Swedish systems of innovation have quite different characteristics. It is argued that these characteristics are embedded in the economic structure and in the socio-institutional set-up and that they have strong and deep roots in the economic history of the two countries.'

Edquist (1997) suggests that anchored to the analysis of a system of innovation should be the historical perspective of the nation. He argues that it is an advantage when studying the processes of innovation, since innovations develop over time. Edquist believes that in their development they are affected by many factors, such as organizations, institutions and other agents that are all co-developed and co-evolved dynamically in line with the economic, political and social development of the country.

THE MEANING OF DIFFERENCE

As Nelson (1993) explores and describes in his work, the national innovation systems between countries can be quite different. Edquist (1997) goes one step further to suggest in line with Porter (1990) that differences exist not only between countries but also between the regional, local and sectoral systems of innovation within the same country. Furthermore, he argues that in some countries raw material-based production is important (e.g., the case of Denmark and Sweden), while in others, knowledge intensive production is more dominant, as is the case for Japan and South Korea where technology policy, human resources, knowledge and competence have been created as a substitute for the lack of natural resources.

It is of great importance to realize that the specifications of the elements of national innovation systems normally differ between countries. As Lundvall (1995: 13–14) argues:

> *The focus upon national systems reflects the fact that national economies differ regarding the structure of the production system and regarding the general institutional set-up. Specifically, we assume that the basic differences in historical experience, language, and culture will be reflected in national idiosyncrasies in: internal organisation of firms, interfirm relationships, role of the public sector, institutional set-up of the financial sector, R&D intensity and R&D organisation … the relationships between these elements are also important … the organisation and strategies of the public sector, including its responsibility for education and R&D, and the financial sector will affect the way firms organise and form networks.*

According to Edquist (1997), one should focus upon the differences between the various systems of innovation at a national, regional, local or sectoral basis. As the author states, without comparisons between existing systems it is impossible to argue that one system is specialized in one way or another: 'Neither can we argue that one country spends much on R&D or that its system performs well – or badly. This is because the notion of optimality is absent from the systems of innovation approaches. Hence comparisons between an existing system and an ideal system are not possible.' (Edquist 1997: 21)

The author suggests that we cannot define an optimal system of innovation since innovation by its nature is based on an evolutionary learning process and is thus subject to continuous change. The system will never achieve equilibrium since, according to Schumpeter, creative destructions alter the equilibrium constantly and, according to Edquist, the evolutionary processes are open-ended and path dependent. It is even impossible to predict if the most optimal course is exploited at all, since we do not know which one it is. Processes, according to the author, change, at least partly, randomly and take a long time. In the notion of a lack of any optimality, it is through the comparison of the systems of innovation that what is good or what is bad, what is a high or a low value for a variable, of the systems of innovation, can be identified and explained. Comparisons thus become crucial for policy making and for the identification of problems and could act as a benchmarking strategy.

UNIVERSITIES – GOVERNMENTS – BUSINESSES

The approach of innovation as a system is based on the idea that innovation processes occur over time and are influenced by many factors. It has been already stated that the concept of innovation systems conveys the idea that innovations do not originate as isolated, discrete phenomena within a firm, but are generated by means of interaction of a number of entities, actors and agents. When innovating, Edquist (1997) argues, firms interact more or less with other organizations, such as customers, competitors, suppliers of inputs – including knowledge and finance, and they do so in the context of certain institutions such as laws, standards, cultural habits, policies, government regulations, rules, and so on. Of course, one should not forget, according to the author, other agents that interact in the process of innovation like universities, schools, training institutes, government laboratories, public and private research institutes, and so on.

It appears, from the material presented above, that one of the important elements that affects business competitiveness and innovative performance centres on the relations between universities and businesses, and the role that institutions, authorities, agents and governments play in triggering and sustaining such relations.

Following the above arguments concerning the core nature of the systems of innovation approach, it appears that the different elements of the system are characterized by high levels of interdependence and interaction, which ultimately determine the innovation processes, for example, 'the long-term innovative performance of firms in science-based industries is strongly dependent upon the interaction between these firms and universities, or other organisations that carry out relevant basic research.' (Edquist 1997: 21) It becomes of major importance then, according to the author, to examine and delineate the relations between the different elements of the system. As he argues, these relations are extremely complex, and most of the time are characterized by reciprocity, interactivity and feedback mechanisms in numerous and continuous loops.

PRODUCT, SERVICE AND PROCESS INNOVATIONS

Another characteristic of the systems of innovation is that it encompasses product/service and process innovations as well as organizational innovations. Scholars in their concepts of systems of innovation explicitly include product and process innovations. Nelson and Rosenberg (1993: 10) stress the importance firm and industrial laboratories dramatize in the process of innovation since they describe them as, 'a facility dedicated to research and development of new or improved products and processes … staffed by university trained scientists and engineers.'

Lundvall (1995: 10) also includes product innovations in his approach to the concept of systems of innovation: 'one way to illustrate how the structure of production and the institutional set-up, together, affect the rate and direction of innovation is to focus upon product innovations, and their roots in the interaction between producers and users.'

According to Edquist (1997), the systems of innovation approach must also include organizational innovation. The author suggests that there are good and solid reasons why the systems approach must give more emphasis to organizational change and innovation, which he argues are sources of productivity, growth and competitiveness. His specific arguments in favour of including organizational innovations in the concept of systems of innovation are:

> *Organisational changes are important sources of productivity growth and competitiveness and they might strongly influence employment; organisational and technological changes are closely related and intertwined in the real world, and organisational change is often a requirement for technological process innovation to be successful; all technologies are created by human beings; they are in this sense 'socially shaped'. And this is achieved within the framework of specific organisational forms. (Edquist 1997: 24)*

THE ROLE OF INSTITUTIONS

One of the most striking common characteristics of the systems of innovation approaches is the emphasis all scholars place on the role of institutions. As Edquist and Johnson (1997) note, the concept of institutions has become increasingly important in innovation theory and is now viewed as a main character in the innovation process. However, the authors suggest that there are many problems with the role of institutions in the systems of innovation mainly because of conceptual vagueness and the fact that various scholars have given different definitions to the term institution. Edquist and Johnson provide their own definition of institutions, which is fairly open and thus allows the institutions to play a twofold role, either as shaping people's cognitions, views and actions, or as a compliant constraint on the decision of agents:

> *In the sense of patterned behaviour: institutions are sets of common habits, routines, established practices, rules, or laws that regulate the relations and interactions between individuals and groups. This definition catches the essence of the classical concept and relates to interactive learning, which is our link between institutions and innovations. (Edquist and Johnson 1997: 46)*

Institutions are of crucial importance for the innovation process as one can surmise from the central role that influential writers on the subject of systems of innovation assign to them:

- For Lundvall (1995: 10), the institutional set-up (of a specific firm, a constellation of firms or a nation) is the second most important dimension of the system of innovation.

- Nelson and Rosenberg (1993: 1) argue that their studies have been carefully designed, developed and written to illuminate the institutions and mechanisms supporting technical innovation in the various countries.

- While Carlsson and Jacobsson (1997: 268) define technological systems as a network or networks of agents interacting in a specific technology area under a particular institutional infrastructure to generate, diffuse and utilize technology.

Edquist (1997) stresses as well the importance and central role of institutions in the process of innovation and argues that their role should be carefully examined in any system of innovation, whether local, regional, sectoral or national. After examining various definitions of the term institutions, as different scholars in the literature present them, he suggests that institutions should be viewed in two main senses, '…one being *things that pattern behaviour* like norms, rules, and laws, and the other *formal structures* with an explicit purpose, i.e. what is normally called organisations.' (Edquist 1997: 26)

Considering the concept of the systems of innovations as presented above, we can argue that exploring entrepreneurship and innovation requires an understanding of the environment within which these concepts exist.

Part 1: References/Bibliography

Aiken, M. and Alford, R. 1970. Community structure and innovation: The case of urban renewal. *American Sociological Review*, Vol. 35, 650–655.

Antoin, M. 1986. *Richard Cantillon: Entrepreneur and Economist*. Oxford: Clarendon.

Baptiste, J.S. 2007. *A Treatise on Political Economy*. New York: Cosimo Classics.

Boulding, K.E. 1985. *The World as a Total System*. Beverly Hills: Sage Publications.

Bower, M. 1965. Nurturing innovation in an organisation, in *The Creative Organisation*, edited by G.A. Steiner. USA: Chicago University Press.

Brooks-Rooney, A., Rees, A. and Nicholson N. 1987. The development of mangers as effective organisational resources: a summary of findings in the wool textiles industry. MRC/ESRC Social and Applied Psychology Unit, University of Sheffield, Memo no. 916.

Carlsson, B. and Jacobsson, S. 1997. Diversity creation and technological systems: A technology policy perspective, in *Systems of Innovation: Technologies, Institutions and Organisations*, edited by C. Edquist. London: Pinter.

Casson, M.C. 1982. *The Entrepreneur: An Economic Theory*. Oxford: Martin Robertson.

Casson, M. 2005. Entrepreneurship and the theory of the firm. *Journal of Economic Behavior & Organization*, 58(2), 327–348.

Cefis, E. and Marsili, O. 2006. Survivor: The role of innovation in firms' survival. *Research Policy*, 35(5), 626–641.

Cole, A.H. 1949. Entrepreneurship and entrepreneurial history, in *Change and the Entrepreneur*, 88–107, reprinted and edited by H.C. Livesay in 1995, *Entrepreneurship and the Growth of Firms*, Aldershot, UK: Edward Elgar, 100–122.

Commission of the European Communities. 2000. Communication from the Commission to the Council and the European Parliament: Innovation in a Knowledge-driven Economy. Available at: http://www.cordis.lu/innovation/en/policy/communications/com2000.htm [accessed 02 May 2011].

Cullen, P. 2000. Contracting, co-operative relations and extended enterprises. *Technovation*, 20, 363–372.

da Silveira, G. 2001. Innovation diffusion: Research agenda for developing Economies. *Technovation*, 21(12), 767–773.

Dollinger, M.J. 1999. *Entrepreneurship Strategy and Resources*. 2nd edn, USA: Prentice Hall.

Drucker, P.F. 1985. *Innovation and Entrepreneurship*. USA: Harper Business.

Edquist, C. 1997. *Systems of Innovation: Technologies, Institutions and Organisations*. London: Pinter.

Edquist, C. and Lundvall, B.A. 1993. Comparing the Danish and Swedish system of innovation. in R.R. Nelson (ed.). *National Innovation Systems: A Comparative Analysis*. New York: Oxford University Press, pp. 265-298

Edquist, C. and Johnson, B. 1997. Institutions and organisations in systems of innovation, in *Systems of Innovation, Technologies: Institutions and Organisations*, edited by C. Edquist. London: Pinter.

Farris, G.F. 1973. The technical supervisor: Beyond the Peter principle. *Technical Review*, 75(April).

Fonseca, J. 2002. *Complexity and Innovation in Organisations*. London: Routledge.

Gartner, W.B. 1988. Who is an entrepreneur? is the wrong question. *American Journal of Small Business*, 12(1), 11–32.

George, G. and Prabhu, G.N. 2003. Developmental financial institutions as technology policy instruments: Implications for innovation and entrepreneurship in emerging economies. *Research Policy*, 32(1), 89–108.

Grupp, H. and Maital, S. 2001. *Managing New Product Development and Innovation: A Microeconomic Toolbox*. UK: Edward Elgar Publishing.

Handy, C. 1985. *Understanding Organisations*. Harmondsworth: Penguin.

Henderson, A.M. and Parsons, T. 1965. *Max Weber: The Theory of Social and Economic Organisation*. 2nd edn, USA: The Free Press.

Howard, M.C. and King, J.E. 1985. *The Political Economy of Marx*. 2nd edn, UK: Longman Group Limited.

Isen, A.M., Daubman, K.A. and Nowicki, G.P. 1987. Positive affect facilitates creative problem solving. *Journal of Personality and Social Psychology*, 71, 1122–1131.

Johnson, B. 1995. Institutional Learning, in *National Systems of Innovation: Towards a Theory of Innovation and Interactive Learning*, edited by B.A. Lundvall, New York: Pinter.

Kanter, R.M. 1983. *The Change Masters*. USA: Simon and Schuster.

Kimberly, J.R. and Evanisko, M.J. 1981. Organisational innovation: The influence of individual, organisational, and contextual factors on hospital adoption of technological and administrative innovations. *Academy of Management Journal*, 24, 689–713.

Kirton, M.J. 1976. Adaptors and innovators: A description and measure. *Journal of Applied Psychology*, 6, 6–10.

Knight, F.H. 2002. *Risk, Uncertainty, and Profit*. Washington, D.C.: Beard Books.

Lehmann, H. and Roth, G. 1993. *Weber's Protestant Ethic: Origins, Evidence, Contexts*. USA: Cambridge University Press.

Lovelace, R.F. 1986. Stimulating creativity through managerial intervention. *R&D Management*, 16, 161–174.

Lundvall, B.A. 1992. *National Systems of Innovation: Towards a Theory of Innovation and Interactive Learning*. New York: Pinter.

Martin, S. and Scott, J.T. 2000. The nature of innovation market failure and the design of public support for private innovation. *Research Policy*, 29, 437–447.

Marx, K. 1971. *Critique of Political Economy*. London: Lawrence and Wishart.

McClelland, D.C. 1961. *The Achieving Society*. Princeton N.J.: D. van Nostrand Company.

McDaniel, B.A. 2000. A survey of entrepreneurship and innovation. *The Social Science Journal*, 37(2), 277–284.

McDonough III, E.F., Athanassiou, N. and Barczak, G. 2006. Networking for global new product innovation. *International Journal of Business Innovation and Research*, 1(1/2), 9–26.

Meyer, A.D. 1982. Adapting to environmental jolts. *Administrative Science Quarterly*, 27, 515–537.

Muller, E. and Zenker, A. 2001. Business services as actors of knowledge transformation: The role of KIBS in regional and national innovation systems. *Research Policy*, 30, 1501–1516.

Nelson, R.R. 1993. *National Innovation Systems: A Comparative Analysis*. New York: Oxford University Press.

Nelson, R.R. and Rosenberg, N. 1993. Technical innovation and national systems, in *National Innovation Systems: A Comparative Analysis*, edited by R.R. Nelson, New York: Oxford University Press.

Nonaka, I. and Kenney, M. 1991. Towards a new theory of innovation management: A case study comparing canon inc. and Apple computer inc. *Journal of Engineering and Technology Management*, 8, 67–83.

Oslo Manual 1997. *Proposed Guidelines for Collecting and Interpreting Technological Innovation Data*. 2nd edn, Brussels: OECD Publishing, European Commission.

Oslo Manual 2005. *Guidelines for Collecting and Interpreting Technological Innovation Data*. 3rd edn, Brussels: OECD Publishing, European Commission.

Parkin, M., Powell, M. and Matthews, K. 1997. *Economics*. 3rd edn, UK: Addison Wesley Longman Limited.

Pelz, D.C. and Andrews, F.M. 1976. *Productive Climates for Research and Development*. Ann Arbor Michigan Institute of Social Research: University of Michigan.

Peters, T.J. 1994. *Crazy Times Call for Crazy Organisations*. USA: Vintage Books.

Peters, T.J. and Waterman, R.H. 1982. *In Search of Excellence: Lessons from America's Best Run Companies*. USA: Harper and Row.

Piperopoulos, G. 2007. *I Communicate Therefore I Exist; Leadership, Communication and Public Relations*. 9th edn, Thessaloniki: Piperopoulos.

Porter, M.E. 1985. *Competitive Advantage: Creating and Sustaining Superior Performance*. USA: The Free Press.

Porter, M.E. 1990. *The Competitive Advantage of Nations*. USA: The Free Press.

Robinson, A.G. and Stern, S. 1997. *Corporate Creativity: How Innovation and Improvement Actually Happen*. 1st edn, USA: Berrett-Koehler Publishers Inc.

Rogers, E.M. 1995. *Diffusion of Innovations*. 4th edn, USA: Free Press.

Rosenfeld, R. and Servo, J.C. 1991. Facilitating innovation in large organisations, in *Managing Innovation*, edited by J. Henry and D. Walker, London: The Open University.

Schumpeter, J.A. 1934. *The Theory of Economic Development: An Inquiry into Profits, Capital, Credit, Interest and the Business Cycle*. London: Oxford University Press.

Schumpeter, J.A. 1942. *Capitalism, Socialism and Democracy*. London: George Allen & Unwin.

Schumpeter, J.A. 1947. The creative response in economic history, in *Essays: Joseph A. Schumpeter*, edited by R. Clemence, USA: Transaction Publishers.

Schumpeter, J.A. 1949. Economic history and entrepreneurial history, in *Essays: Joseph A. Schumpeter*, edited by R. Clemence, USA: Transaction Publishers.

Stevenson, H.H., Roberts, M.J. and Grousbeck, H.I. 1989. *New Business Ventures and the Entrepreneur*, Homewood Ill: Irwin

Swedberg, R. 1998. Max Weber's vision of economic sociology. *Journal of Socio-Economics*, 27(4), 535–555.

Torrance, E.P. and Horng, R.G. 1980. Creativity and style of learning and thinking characteristics of adaptors and innovators. *The Creative Adult and Child Quarterly*, 5, 80–85.

West, M.A. and Farr, J.L. 1990. *Innovation and Creativity at Work: Psychological and Organisational Strategies*. UK: John Wiley & Sons Ltd.

Wolfe, R.A. 1994. Organisational Innovation: Review, critique and suggested research directions. *Journal of Management Studies*, 31(3), 405–431.

Zaltman, G., Duncan, R. and Holbek, J. 1973. *Innovations and Organisations*. USA: Wiley.

PART 2

Small and Medium-Sized Enterprises and the Evolution of Competition

Prolegomena of Part 2

In the first part of the book, we introduced the concepts of entrepreneurship, innovation and systems of innovation. We discussed also the link between entrepreneurship and innovation and delineated the theoretical framework for understanding these concepts. This second part of the book focuses on small and medium-sized enterprises (SMEs). The aim is to attempt a generic understanding of the characteristics of SMEs, as found in the literature and in various research studies. In the following chapters we delineate the theoretical framework for understanding SMEs innovative capabilities, the central role of entrepreneurs, the changing nature of competition and the advancement of information and communication technologies and how these affect the way SMEs organize their operations and compete. Furthermore, we examine the characteristics, motives and aspirations of ethnic and female entrepreneurs, who are widely considered to be critical elements in the structures of western economies and the revival of the small business population. Moreover, we address and attempt to answer the issues of how and why business networks and strategic alliances affect SMEs' competitiveness and innovative performance. We also bring forth the concept of *open innovation* which, in the last few years, has been proposed as a new paradigm for the management of innovation. In the closing section of this second part of the book I present a hypothetical model for enhancing the competitiveness and performance of the SME by properly utilizing employees' creative potential, emotional intelligence, tacit knowledge and innovative ideas.

The role of SMEs in the innovation process has become an important component of many policy-making decisions in the European Union (EU) in the first decade of the twenty-first century. The important role of SMEs in the economic and social infrastructure of the European Union and its member states was clearly illustrated by the establishment of, *The Observatory of European SMEs* by the European Commission, two decades ago in December 1992. Its primary goal is to improve the monitoring of the economic performance of SMEs in Europe, and to provide information on SMEs for policy makers, at national and European levels, researchers and to SMEs themselves (European Commission 2002).

According to Goffee and Scase (1995), small businesses have been viewed as being of little importance in market economies, which have been for the most part dominated by large, national and multinational enterprises. Traditionally, whereas large enterprises have been equated with government lobbying, manipulating prices and direct and indirect dictation of market forces, the opportunities for small businesses would tend to be limited. In the conditions of the 1990s, the attitudes towards small businesses have changed, as the authors argue:

> Small business and entrepreneurship are no longer seen as marginal to modern economies. Both government macroeconomic policies and corporate thinking now reflect small business values ... opportunities for setting up small business ventures are now greater than in the earlier post-war decades ... entrepreneurship is now more important than in the past, while equally, many medium-sized enterprises stem from very small-scale entrepreneurial origins. (Goffee and Scase 1995: 1-3)

SMEs comprise the largest portion of businesses in most developed and developing economies, offer the greatest potential for employment creation and contribute positively to economic growth, competitiveness and productivity (Tether 2000, Samitas and Kenourgios 2005, Piperopoulos and Scase 2009). It is estimated that, currently, there are over 23 million enterprises employing one or more persons, operating in Europe and representing 99 per cent of all EU companies and providing jobs for some 75 million people (Schmiemann 2008). The definition of an SME according to the European Union is an enterprise employing less than 250 employees whilst having an annual turnover of no more than €50 million.

According to the European Commission (2005), on average, a European SME employs 6.8 persons (on EU-27 level). Nevertheless, this varies between two persons in microenterprises, and over 1,000 in large enterprises. Turnover per enterprise varies between €200,000 for an SME and €255 million in large enterprises. Thus, while SMEs export only 13 per cent of turnover, only 7 per cent represents export activities of microenterprises, while large scale enterprises' (LSEs) share of exports in turnover amounts to 21 per cent. However, because SMEs act as subcontractors, supplying goods and services to large exporting enterprises, the indirect exports of SMEs are far more significant than what was statistically unveiled.

The European Commission (2002: 6) that convened in Lisbon, more than a decade ago in March 2000, highlighted the importance of SMEs for every country and for the EU as a whole, by placing enterprises that operate in the EU markets at the heart of the strategy: 'reaching the objective of becoming the most competitive and dynamic knowledge-based economy in the world, capable of sustainable economic growth, more and better jobs and greater social cohesion will ultimately depend on how successful enterprises, especially small and medium-sized ones, are.'

4

Characteristics of Small and Medium-sized Enterprises

Types and Definitions of SMEs

There is no single definition of a small firm, mainly because of the wide diversity of businesses. This is because a small firm in, say, the petrochemical industry is likely to have much higher levels of capitalization, sales and possible employment than a small firm in the car repair industry (Storey 2000). One of the best descriptions of the key characteristics of a small firm that has been used extensively by governments and scientists around the world, according to management literature, is the one used by the Bolton Committee in its 1971 *Report on Small Firms*. The *economic* definition regarded firms as small if they satisfied the following three criteria:

- They had a relatively small share of their market place.

- They were managed by owners or part-owners in a personalized way and not through a formalized management structure.

- They were independent businesses, in a sense of not forming part of a larger enterprise.

Three key issues immediately emerge from this definition. How can anyone measure the relative size of a company by its market share? What does the Bolton Committee see as an independent business? What does the committee mean by a formalized management structure?

According to Burns (1996), the Bolton Committee sees the characteristic of a small firm's share of the market as not being capable of influencing the prices or national quantities of goods sold to any significant extent. The author argues that personalized management implies that the owner actively participates in all decision making and all aspects of the management of the business. And as far as the independence of the business is concerned, Burns argues that the Bolton Committee explains independence as being free from outside control of any kind; even small subsidiaries, although autonomous in many ways, still have to refer major decisions to a higher authority.

The Bolton Report (1971) also adopts a number of different statistical definitions. It recognizes that size is relevant to sector, that is, a firm of a given size could be small in relation to one sector where the market is large and there are many competitors, whereas a firm of similar proportions could be considered large in another sector with fewer players and/or generally smaller firms within it. Similarly, it accepts that it may be more appropriate to define size by the number of employees in some sectors, and more appropriate to use turnover in others. It is most usual to measure size according to numbers of full-time employees or their equivalent. The statistical definitions of the Bolton Committee are the following:

Table 4.1   Bolton Committee's statistical definition of a small firm

Sector	Definition
Manufacturing	200 employees or less
Construction	25 employees or less
Mining and quarrying	
Retailing	Turnover of £50,000 or less
Miscellaneous	
Services	
Motor trades	Turnover of £100,000 or less
Wholesale trades	Turnover of £200,000 or less
Road transport	Five vehicles or less
Catering	All excluding multiples and brewery-managed houses

Source: Storey 2000: 9

According to Storey (2000), the aim of the statistical definition was threefold:

- First, the Bolton committee wanted to quantify the current size of the small firm sector and its contributions to national aggregates such as the gross domestic product (GDP), employment figures, exports and innovation.

- Second, the purpose was to compare the extent to which the small firm sector changes its economic contribution over time.

- Third, the statistical definition enables comparisons between the contributions of small firms in one country with that of other nations.

The Bolton Committee's statistical and the economic definitions proved to be incompatible in some ways. For example, how could a firm with 200 employees be managed in a personalized way without having supervisors, different layers of managers and delegation of authority?

Leaving aside the obvious incompatibility and certain question marks of how some elements of the definitions can be measured, the Department of Trade and Industry in the United Kingdom, for statistical purposes, usually employs the definitions below, following the proposition of the Bolton Committee of 1971:

1.   Micro firm: 0–9 employees

2.   Small firm: 0–49 employees (includes micro)

3.   Medium firm: 50–249 employees

4.   Large firm: over 250 employees.

EUROPEAN COMMISSION'S DEFINITIONS OF SMES

According to Storey (2000), the European Commission, in aiming to overcome the various problems with the definitions analyzed earlier and others found in the management literature, decided that the term *small and medium-sized enterprise* should be coined. According to the author, the SME sector is itself disaggregated into three components:

- Microenterprises: those with 0–9 employees.

- Small enterprises: those with 10–99 employees.

- Medium enterprises: those with 100–499 employees.

Furthermore, under the Fourth Framework Programme, in order for an enterprise to be considered as an SME, it must have an annual turnover of no more than €38 million and not be more than one-third owned by an organization larger than an SME (based on turnover and number of employees), unless it is a financial investor, for example, a bank or venture capitalist.

In April 1996 the European Commission circulated a communication in an attempt to set out a single definition of an SME to overcome a number of problems with the existing definitions. The Commission proposed a recommendation outlining a new common definition for SMEs (OECD 2000) which it decided to roll out across community programmes and proposals. The communication also included a (non-binding) recommendation to member states, the European Investment Bank and the European Investment Fund encouraging them to adopt the same definitions for their programmes. On 6 May 2003 the European Commission, taking into account the economic developments since 1996 and the lessons drawn from the application of the definition, revised its SME definition as follows:

Table 4.2   European Commission SME definitions

Criterion	Micro	Small	Medium
Headcount: Annual Work Unit (AWU) It includes full-time, part-time and seasonal staff	<10	<50	<250
Annual turnover	≤€2 million	≤€10 million	≤€50 million
Annual balance sheet total	≤€2 million	≤€10 million	≤€43 million

Source: European Commission 2005: 14

As from 1 January 2005, according to the European Commission (2005), to be considered an SME under the new definition, an enterprise must fulfil the following criteria:

1. Have no more than 250 employees.

2. Have an annual turnover of no more than €50 million or an annual balance sheet total of no more than €43 million.

In summary, it appears that there is no uniformly, satisfactory definition of small and medium-sized enterprises. Nevertheless, the new definition set up by the European Commission has the advantage of being used in several programmes and surveys, which ultimately enhances the comparability of SMEs' performances and characteristics between the different member states. Furthermore, it provides also for three sub-categories, namely micro, small and medium-sized enterprises. In this book, we are using the definition of an SME as proposed by the European Commission (2005) and presented above.

The Characteristics of an SME

European firms, both SMEs and large scale enterprises (LSEs), face the double challenge of being confronted both with the increase in global competition and the features related to the single European market. Having defined an SME, the next step in the set up of the theoretical framework of SMEs is to identify the characteristics that distinguish them from large enterprises and multinational alliances. Several research studies and extensive management literature have been devoted to exploring and understanding the characteristics of SMEs, scrutinizing, for example, the management styles, the roles of entrepreneurs and their business constraints. It should be noted that different scholars and research studies assign greater or lesser importance to the various characteristics of SMEs and how these affect their everyday operations, their potential for growth and competitiveness and ultimately their capability to be innovative.

In this section of Chapter 4, an attempt is made to list and explore in some detail the most significant characteristics that SMEs appear to have in common. We begin our analysis with a perception that small and medium-sized enterprises, and in particular innovative SMEs, are an important source of employment creation. Most economic structures, and the European Union itself as we have already mentioned, are largely composed of SMEs, and despite the presence of large enterprises, most employment is concentrated in this group. Hence, we choose to study entrepreneurship, innovation and business clustering within SMEs, which are characterized as the backbone of the European economy. SMEs' capacity to become and/or remain competitive and innovative affects their ability to create employment:

> When a steelwork closes, or a large industry contractor shuts, it is the small and medium sized firm sector, which is seen as the source of new employment opportunities for the redundant workforce. Former

unskilled employees become self-employed taxi drivers, window cleaners and small garage employees. Draughtsmen, precision engineering fitters and computer specialists become self-employed in their own trades. Where major job shedding takes place, the SMEs sector is seen to be the way in which the local economy can create its own employment by 'pulling itself up by its own boot-straps'. (Storey 2000: 160)

The major shift in public policy focus, during the early 1980s, towards the promotion and development of new small firms as the vehicle for job creation was ignited by Birch's (1979) startling findings that small firms (with fewer than 20 employees) were responsible for more than 66 per cent of all new jobs created between 1969–1976 in the USA. Birch's work ensured that the SME sector would remain a key focus for policy makers, politicians and academics. During the 1980s Pavitt et al. (1989) argued that the role of SMEs in the innovation process and in economic growth made them a central element in policy making across the European Union economies. In the dawn of the twenty-first century, according to Asquith and Weston (1994), in OECD countries, over 95 per cent of enterprises were SMEs, providing 60–70 per cent of jobs, while half of the US GDP in 1999 was attributed to small businesses, which contributed for about 58 per cent of the 1999 employment figures (Hausman 2005). As we have already discussed, the latest data estimates over 23 million enterprises (with one or more employees) operating in Europe, representing 99 per cent of all EU companies, providing jobs for some 75 million people and verifying the dominant position of SMEs in Europe and around the world (Schmiemann, 2008).

According to Storey (2000), from studies in the United Kingdom and the USA, four main conclusions emerge for the quantity of jobs created by SMEs. The first is that small firms make a disproportionately large contribution to job creation in the economy. According to the author, in the period 1976–88 the US Small Business Administration reported that firms with less than 20 employees provided 37 per cent of employment creation, at a time when they represented only 19 per cent of total employment. His second finding was that there were differences in the pattern of employment creation, varying according to firm size in both countries. Irrespective of the trade cycle, it appears that SMEs make a more consistent contribution to job creation whereas large firms make weak or negative contributions when job change and the trade cycle is negative or low, but do make a major contribution when the net job change and the trade cycle is high and positive. It should be mentioned here that job change refers, according to the author, to the difference between new jobs and job losses (new jobs – job losses = net job change, Storey 2000: 162).

While it is evident that in aggregate terms SMEs play an important role in local and national economic development, only a small portion of enterprises from the total SME population are responsible for the majority of positive effects in terms of innovation, new product development, R&D and thus jobs and wealth creation, and could be classified as belonging to the 'high growth' sector (Thwaites and Wynarczyck 1996, Wynarczyck 2010).

According to Tether (2000), the findings from a UK based study and several other studies of European new and small firms suggest that even amongst the fastest growing innovative and technology sectors, the absolute number of jobs created within each individual firm over a decade tends to be modest and counted in the hundreds rather than, as the general perception goes, in thousands. Tether (2000: 110–111) identifies the following four key factors:

1.   *Innovative* or technology-based new and small firms are more likely to create employment than similar firms in the general population.

2.   The *average rate of employment creation* within an individual innovative or technology-based new or small firm tends to be modest. According to the author, the average employment growth of such firms tends to be less than ten jobs per year.

3.   The growth amongst innovative and technology-based new and small firms tends to be concentrated in a few firms. Only a handful of firms will be responsible for most of the new jobs created over a period of a decade or so, while he also argues that 10 per cent of the firms studied were responsible for half the new jobs created by a group of 149 firms over a decade. It is worth noting though that this pattern of growth is also characteristic, according to research studies, for firms in more conventional industries.

4.   Even amongst the fastest growing innovative and technology-based new and small firms *the absolute number of jobs created over a decade tends to be modest*. The author argues that in the USA, corporations like Microsoft, Dell, Gateway, Intel and Apple were established in the last 30 years and are now in the Fortune 500 list of the largest companies. Unfortunately, though, there is little evidence of such

growth in Europe. Two distinguishable examples are SAP, the German software company established in 1972 that has now over 7,000 employees and Dyson Appliances Ltd in the UK, which was based on a novel vacuum cleaner and is currently employing several thousands of employees.

Management and Organizational Structure of SMEs

An important characteristic of SMEs is their management and organizational structures. As the quotation that we present below describes, the differences between SMEs and large enterprises are so significant that they oblige us to explore their idiosyncrasies in some detail. It is useful to point out that even among SMEs there are important differences, such as those concerning size-class patterns that determine how they are organized and managed. The analysis that follows depicts several issues related to the development and growth of an SME and introduces the central role of the entrepreneur in the inception, survival, growth and management of the enterprise:

> *The differences in the administrative structure of the very small and the very large firms are so great that in many ways it is hard to see that the two species are of the same genus. (Storey 2000: 121)*

Storey (2000) proposes a five-stage model through which a small company evolves to become a bigger one and how this affects its administrative structure as presented in Table 4.3. It should be made clear that the author does not imply by any means that all firms begin from stage one and move to stage five. The model merely describes some of the characteristics of firms rather than tries to predict how they will progress during their life span. This suggestion is even more real since the majority of businesses will not survive to go even beyond stages one and two. The point where we should focus our attention is on the three components that describe an SME: the management role, the management style and its organizational structure.

Table 4.3   Storey's five-stage evolution model

Stage	Top management role	Management style	Organization structure
1. *Inception*	Direct supervision	Entrepreneurial, individualistic	Unstructured
2. *Survival*	Supervised supervision	Entrepreneurial, administrative	Simple
3. *Growth*	Delegation/co-ordination	Entrepreneurial, co-ordinate	Functional, centralized
4. *Expansion*	Decentralization	Professional, administrative	Functional, decentralized
5. *Maturity*	Decentralization	Watchdog	Decentralized functional/ product

Source: Storey 2000: 121

GREINER'S MODEL OF ORGANIZATIONAL DEVELOPMENT

Greiner (1972) argues that while organizations grow they progress through five distinguishable phases of development, each of which is characterized by a relative calm period that ends with a management crisis. The future survival and success of the company lies within their organization and their evolving stages of development. As the author argues, the organization's particular history determines its future rather than external forces. Each phase of organizational development is characterized by both an evolution and a revolution, for example, centralized practices lead to demands for decentralization that the author defines as follows:

> *Evolution is used to describe prolonged periods of growth where no major upheaval occurs in organization practices and revolution is used to describe those periods of substantial turmoil in organization life.* (Greiner 1972: 1)

According to Greiner (1972), each phase is both an effect of the previous cause and a cause for the next phase. Five key dimensions emerge as essential for building a model of organization development:

1. Age of the organization

2. Size of the organization

3. Stages of evolution

4. Stages of revolution

5. Growth rate of industry.

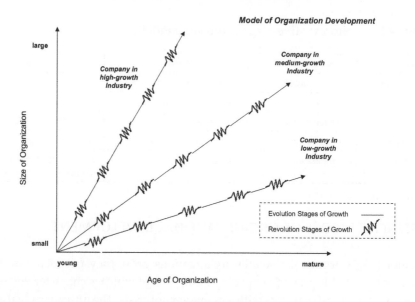

Figure 4.1   Model of organization development
Source: Greiner 1972

The combined effects of the proposed five key dimensions are illustrated in the figure above. According to Greiner, the same organization practices are not maintained throughout a long time-span. The passage of time contributes to the institutionalization of managerial attitudes, while management problems and principles are rooted in time. Furthermore, the company's problems and solutions tend to change as the number of employees, the sales volume and the turnover increases. The increased size can amplify problems of co-ordination and communication among employees as new functions emerge and levels in the management hierarchy multiply and jobs become more interrelated. As we have defined above, the stages of *evolution* describe the prolonged periods of growth where only minor modifications are necessary for maintaining growth under the same management principles. A serious upheaval of management produces turbulent times, which represent the periods of *revolution* as described above. Traditional management practices that functioned positively for the past few years and were appropriate for a smaller size are becoming obsolete and inappropriate to follow and manage the growth of the company. According to Greiner (1972), during such periods of crisis, a number of companies fail, particularly those unable to abandon past practices as the following quotation/ example illustrates. The critical task for management is to find a new set of organizational and management practices that will be the basis for managing the next evolutionary period, otherwise the company will fail. As the author argues:

> Key executives of a retail store chain hold on to an organization structure long after it has served its purpose, because their power is derived from this structure. The Company eventually goes into bankruptcy. (Greiner 1972: 1)

These revolutionary new practices, as the company grows, will eventually become inadequate and force the next revolutionary period. Companies, therefore, experience the irony of seeing a major solution in one time-period become a major problem later. The rate at which the company experiences these phases is closely related to the market environment of the industry. Greiner (1972) claims that in a rapidly expanding market the company will have to employ more personnel rapidly, hence the need for new organization structures and revolutionary periods. On the other hand, a company might prolong its growth by choosing deliberately not to grow as quickly as it could.

With the above framework in mind Greiner examined in depth the five specific phases of evolution and revolution. A prevailing management style used to achieve growth characterizes each evolutionary period, while its revolutionary period is characterized by a management problem that has to be solved before growth can continue, as we can see in Figure 4.2 and Table 4.4.

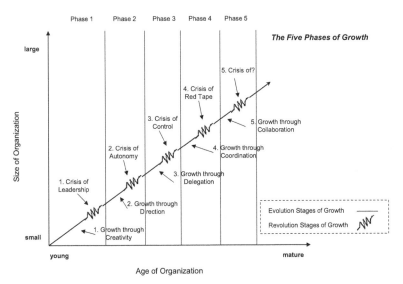

Figure 4.2   The five phases of growth

Source: Greiner 1972

Table 4.4   Organizational practices during evolution in the five phases of growth

Category	Phase 1	Phase 2	Phase 3	Phase 4	Phase 5
Management Focus	Make and sell	Efficiency of operations	Expansion of market	Consolidation of organization	Problem solving and innovation
Organization Structure	Informal	Centralized and functional	Decentralized and geographical	Line-staff and product groupings	Matrix of teams
Top Management Style	Individualistic and entrepreneurial	Directive	Delegative	Watchdog	Participative
Control System	Market result	Standards and cost centres	Reports and profit centres	Plans and investment centres	Mutual goal setting
Management Reward Emphasis	Ownership	Salary and merit increases	Individual bonus	Profit sharing and stock options	Team bonus

Source: Greiner, 1972

Both models demonstrate how the management style adopted by the owner-manager must change if they are to pass successfully through the different phases of growth. Their arguments could be confirmed by the data presented by the Observatory of European SMEs, which depicts SMEs as placing differing emphasis on business policies according to their size, as illustrated in Table 4.5.

Table 4.5   Main focus of business policy, by size-class (percentage of SMEs)

	Number of employees			Total
	0–9	10–49	50–249	
Struggle to survive	21	14	8	20
Consolidation	21	21	18	21
Growth	29	30	38	29
Higher profits	9	12	14	9
Higher quality	11	14	12	11
Innovate	7	7	8	7
Other/no answer	2	2	2	2
Total	100	100	100	100

Source: European Commission 2002: 17

Micro firms are most usually entangled with a 'struggle to survive' while larger SMEs tend to place more emphasis on other business policies, such as higher profits and higher quality of products or services. The importance of growth as a business policy tends to increase by size, from about 30 per cent of micro and small enterprises, to about 38 per cent for medium-sized enterprises (European Commission 2002).

We have already mentioned that the dominant size-class of enterprises in the EU is the SME; moreover, though, we should point out that according to the European Commission (2002), the dominant size-class within the SMEs' sector is the microenterprise. According to the above survey data and the theories of growth we have presented, organizations of this size have somewhat formless organizational structures with the entrepreneur being the central figure and most of the times the founder and/or manager of the company.

The growth models presented above and the empirical data from the Observatory of European SMEs 2001 survey (European Commission 2002) also presented in the tables above depict a clear relation between the size of an enterprise and its management and organizational policies. In many ways the growth models presented by Storey (2000) and Greiner (1972), earlier, are best used as predictors of problems that the firm is likely to face as it grows and therefore what management should be aware of if it wishes the company to continue its growth at different stages of development. This does not imply that these growth models are rendered obsolete but rather that they can be used as tools by the entrepreneurs/owners/managers to identify the particular phase a firm is in and be able to understand the major issues that they need to address, not only in that stage, but also in the next stages of its development.

5

The Small and Medium-Sized Enterprise and the Entrepreneur

The Role of the Entrepreneur/Owner/Manager

Several researchers in their studies give special emphasis to the influential role of the entrepreneur in affecting the performance, survival and growth of the firm particularly when the firm is small, as we explored briefly in the previous chapter. The idea we bring on stage in this chapter of Part 2 is that the basic role played by the entrepreneur/owner/manager is one of the major determinants of SME competitiveness. This turns out to be so because the concentration of decision-making power in the entrepreneur/owner/manager in an SME environment consequently affects the firm's overall strategy. The central and dominating position of the entrepreneur in a business, especially at its first stages of development while it is still a micro or small enterprise, is highlighted in the work of Storey (2000) and Greiner (1972) and their growth models as presented in Chapter 4.

As we examined in Part 1, an entrepreneur, according to Schumpeter (1942), is everyone who carries out new combinations: Schumpeter defines carrying out new combinations as, new products, new services, new sources of raw material, new methods of production, new markets and new forms of organization. The focus is on the producer and it is here that the *entrepreneur* enters the stage. Schumpeter (1942: 65) defines production as the combinations of materials and forces that are within our reach. All components that the entrepreneur needs for their product or service, whether physical or immaterial, already exist and are in most cases readily available. The basic driving force behind structural economic growth is the introduction of new combinations of materials and forces, not the creation of new possibilities:

> *The new combinations are always present, abundantly accumulated by all sorts of people. Often, they are also generally known and being discussed by scientific or literary writers. In other cases, there is nothing to discover about them, because they are quite obvious ... it is this 'doing the thing', without which possibilities are dead, of which leader's function consists ... it is, therefore, more by will than by intellect that the leaders fulfil their function, more by authority, personal weight, and so forth than by original ideas. (Schumpeter 1942: 88–89)*

In his work, *Innovation and Entrepreneurship*, presented in some length in Part 1, Drucker (1985) argues that some researchers use the term entrepreneurship to describe either small businesses or new businesses. However, the author argues in line with Schumpeter, that a great number of well-established, large companies engage in successful entrepreneurship, and he thus believes that entrepreneurship should refer not to an enterprise's size or age but to a certain kind of activity. Entrepreneurship is a special characteristic of an individual or an organization. Innovation is at the heart of entrepreneurship, the effort to create purposeful, focused change in an enterprise's economic or social potential (Drucker, 1985).

According to Goffee and Scase (1995), the entrepreneurs are these owner-managers that exercise control over their businesses through directly imposed but mostly unwritten guidelines and instructions. They may employ as many as 50 or 60 staff, or even much more, according to their ability to exercise control through informal, face-to-face processes rather than according to formalized structures and job descriptions. Nevertheless, in SMEs there may be different layers of managers, supervisors, job descriptions and so on, but the distinguishable characteristic of the entrepreneur is that he will retain almost total control and remain the centre of the decision-making web (Aaboen et al. 2006). Such enterprises are sculptured around the *personalities* of their owner-managers and their growth potential, and financial viability is highly dependent upon the proprietors' preferences, energies, talents and plans.

Entrepreneurial Competencies and Competitiveness

The role and personality of the entrepreneur/manager/owner of the small firm and their strategic decisions are in direct relationship with the competitiveness and innovative performance of the SME (Hoffman et al. 1998, Hausman, 2005). According to recent research results in 305 small tourism firms in Israel, the entrepreneurial human capital and particularly the managerial skills were the strongest contributors to both short-term and long-term business performance and growth (Haber and Reichel 2007).

In their research, Man et al. (2002) focus on the concept of competitiveness and the competency approach and develop a conceptual model to link the characteristics of SMEs' owner-managers and their firm's performance. Competitive scope, organizational capabilities, entrepreneurial competencies and performance are the four components of the model. According to the authors, the focal point of the model concentrates on the entrepreneurial tasks that link the different competency areas with the constructs of competitiveness. The entrepreneur's managerial skills and technical know-how, their demographic, psychological and behavioural characteristics are often cited as the most influential factors related to the performance of an SME; particularly since quite often small firms or even medium-sized companies have a dominating entrepreneur who is most likely to be the founder of the business. The relationship is also affected by many industrial, environmental, firm-specific characteristics and firm strategies (Man et al. 2002).

Earlier, Burns and Harrison (1996) had suggested that when the personal characteristics of the owner/manager of the company are problematic and interact with managerial deficiencies, they tend to produce weaknesses in the firm and potentially lead it to failure.

As shown in the following figure, *competitiveness* is conceptualized as having three dimensions, namely *potential*, *process* and *performance*. From the model below, we distinguish between three key aspects that affect SMEs' competitiveness, internal firm's factors, external environment and the influence of the entrepreneur, all of which in turn affect the performance of the SMEs (Man et al. 2002).

The authors argue that merely the possession of the following competencies does not make an entrepreneur competent. Competencies can only be demonstrated by a person's behaviour and actions, which in turn correspond to the dynamic characteristic of competitiveness.

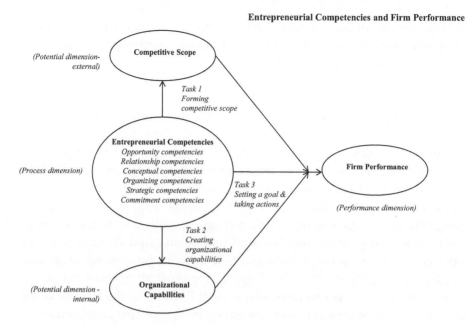

Figure 5.1   Entrepreneurial competencies and firm performance

Source: Man et al. 2002

Man et al. (2002: 132) delineate the entrepreneurial competencies as follows:

1. *Opportunity competencies. Competencies related to recognizing and developing market opportunities through various means.*

2. *Relationship competencies. Competencies related to person-to-person or individual-to-group based interactions, e.g. building a context of cooperation and trust, using contacts and connections, persuasive ability, communication and interpersonal skills.*

3. *Conceptual competencies. Competencies related to different conceptual abilities, which are reflected in the behaviour of the entrepreneur, e.g. decision skills, absorbing and understanding complex information, and risk-taking and innovativeness.*

4. *Organising competencies. Competencies related to the organization of different internal and external human, physical, financial and technological resources, including team-building, leading employees, training and controlling.*

5.   *Strategic competencies. Competencies related to setting, evaluating and implementing the strategies of the firm.*

6.   *Commitment competencies. Competencies that drive the entrepreneur to move ahead with the business.*

The authors in their study concluded that the organizing, relationship and conceptual competencies of the entrepreneur are positively related to the organizational capabilities of an SME. They focused upon the competencies of the entrepreneur and found a positive relationship between the firm's long-term performance and the strategic and commitment competencies. The authors suggest that in order for the entrepreneur to ensure the competitiveness and survival of the firm they must set the direction for the company since it is often the entrepreneur/owner/manager of the SME that leads the strategic planning process. The entrepreneur also needs to be persistent and committed to the task in order to enhance the performance of the firm and motivate their employees through inspiration. Of course, one can argue that the same competencies and characteristics are present in the majority, if not all, of the high-performing firms, irrespective of their size. If we recall the definition by Schumpeter and Drucker on entrepreneurship, this makes good sense since entrepreneurship is not solely equated with new and small firms, but rather it constitutes an activity. The important point in this section though, as we also stressed above, is that the new, the micro and the small business that is most often created by an entrepreneur will be largely affected by their personality and organizational/management abilities. Goffee and Scase (1995), as well as Greiner (1972), argue the entrepreneurs might decide to keep their business small so that they can control it or they may decide or be forced to pursue a growing strategy. In the latter case, it is again the qualities of the entrepreneur that will play a decisive role in the future survival and growth of the company. If the entrepreneur decides to review their business and personal life strategies, delegate more authorities and responsibilities, the company may grow, otherwise it might fail.

Constraints on the Survival and Growth of SMEs

It is an abiding perception that SMEs compared with larger enterprises often face difficulty in surviving and growing. Authors like Storey (2000), Burns and Harrison (1996), argue that often the managers/owners of SMEs have difficulties in coping with the multiplicity of external and internal demands placed on them once the enterprise has grown in size. Moreover, they argue that failure is endemic to the small business sector especially during their first stages of establishment and growth.

We attempt to enhance our understanding of how SMEs operate in the business world by exploring and delineating the multiple and often interrelated obstacles that SMEs often face in today's economies that hinder their growth and prosperity, or even lead them to 'Chapter 11' (i.e. bankruptcy), according to management literature and extensive research studies. Because of the variety and complexity of some of the obstacles SMEs are facing, we shall explore in depth only the most important and relevant to the concepts of entrepreneurship, innovation and business clustering/networks, as found in management literature; that is, the *managerial deficiencies* and *entrepreneurial characteristics* and the *limited access to finance*.

Previously, we investigated the importance and the central role of the entrepreneur for the SME. It was argued that the personal characteristics of the entrepreneur would to a large degree affect the performance of the company, its survival and success. According to Burns and Harrison (1996), the personal characteristics and qualities of the entrepreneur/manager that can, on one hand lead a company to success can, on the other hand, lead it to failure. Storey (2000: 105) argues the following in his work in understanding the small business sector:

> It would appear that the owners of young firms were more likely to suffer from inadequate funding, poor products and inefficient marketing. As their companies aged, however, they are more likely to be buffeted by strategic and environmental shocks for which they did not have the managerial skills to respond.

Moreover, Burns and Harrison (1996) suggest that when the personal characteristics of the owner/manager of the company are problematic and interact with managerial deficiencies, they tend to produce weaknesses in the firm and potentially lead it to failure. The authors (1996: 69–70) provide a list, without further elaboration, of the personal characteristics and managerial deficiencies that could lead to failure of the SME, which are as follows:

PERSONAL CHARACTERISTICS

1. Exaggerated opinion of business competency based upon knowledge of some skill

2. Limited formal education

3. Inflexible to change and not innovate

4. Uses own personal taste and opinion as the standard to follow

5. Decisions based on intuition, emotion and non-objective factors

6. Past, not future, orientation

7. Little reading in literature associated with business

8. Resistance to advice from qualified sources but, paradoxically, accepts if from the least qualified.

MANAGERIAL DEFICIENCIES

1. Cannot identify target market or customers

2. Cannot delineate trading area

3. Cannot delegate

4. Believes advertising is an expense, not an investment

5. Only rudimentary knowledge of pricing strategy

6. Immature understanding of distribution channels

7. No planning

8. Cannot motivate

9. Believes the problem is somebody else's fault and a loan would solve everything.

Goffee and Scase (1995) emphasize in their work, *Corporate Realities*, that managers, scientists, professionals and other experts are attracted to entrepreneurship because of personal motives and usually the employment autonomy and independence, which they hope to enjoy. On the other hand, as we have discussed earlier in this chapter, as the company grows over the course of time it requires the adoption of new managerial and organizational practices that the entrepreneur might not be able to adopt, or they might be reluctant to relinquish to their personal control over the company. According to the authors, among traditional craft enterprises there is a reluctance to move beyond a size at which face-to-face managing and working is possible. In such a working environment, the owner/manager can have a direct control of staff and the company. To shift from this management style to adopting rules, procedures, delegation of authority and responsibility requires entrepreneurs to develop management competencies. It is in this stage that many of the new and small businesses fail to grow or survive, as Goffee and Scase (1995: 43–44) vividly point out in the following extract from a survey of small business owners:

> *Everybody says you've got to delegate but once you leave your hand off the button then your business will start sliding. The main thing is to be on top of it all the time, in touch with every section and really on the ball. If you get to the size where you have to delegate, you've got to work with the person involved so that his mind works like yours and he's totally trustworthy. Personally, I don't want to get to that size. I don't want to get to the point where I don't know where the money's coming from and how different jobs are going. I don't want to get to the stage where I have to take somebody else's word for how the job is going.*

Furthermore, Goffee and Scase explain that often in small businesses employers and employees work so closely with each other that they develop flexible and broadly defined skills, which complement each other and which enhance the overall performance of the company. In the process of business expansion, the restructuring of job specifications and relationships can create discomfort and low motivation in staff, also resentment and deterioration of trust relations between the employer and the employees as well as among colleagues. Many of the entrepreneurs according to the authors do not possess the necessary managerial skills and competencies to steer the business towards the fundamental changes in the nature and organization of their business practices. In such cases, the owner-manager will in due course become overloaded with strategic and operational matters, so that the business controls are neglected and the firm starts to face financial difficulties.

Goffee and Scase (1995) suggest still another category of entrepreneurs and business owners: the people with creative talents that usually have little desire to exercise control over other people. These professional, creative proprietors are more interested in exercising their personal talent and abilities to deliver state of the art professional, quality services or products and get personal recognition. These kinds of businesses are unlikely to have a business plan, since most of the time demand and expansion will be random and customer driven.

Business Constraints of SMEs

So far, in our analysis we are exploring some of the obstacles that start from within the SME, such as management deficiencies and entrepreneurial incompetence. It is an enduring perception of manager practitioners and policy makers around the world that SMEs often face economic, institutional and legal obstacles that are beyond their immediate influence. The Gallup Organisation (2007) conducted a survey, for the Eurobarometer team of the European Commission and the Observatory of European SMEs, on 16,339 SMEs from the 27 member states of the European Union: they asked small business owners to assess whether or not they had faced any of the business constraints over the period 2005–2007, as shown in the following table:

Table 5.1   Constraints on business performance of SMEs

Limited demand	46%
Problems with administrative regulations	36%
Lack of skilled labour	35%
Labour force too expensive	33%
Problems with infrastructure (e.g. roads, gas, electricity, communications, etc.)	23%
Limited access to finance	21%
Implementing new technology	17%
Implementing new forms of organization	16%
Lack of quality management	11%

Source: Gallup Organisation 2007: 16

The most important business constraint for 46 per cent of the European SMEs in the sample was the limiting purchasing power of consumers. Beyond the constraint of a limited demand, three problem areas emerged as affecting most European SMEs: problems with administrative regulations (36 per cent), the scarcity of skilled labour (35 per cent) and the increased cost of appropriate human resources for the firm (33 per cent). As shown in the table above, two more external (to the organization) variables, such as the infrastructure of a country (23 per cent) and the limited access to finance (21 per cent), acted as an obstacle to the growth of the SME and its survival.

Extensive empirical researches and theoretical views from influential scholars (Gallup Organization 2007, European Commission 2002, Storey 2000, Pissarides 1999, Burns and Dewhurst 1996) indicate that *access to finance* is one of the dominant obstacles to the growth and survivability of the SME. According to Pissarides (1999: 522) and the European Bank for Reconstruction and Development (EBRD):

> *SMEs are penalised moreover by the fact that in any type of economy they face higher rates on loan finance than their larger counterparts, partly because banks consider the credit risks applying to SMEs higher than those applying to larger firms, and partly because SMEs are generally unable to offer adequate collateral. Only those SMEs that were successful in identifying a niche in the market in which high returns could be obtained can afford to pay the high interest rates. The rest will rely on reinvested profits, reorient their products/markets, or die.*

6

Ethnic and Female Entrepreneurs and Small Business Owners

Ethnic Entrepreneurship[1]

Ethnic entrepreneurship appears nowadays in a variety of nations and cultural settings. Entrepreneurs from specific ethnic communities are a part of the business landscape in most countries of the world, attracting a good deal of scientific attention (Wauters and Lambrecht 2008, Morawska 2004, Ram and Smallbone 2003, Engelen, 2001). Enclaves of ethnic minority businesses (EMBs) can be found in the USA and other countries of the West (Portes and Shafer 2007). East Indians in Edison, New Jersey; Cubans in Miami; Koreans in Chicago and Los Angeles; and Chinese in San Francisco and Vancouver are among a new wave of immigrants who have turned to self-employment and entrepreneurship as a way of overcoming block mobility in the labour market, or as a key tool that has allowed them to carve a socially respectable and economically viable position in the host societies or as an affirmation of an ethnically specific inclination for entrepreneurship (Portes and Shafer 2007, Corsino and Soto 2005, Ram and Smallbone 2003, Hiebert 2002, Light 1972). Kloosterman and Rath (2001) argue that the immigrant entrepreneur may not come up with the introduction of a new product or service and make a profit out of it, but instead in much more modest ways they open up a business to serve, for instance Indian foods, to the white population:

> *I am a professional businessman, you fool, not a professional Pakistani.*
> *I make money, not gestures, commented a particularly ruthless ethnic*

1   The section on ethnic entrepreneurship is based on my paper: Piperopoulos P. 2010. Ethnic minority businesses and immigrant entrepreneurship in Greece. *Journal of Small Business and Enterprise Development*, 17(1), 139-158. The paper received the *Highly Commended Paper Award* at the Literati Network Awards for Excellence 2011, by Emerald Group Publishing Ltd.

entrepreneur in Hanif Kureishi's 'My Beautiful Launderette'. (Ram 1997: 149)

Ethnic entrepreneurship is widely considered a critical element in the structures of western economies and the revival of the small business population, while EMBs have demonstrated a remarkable increase in their numbers during the last two decades (Ram 2007, Engelen 2001, Teixeira 2001, Light and Karageorgis 1994). According to Heilman and Chen (2003), in 1998, 898,000 new firms were established – the highest number ever, representing a 1.5 per cent increase from 1997 (US Small Business Administration 1999). As the authors argue, from 1982 to 1998, the number of business tax returns filed in the USA increased by 73 per cent, totalling 24.8 million in 1998. During the same time-period (1982–1997), the number of businesses owned by ethnic groups more than doubled, reaching an estimated 3 million businesses, providing jobs to nearly 4.5 million workers and generating $591 billion in revenues. Furthermore, approximately 14 per cent of the labour force of 216 metropolitan areas investigated was employed in ethnic niches (Wilson 2003).

Basu and Altinay (2002) argue in their research that immigrant entrepreneurs own over 50 per cent of new business start-ups and 7 per cent of all small businesses in London. According to Basu (2004), it is estimated that over two-thirds of all worldwide businesses are owned or managed by families, while in the United States and Europe the percentage of family owned/managed businesses rises to 80 per cent. A recent survey by the Small Business Service (SBS, 2004) in the UK showed that in 2004 more than 250,000 small businesses were owned and operated by immigrant entrepreneurs, representing over 11 per cent of all new business start-ups.

Starting up an Ethnic Minority Small Business

It is an undisputable general assumption that the vast majority of immigrants leave their home countries in search of a better life for them, their families and their children (Singh and DeNoble 2004). A careful review of current ethnic entrepreneurship literature, however, suggests several different reasons for its appearance and development within an overall modern business and professional ethos. Indeed, there is much debate in literature about the self-employment entry motives and their business aspirations (Basu 2004, Kloosterman 2003, Phizacklea and Ram 1995). Entrepreneurship among immigrants may arise from lack of suitable labour market opportunities (especially due to language barriers and ethnic/race discrimination), desire to amass wealth and return to one's homeland, from business opportunities created by a growing community of co-ethnics, the potential for earnings advantage, upward social mobility in their host society, investment in family futures or as a result of an entrepreneurial cultural predilection, heritage and attitude (Singh and DeNoble 2004, Basu 2004, Sanders and Nee 1996, Phizacklea and Ram 1995, Zhou 1992, Aldrich and Waldinger 1990, Light 1972).

Ethnic entrepreneurs are generally described in the literature as sojourners who work harder, save money, spend less by living frugally, have preferential access to limited, low cost funding from family and community resources and use social networks to find market opportunities as well as cheap labour (Barrett et al. 1996). Scanning the pertinent literature on ethnicity and entrepreneurship, we identify and cluster four main approaches that contribute to the understanding of the process of starting up an ethnic minority business and becoming self-employed: (a) the cultural thesis, (b) the block mobility thesis, (c) the opportunity structures thesis and (d) the ethnic resources thesis.

THE CULTURAL THESIS

Ethnic entrepreneurs exhibit a strong trader's instinct and often migrate with the explicit goal of starting up a business in the host society, using extensively formal and informal networks and mechanisms (Wauters and Lambrecht 2008, Chaudhry and Crick 2004, Marger 2001, Morrison, 2000). In the *cultural thesis*, special skills, cultural predilection, personal motivations, values, attitudes, aspirations for achievement and heritage that the migrant entrepreneur brings to the host society are often translated into entrepreneurial activities and behaviour around particular business environments (Sriram et al. 2007, Corsino and Soto 2005, Singh and DeNoble 2004, Ram and Carter 2003, Morrison 2000, Boyd, 1998).

Extensive empirical evidence emphasizes that specific ethnic communities like Chinese, Koreans, Jews, South-Asians and Cubans establish and operate successful EMBs because of their particular cultural approach to entrepreneurship (Raijman and Tienda 2003, Ram 1997, Light and Bonacich 1988, Light 1972, 1985). According to the cultural thesis, traditional values and socio-cultural backgrounds of immigrant/ethnic entrepreneurs explain not only differences in the self-employment rates among immigrant entrepreneurs and the native population but also differences among minority groups themselves (Teixeira 2001, Light and Bonacich 1988, Waldinger 1986, Light 1972). In addition, ethnic minorities who had been self-employed or at least had some previous experience and training in small businesses in their countries of origin are usually more inclined towards self-employment (Basu and Altinay 2002, Hammarstedt 2001).

THE BLOCK MOBILITY THESIS

In the *block mobility thesis*, ethnic groups who are disadvantaged in the labour market due to racial discrimination, negative events, low education and qualifications, redundancy, underpaid salaried work or language difficulty concentrate their entrepreneurial activities into marginal niches in the economy that help their members not only to overcome such barriers but also to provide them with an avenue of upward social mobility (Wauters and Lambrecht 2008, Chaudhry and Crick 2004, Kontos 2003, Kloosterman 2003, Basu and Altinay 2002, Hammarstedt 2001, Basu and Goswami 1999, Light, 1972).

Immigrant individuals may encounter negative experiences within traditional organizational settings, cultural barriers that block their advancement in mainstream economic markets that may push them out of organizations and channel them into entrepreneurship as an alternate route to personal success and economic prosperity (Ram 2007, Hussain and Matlay 2007, Ram and Carter 2003, Heilman and Chen 2003, Teixeira 2001, Barrett et al. 1996). Despite the efforts of corporations around the world to provide access for immigrants through recruitment programs and policies, ethnic workers often are not placed (if they are accepted at all by employers) in visible and demanding jobs that provide them with an opportunity to advance up the corporate hierarchy, nor are they given on-the-job training to build new skills (Sriram et al. 2007, Heilman and Chen 2003). These disadvantaged groups are forced to accept whatever residual jobs are available once groups higher up in the queue have made their selection (Chaudhry and Crick 2004, Wilson 2003).

Phizacklea and Ram (1995) argue that racial discrimination factors push immigrants towards self-employment, since the most often stated reasons for setting up EMBs in France and Britain were cited as: difficulties in securing employment and limited opportunities to find any work. Heilman and Chen (2003) quote in their work that in comparison to whites, blacks receive lower ratings on both relationship and task components of performance and receive less encouraging appraisals for promoting purposes from supervisors. Hence, entrepreneurship, according to the block mobility thesis, is seen principally as an escape route from unemployment, low wages or restrained labour market opportunities (Sriram et al. 2007, Singh and DeNoble 2004, Kloosterman 2003, Hammarstedt 2001, Teixeira 2001). Entrepreneurship and self-employment holds the promise that individuals' career achievement will depend on their own qualities and efforts, and not on the prejudice of others in the corporate work setting, while it will also be a route of assimilation and a way of making it in the host country (Wauters and Lambrecht 2008, Constant and Shachmurove 2006, Heilman and Chen 2003, Razin 2002).

THE OPPORTUNITY STRUCTURES THESIS

In the *opportunity structures thesis*, immigrant entrepreneurs who have knowledge of the specific needs and heritage of their co-ethnic consumers are allured to entrepreneurship and self-employment by moving into niche, saturated spatial markets that require low financial or human capital, and are largely ignored by mass retailing enterprises due to security problems or low purchasing power of the unattractive and poorer minority areas (Sriram et al. 2007, Raijman and Tienda 2003, Barrett et al. 2001, Iyer and Shapiro 1999, Ram 1997).

Cultural-based tastes for particular goods and services (e.g., ethnic food products) generate special consumer demands and entrepreneurial opportunities that mostly merchants from a particular ethnic group can satisfy, due to the inside knowledge that the group has (Wauters and Lambrecht 2008, Jamal 2005, Singh and DeNoble 2004, Basu and Altinay 2002, Hammarstedt 2001, Boyd 1998).

The opportunity structures thesis argues that immigrants usually create enclaves by concentrating in specific geographic areas which provide opportunities for EMBs to act as a training system for the young ethnic entrepreneurs, generate network linkages and informal communications of market opportunities and an evolving cadre of ethnic business institutions (Chaudhry and Crick 2004, Hammarstedt 2001, Basu and Goswami 1999, Light 1972). According to relevant research these EMBs which show a preference for ethnic enclaves focus on low-order retailing, services, the garment industry, catering, grocery stores, confectioners, newsagents and tobacconists and other low-rewarding sectors of the economy (Ram et al. 2003, Rath 2002). Immigrant entrepreneurs usually avoid the mainstream market and focus on ethnic, closed markets that exhibit minimum interethnic competition, are characterized by import/export and retail of ethnic goods or where governmental policies favour small business development (Corsino and Soto 2005, Singh and DeNoble 2004).

THE ETHNIC RESOURCES THESIS

In the *ethnic resources thesis*, social capital provides a vital and reliable source of labour (low cost and highly committed workforce) for EMBs, access to training, credit and capital, valuable market and business information about opportunities and threats that would otherwise be inaccessible (due to time and resource limitations) to immigrant entrepreneurs (Deakins et al. 2007, Fong et al. 2005, Raijman and Tienda 2003, Marger 2001, Park 1997, Sanders and Nee 1996, Light 1984). In fact several scholars suggest that ethnic entrepreneurs (Asians, Koreans, Chinese, Japanese and Cubans, among others) make use of extensive networks of identity, family and community resources (in other words, ethnic social capital) to acquire business information and inside knowledge of market opportunities that facilitate business start-ups (Sriram et al. 2007, Fong et al.2005, Chaudhry and Crick 2004, Raghuram and Hardill 1998, Sanders and Nee 1996, Portes and Sensenbrenner 1993, Aldrich and Waldinger 1990, Light and Bonacich 1988, Light, 1972).

Ethnic resources (i.e,. social ties/networks, kinship, family, ethnic communities) are vital at the business start-up phase, when immigrant entrepreneurs need to gain access to scarce financial and human resources, especially in the absence or insufficiency of external sources (Deakins et al., 2007, Singh and DeNoble 2004, Galbraith 2004, Jan Nederveen 2003, Raijman and Tienda 2003, Ram and Carter 2003, Ram et al. 2003, Light and Bonacich 1988). In several pieces of research scholars suggest that, in their majority, EMBs have never used or had access to any forms of business and financial support from banks and other financial institutions and hence had to rely on personal savings and ethnic social resources (Hussain and Matlay 2007, Ram and Carter 2003, Ram et al. 2003, Ram and Smallbone 2003a, Smallbone et al. 2003, Barrett et al. 2002).

Economic and social niches in the host society provide immigrants' self-employment opportunities (through social networking and family ties) and more unprejudiced compensation than immigrants who work in local enterprises and industries (Marger 2001, Waldinger 1996). Immigrant workers employed in EMBs can gradually acquire the necessary skills, experience and capital to secure their living in the local community (Waldinger 1999).

A further review of the pertinent literature suggests that ethnic businesses are, in their majority, owned and managed by members of a single family (Basu and Goswami 1999, Iyer and Shapiro 1999). Family background plays a two-fold role in entrepreneurship. First, the new-entrepreneur has previous experience of the effect of entrepreneurship from his/her own family and second, family support (capital and human) can be critical to the creation, sustenance and development of EMBs (Basu 2004, Deakins 1996).

The following table summarizes the main arguments for the four theories, explored above, which contribute to the understanding of self-employment entry motives and aspirations of ethnic small business owners/entrepreneurs.

Table 6.1   Four theories for the development and appearance of ethnic entrepreneurship

The cultural thesis	• Explicit goal of migration for ethnic entrepreneurs is to start up a business in the host society. • Special skills, cultural predilection, personal motivations, values, attitudes, aspirations for achievement and heritage are translated to entrepreneurial activities. • Ethnic minority entrepreneurs have previous experience in entrepreneurship/self-employment in their countries of origin.
The block mobility thesis	• Negative experiences and cultural barriers block immigrants' advancement in mainstream economic markets. • 'Push' towards entrepreneurship due to racial discrimination. • Entrepreneurship is an escape route from unemployment, low wages or restrained labour market opportunities.
The opportunity structures thesis	• Immigrants have the knowledge of the specific needs and heritage of their co-ethnic consumers. • Establish small businesses into niche, saturated spatial markets that require low financial or human capital. • Cultural-based tastes for particular goods and services (e.g., ethnic food products). • Import/export and retail of ethnic goods. • Small businesses act as a training system for the young ethnic entrepreneurs; generate network linkages and informal communications of market opportunities.
The ethnic resources thesis	• Ethnic entrepreneurs make use of extensive networks of identity, family and community resources to acquire business information and inside knowledge of market opportunities. • Immigrants most of the times have to rely on ethnic social resources and personal savings at the start-up phase. • Ethnic businesses are, in their majority, owned and managed by members of a single family.

A Combination of Push and Pull Towards Self-Employment

According to my research (Piperopoulos 2010), the three theories of 'block mobility', 'opportunity structures' and 'ethnic resources' complement each other in explaining the process of starting up an ethnic minority business and becoming self-employed, while the 'cultural thesis' seems to stand on its own.

As my research brings forth, an immigrant entrepreneur is pushed to self-employment due to race discrimination or restricted opportunities to work, but once he reaches the decision to establish an EMB, he will then rely on ethnic resources (human and/or capital), employ family members and use inside knowledge to spot an opportunity in the business landscape. On the other hand, an ethnic entrepreneur is pulled to entrepreneurship by an opportunity he sees to serve a specific consumer demand (e.g., ethnic foods or retail/wholesale of ethnic products). However, this entrepreneur will also use ethnic resources and family support even after they have established an EMB, while at the same time, this kind of an entrepreneur also reported that they were unsatisfied by the low-paid, limited career advancement jobs. Hence, in a way these entrepreneurs are both pulled and pushed towards self-employment.

The findings of my research also revealed a small percentage (less than one out of ten) of immigrants that have cultural predilections towards entrepreneurship and who will most likely seek finance, rely less on family support and participation and probably start up a scientific/artistic/professional EMB (e.g., IT shops, accountant services, educational services, etc.). These entrepreneurs have different motives and aspirations towards becoming self-employed and usually have higher education training than their co-ethnic or other immigrant entrepreneurs.

Female Entrepreneurs

Despite the general thrust towards entrepreneurship and self-employment, as we have been discussing so far in this book, the research and dissemination of information and scientific knowledge about female entrepreneurship has not kept pace with the impact these self-employed women appear to have had on economies. Small firms owned by women entrepreneurs are a growing phenomenon in today's world economies. Female entrepreneurs in the USA increased from 1.5 million in 1972 (nearly 4.6 per cent of all businesses) to 2.1 million in 1979, 3.5 million in 1985, 9.1 million in 1999 and climbed to 10.1

million firms (almost 37 per cent all businesses), employing 13 million people and generating $1.9 trillion in revenue in 2008 (Petridou et al. 2009, Greene et al. 2003). Furthermore, it is estimated that female entrepreneurs account for 25 per cent of all businesses from Asian economies to Eastern European economies, around a third of all businesses in the UK and 26 per cent in France (Sarri and Trihopoulou 2005, Fielden et al. 2003, Orhan and Scott 2001, Jalbert 2000).

Scanning the pertinent literature on female entrepreneurship, the primary focus of the majority of research reports and scientific articles is on the motives and reasons women have for establishing new ventures: their education background and previous experiences; their personal characteristics; business networking and performance, as well as the barriers they face in the start-up phase; and the access to initial funding (Benschop and Essers 2007, Martin and Wright 2005, Hisrich and Drnovsek 2002, Carter et al. 2001, Aldrich 1989).

PERSONAL ATTRIBUTES

Educational and professional experiences play a significant role in shaping women's attitudes towards self-employment. Their inclination towards human and social sciences and liberal arts, as well as their previous work experience (usually in the private sector) influences the way women embark upon entrepreneurial activities and mostly propels them towards traditional service professions, retail and trade (Brush 1992, Hisrich and Brush 1983, 1984). Investigating the relevant literature on female entrepreneurship, we conclude that the average, self-employed woman is between the ages of 35 and 54, is married with children, has prior work experience in the private sector and a college degree, or at least high school level education (Weeks 2001, Devine 1994).

MOTIVATIONS

Empirical research on the subject of female-owned small businesses seems to validate, equally, pull as well as push reasons that lead women towards entrepreneurial activities. Women reported positive pull reasons to start up a business such as: looking for job satisfaction and a personal challenge; independence; a need for achievement; flexibility between their personal and family life; and freedom on how they manage and control their time and making their own decisions (Carter et al., 2001, Shabbir and Di Gregorio 1996, Ljunggren and Kolvereid 1996, Scott 1986, Schwartz 1976). On the other hand, push reasons such as: the need to generate more income for the family; become independent from their spouses; divorce or relocation; death of a family member; dissatisfaction with a previous employer; and inequality or low wage earnings are equally important in explaining why women set up a business (Weeks 2001, Boden 1999).

INITIAL FINANCING

Early research on female entrepreneurs suggested that they might encounter credit discrimination during the initial capital accumulation process and funding for their business, since lending institutions perceived women to have less chances of success than their male colleagues (Buttner and Rosen 1988, Hisrich and O'Brien 1981, Schwartz 1976). Access to capital during the 1980s was identified as a major obstacle to female entrepreneurship. In more recent and larger scale comparative researches, gender discrimination in accessing start-up capital could not be confirmed. Studies in Canada and Holland found no significant differences in the proportion of capital females and males can acquire from banks and small business supporting institutions (Verheul and Thurik 2001, Haines et al. 1999). Furthermore, Coleman's (2000) research of 4,500 respondents concerning possible differences by lenders and banks to male and female entrepreneurs revealed no signs of gender biased access obstacles in obtaining loans and start-up capital.

SOCIAL NETWORKS

The initial decision to set up a business and mobilize the necessary resources, get support and develop a business relies largely on the informal sources and the personal network that the entrepreneur has. Empirical results for female entrepreneurial networking activities are not conclusive and it has yet to be confirmed if these informal networks are actually effective in affecting women's decision to turn to self-employment (McManus 2001, Carter et al. 2001, Greve 1995). Aldrich et al. (1989) suggest that women's networks are organized around their family, their work and their social life. Research in Northern Ireland provides some evidence that male and female entrepreneurs rely more or less on similar types of networks, while in a Hong Kong-based study the findings revealed that female business owners value network information for their entrepreneurial aspirations more than their male colleagues (Chan and Foster 2001, Cromie and Birley 1992).

Need for More Research and Support

Despite an admitted lack of theories, knowledge and statistical data from both academic research studies and national and international research and policy bodies on female entrepreneurship, in the last two decades women-owned businesses are increasingly becoming a significant part of local and national economies:

> *According to the available data, between one-quarter and one-third of the formal sector businesses are owned and operated by women. In the USA 38 per cent of businesses are owned by women (1999), in Finland, 34 per cent (1990), in Australia (1994) and Canada (1996), 33 per cent, in Korea, 32 per cent (1998) and in Mexico, 30 per cent (1997). (Levent et al. 2003: 1134)*

One of the key conclusions of the European Forum of Female Entrepreneurship was the immediate need to stimulate and support female entrepreneurship, as well as the need to carry out research that would provide data which is more reliable and on a greater scale than the current, limited qualitative research (Sarri and Trihopoulou 2005, European Commission 2003).

7

Business Networks, Strategic Alliances, Open Innovation and the SME

World Wide Web and the SME

The reasons behind our investigation and presentation of some of the most common characteristics of SMEs, as found in literature and research studies, derives both from the need to set up the theoretical framework for SMEs, as stated at the beginning of this second part of the book, and the need to introduce, explore and suggest how and why networks, co-operative alliances and other forms of co-operation can enhance the innovative abilities of SMEs and their competitiveness. This becomes particularly significant in the era of information and communication technologies and the increased internationalization of competition. In the last section of this chapter we bring forth the concept of open innovation which, in the last few years, has been proposed as a new paradigm for the management of innovation.

In the era of the Internet boom, Dierckx and Stroeken (1999) studied the relationship between information technology and innovation in SMEs on behalf of the Dutch Council for Small and Medium-Sized Enterprises. Amongst other findings, the authors argue that information and communication technology (ICT) can lead to new organizational structures which are flatter and more flexible and also to new forms of labour such as teleworking, freelance work and other new, independent and mobile forms of work. Thus, in the ever increasing competitiveness and internationalization of the market place, information and communication technologies, if ignored, may become a significant threat to a company. In contrast, the same ICT in the hands of a firm that knows how to anticipate and use them can prove to be valuable opportunities for growth and survival.

Moreover, the advent of the World Wide Web and electronic businesses during the first decade of the twenty-first century, as one would expect, opened up new perspectives for SMEs as it made electronic communication affordable to even the smallest of companies. Companies can send and receive electronic data interchange (EDI) messages to customers and suppliers through the Internet, or via emails and they can also distribute and share information to the parties of interest (for example customers) through web pages (Stefansson 2002).

The most common information and communication technologies used by SMEs are, according to the European Commission (2002), mobile phones, stand-alone PCs, network of PCs, email and electronic data interchange, intranet, Internet connection and an own websites. A size-class pattern in the percentage share of SMEs that are using various types of ICT emerged from this research. Microenterprises (0–9 employees) seem to be slower or more reluctant in adopting ICT. According to the European Commission (2002), nearly 30 per cent of microenterprises do not have an Internet connection, and another 41 per cent do not even have a stand-alone PC. Moreover, only about 17 per cent are using intranet and 37 per cent have their own website. On the other hand, larger SMEs seem to extensively use ICT, as 75 per cent have their own websites, 92 per cent have an Internet connection and nearly 90 per cent have PCs and an installed network within the company.

Despite the obvious size-class pattern, it is interesting to note that microenterprises seem to be rapidly catching up with the rest of the SMEs, at least as far as access to the Internet is concerned. According to the European Commission (2002), during the year 1999, only 40 per cent of microenterprises had access to the World Wide Web, while in the year 2001, the figure had risen to 70 per cent. Furthermore, the large differences that existed between the different sectors of the economy in 1999 (the survey involved the following sectors: manufacturing, construction, wholesale, retail, transportation/ communication, business services and personal services) have considerably reduced. In 2001, nearly 70 per cent of SMEs in all sectors had access to the Internet, while business services scored considerably higher, reaching more than 80 per cent of enterprises having access.

The increasing number of SMEs connecting to the World Wide Web every year is a clear indication that they understand the need to use that form of ICT as effectively and as efficiently as possible to increase their competitiveness. Around 65–75 per cent of SMEs use the Internet for distribution of information on products, but even more important to note, about 40 per cent use it to receive orders and another 17 per cent to deliver their products to their customers (European Commission 2002).

After what has been said for SMEs in the preceding pages, the question that now arises is how can SMEs become more competitive and, furthermore, how can they survive the internationalization of business activities, also attributed to the advent of ICT? Should SMEs and, consequently, their entrepreneurs and/or managers proceed to alter their strategic orientation and organizational policies towards co-operative agreements and strategic alliances? And if so, what would be the reasons? In the following pages, we attempt a first glance at how business networks, strategic alliances and the open innovation paradigm can affect the competitiveness of SMEs and their innovative capabilities. We establish a theoretical framework to function as a springboard for the investigation and presentation of the concepts of industrial districts, networks and business clusters that are the primary focus of evaluation and analysis in Part 3 of this book.

The Evolution and Internationalization of Competition

This part of the chapter starts with the introduction of the concept of the evolution of competition and how it affects SMEs' operations and competitiveness. We then discuss the emerging ways for an SME to retain its competitiveness and address the issues of *networking, strategic alliances* and *collaborations* between enterprises as well as *open innovation*. Furthermore, we explore the historical roots of business networks and strategic alliances, and attempt to explain why companies, particularly SMEs, should engage themselves in such activities and pursue co-operative strategies, which will positively affect their innovative performance and competitiveness.

The concept of *evolution of competition* describes the escalating internationalization of business activities. For example, the unification of 17 out of the 27 member states of the European Union under a single monetary unit (and new legalization) opened up markets for enterprising member states that now have the possibility to compete and seek opportunities not only within the limits of their countries but also into the unified European market. On the other hand, internationalization poses several threats for the companies that have to realize now that competition could strike not only from other companies located in a certain geographical proximity but potentially from any company operating in the EU. Internationalization or, as otherwise stated, globalization is the evolution of competition. According to Castro et al. (2000), globalization released firms from physical and geographical constraints and from national regulatory frameworks. The authors (2000: 193) suggest that globalization is the outcome of three main processes:

1.   The substantial decline of transport costs.

2.   The rapid development of telematics, which is the combination and joint development of telecommunication and information technologies.

3.   The gradual removal of barriers to trade and to the circulation of capital.

Narula and Hagedoorn (1999) refer to globalization as the increasing similarity in consumption and income levels across countries and the simultaneous increase in cross-border activities of enterprises from these countries. The authors suggest that globalization is mainly associated with the triad of the industrialized countries, the USA, Europe and Japan, and that its effects vary across industries and is particularly heightened in sectors that are capital and knowledge intensive, as well as in sectors that depend on fast evolving technologies.

The internationalization of competition is strongly illustrated in the survey results of the Gallup Organization (2007) for the European Commission and the Observatory of European SMEs. According to the results (2002), 60 per cent of the managers of SMEs stated that competition has intensified during the two year period, 2005–2007. The perception of increased competition is most widespread among SMEs in trade (65 per cent), transportation/logistics/communication (65 per cent) and the financial (64 per cent) sectors.

In response to the intensified competition, SMEs' managers were asked to outline their strategies for coping with the tighter competition, as shown in the table below.

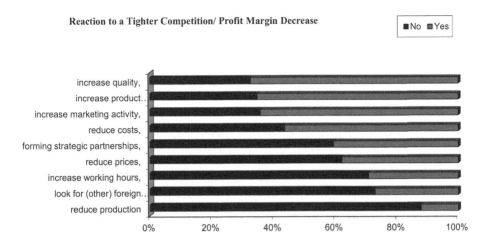

Figure 7.1   Reaction to a tighter competition/profit margin decrease
Source: Gallup Organization 2007: 63

According to the figures, the primary strategy for SMEs in the EU is to put more effort in to the quality of their products/services (64 per cent) and increase product differentiation and look for market niches (62 per cent). In response to the tighter competition, 61 per cent would increase marketing efforts and 53 per cent would cut costs. The fifth solution/strategy adopted by SMEs to overcome the intensified competition is to form alliances with other companies (38 per cent).

INTERNET AND ELECTRONIC MARKETS

The soaring power of computer technology has spawned powerful communication networks that organizations can use to access vast storehouses of information from around the world and to co-ordinate activities across space and time. The world's largest and most widely used network is the Internet. The Internet is becoming the foundation for new business models, new business processes and new ways of distributing knowledge. Traditional firms are finding they can use the Internet to organize suppliers, manage production and deliver to customers. Internally, companies can use the Internet and networking technology to conduct more of their work electronically, seamlessly linking factories, offices and sales forces around the globe. The Internet has created a universal platform for buying and selling goods. This digital integration both within the firm and outside, from the warehouse to the executive suite and from suppliers to customers is changing the organization and management of business firms.

As early as the beginning of the 1990s, the Internet was fundamentally changing the worldwide patterns of commerce:

> *In 1994, Ford announced that it was merging all its activities, distributed among 30 countries, into a single global operation. It electronically merged its seven automotive design centres on four continents. Ford developed its world car and split vehicle development by vehicle type, not geographic market. At about the same time, IBM reorganised itself by industry type, instead of geography ... large companies are shifting from being geographically specific and product diversified to being product specific and geographically diversified. (Martin 1996: 17)*

According to Laudon and Laudon (2001), the Internet has internationalized the business world and marketplace. The Internet is creating new ways of conducting business electronically since it is providing the underlying technology for it. The Internet can link thousands of organizations into a single network, creating vast electronic marketplaces. An electronic market links together numerous buyers and sellers, producers and customers to exchange information, knowledge, products and services and payments. As the authors argue, through computers and the Internet, the typical marketplace transactions such as selecting suppliers, establishing prices, ordering goods and paying bills have lowered costs and increased speed. The transactions are made electronically regardless of the location of the suppliers, the buyers, the company and the customers and so on.

The Internet has allowed in great part for the internationalization of competition. In the traditional sense of a marketplace, typically geographically oriented, corporations knew who their competition was. In today's Internet market, much unexpected competition can come from anywhere because it depends on knowledge that can be transmitted anywhere and because of the elimination of national boundaries. The Internet is used to find the lowest possible price of goods and services, to link cheap labour countries to western societies, to use low salary designers, educated workers and experts from around the globe in order to create competitive advantages for the company.

Business Networks and Strategic Alliances

One of the policy approaches to improving the industrial competitiveness and innovation of small and medium-sized enterprises (SMEs) is that this can be accelerated through inter-firm collaboration (Piperopoulos 2007). High costs of new product, market and technology development may act as barriers to the innovative capabilities and performance of small firms (Aaboen et al. 2006). When SMEs share competencies and knowledge it becomes possible to tackle jobs that no single SME could tackle alone. In the best cases, the assembly of core competencies from different SMEs enables them to build a team of organizations and individuals who together have the highest level capabilities and to collaborate and compete in markets that they would be unable to pursue if they operated solely and independently. Networks provide firms with access to knowledge, resources, markets and technologies (Inkpen and Tsang 2005). This is increasingly essential for excellent competition and innovation.

As we have discussed in the previous part of this chapter, today's networks, the Internet, video conferencing and computerized tools make possible flexible but tightly coupled linkages between corporations. Companies are increasingly using information systems and the Internet for strategic advantage by entering into strategic alliances with other companies in which both firms co-operate by sharing resources or services. Such alliances are often information partnerships in which two or more firms share data for mutual advantage. They can join forces without actually merging:

> American Airlines has an arrangement with Citibank to award one mile in its frequent flier program for every dollar spent using Citibank credit cards. American benefits from increased customer loyalty, whereas Citibank gains new credit card subscribers and a highly creditworthy customer base for cross marketing. (Laudon and Laudon 2001: 60)

Some companies are extending their enterprise systems beyond the boundaries of the firm to share information and co-ordinate business processes with other firms in their industry. Industrial or business networks link together the enterprise system of firms in an entire industry. Internet technology has fuelled the growth of industrial and business networks because it provides a platform where systems from different companies can seamlessly exchange information. According to Laudon and Laudon (2001: 91):

> *Procter & Gamble (P&G) the world's largest consumer goods company has been developing an integrated industry-wide system that coordinates the grocery store point-of-sale systems with grocery store warehouses, shippers, its own manufacturing facilities, and its supplier or raw materials. This single industry-spanning system effectively allows P&G to monitor the movement of all its processes from raw materials to customer purchase. Typically, there are two kinds of industrial networks. Vertically organised industrial networks as the one just described and horizontally organised industrial networks that link firms across an entire industry. For example, General Motors, Ford and Daimler-Chrysler created a common Internet purchasing system to help them obtain parts and other goods on-line from suppliers, in order to reduce costs and save time from their cooperation.*

Strategic alliances are increasingly gaining favour over go-it-alone strategies for organizations in order for them to achieve fast economical growth (Hoffmann and Schlosser, 2001). The new competition, according to Rosenfeld (1996), is among alliances of firms and not among individual firms. According to the literature and empirical studies (Hoffmann and Schlosser 2001, Narula and Hagedoorn 1999, Prabhu 1999), co-operative alliances are particularly acute in sectors that are capital and knowledge intensive, as well as in sectors that depend on fast evolving technologies. The scholars suggest that this phenomenon is most prominent in industrial sectors where new product developments are high and where access to new technology is vital. Prabhu (1999), for example, argues that 60 per cent of Japanese firms expected to be highly dependent on external technology sources and half of the major US firms are expected to increase their participation in joint ventures and alliances primarily for access to new technology. Moreover, Hoffmann and Schlosser (2001) suggest that alliances are most important manoeuvres in industries like information and communication technologies, manufacturing and trade and services.

Small Firms Networks

Before the evolution of competition as described earlier and the advancement of ICT, the case of inter-firm collaboration, which could be assigned the role of catalyst, was noted, among other places, in Europe and specifically in northern Italy in the 1970s where it was common for small, artisan firms to band together and to stake out remarkable strong market positions, even in traditional industrial markets. These family-owned manufacturing companies owe much of their success to their interdependencies, collective vision, tightknit infrastructure of trade and business associations and membership service centres as Rosenfeld (1996) points out. Perrow (1992: 455–456) identifies the Small Firms Network (SNF) accordingly:

> *The firms are usually very small – say 10 people. They interact with one another, sharing information, equipment, personnel, and orders, even as they compete with one another. They are supplied by a smaller number of business service firms (business surveys, technical training, personnel administration, transport, research and development, etc.) and financial firms. There are, of course, suppliers of equipment, energy, consumables, and so on, as well as raw material suppliers. Finally, while producers may do their own marketing and distribution, it is more common for there to be a fair number of quite small distributors, which is especially striking because SFNs typically export most of their output. The small firms are surrounded by an infrastructure that is essential for their survival and for their economies of network scale: local and regional government provides roads, cheap land, educational services, and even financing; trade associations provide economic information, training, financing, and marketing services; and both of these along with unions monitor unfair business and labour practices. SFNs do not exist in heavy industry or extractive industry, and in final assemble for large goods such as autos we have the nondependent subcontracting form rather than a true SFN. SFNs are said to exist in clothing, food, light machinery, electronics and small-to-medium-sized electronic goods, ceramics, furniture, auto components, motorcycles, small engines, machine tools, robots, textile and packaging machinery, mining equipment, industrial filters, and agricultural machinery. But it is not clear from the literature that in all cases networks of small firms are involved, though networks exist in most … a well-known example would include the textile firms in Prato and Modena in Northern Italy.*
> *(Perrow, 1992: 455–456)*

The success of the noted co-operation amongst a variety of northern Italy firms soon forced governments in many other countries to adopt the underlying environment and the infrastructure that was necessary for encouraging co-operation between SMEs. According to Rosenfeld (1996), in 1989 the Danish Technological Institute developed a programme that was immediately adopted by the Ministry of Trade and Industry that was based on three features:

1.   Training programmes for people that would facilitate co-operative ventures and for people that would identify opportunities.

2.   Publicity campaign.

3.   Encouragement of three or more firms to co-operate in the design, development and implementation of activities by providing them the necessary funds.

According to the author, Denmark has created what has nowadays been commonly accepted as the international term for these kinds of *co-operation networks*. The author goes on to suggest that the Denmark case, in conjunction with the Italian case, inspired other countries such as Spain, the United Kingdom and Portugal to implement similar programmes for SMEs' networking. In fact, in Europe, several government agencies and private foundations have since experimented with and consistently tried to support, stimulate and accelerate different forms of inter-firm collaboration, or as otherwise stated business networks. The assumption behind such efforts and programmes is that co-operative behaviour will help SME firms to first survive in their market place, innovate through collaborative research and development projects and shared knowledge, and then successfully compete with larger enterprises.

According to Goffee and Scase (1995), the aim in the business world is to combine operational efficiency and cost effectiveness, attributes commonly associated with large-scale organizations, with flexibility, responsiveness and innovation, characteristics conventionally linked with smaller enterprises. The ideal for the authors (1995: 159) is to achieve global organization and local responsiveness simultaneously:

> Networks are faster, smarter and more flexible than reorganisations or downsizing ... in effect, a network identifies the 'small company inside the large company' and empowers it to make the four-dimensional trade-offs – among functions, business, units, geography and global customers – that determine success in the marketplace.

The authors argue that organizations are, or at least should be, focusing upon areas of core strength and competence and spinning off, outsourcing and subcontracting all other activities. In this business network, organizational changes and strategies will depend on forming alliances and empowering relations with small businesses that would form a constellation around the core enterprise where boundaries are ambiguously defined and constantly shifting.

Hoffmann and Schlosser's Strategic Alliance Theory

Co-operation has been studied from a number of different perspectives. According to Hoffmann and Schlosser (2001: 358–359), the three most prominent theories that explain the potential reasons for an SME to form a co-operative alliance are:

1. The *transaction cost* theory recommends choosing the organizational mode that minimizes the sum of fixed and continual transaction costs. In the case of medium-asset specificity, alliances are considered the most transaction-cost-efficient organizational form.

2. The *resource-based* view of the firm explains firms as bundles of resources, that is, of all assets and capabilities a company possesses. From this perspective, alliances arise when a firm needs additional resources that cannot be purchased via market transaction and cannot be built internally with acceptable cost (risk) or within an acceptable amount of time.

3. According to the emerging *knowledge-based* theory of inter-firm collaboration, alliances provide the best context for creating value by exchanging or combining dispersed knowledge. Firms that face high environmental uncertainty especially can utilize alliances to enhance and speed organizational learning, reshape their environment and reduce strategic uncertainty.

In their study, Hoffmann and Schlosser (2001) examined several attributes of the strategic alliances of SMEs in the Austrian economy. According to the authors, more than 99 per cent of Austrian companies are SMEs, which represents the typical structure of any western type of economy. These companies represent almost 60 per cent of the total turnover of all Austrian companies and employ more than 65 per cent of all workers. In Austria SMEs needed to adjust to the market conditions and competitive situations, particularly due to the unification of the European Union and the globalization of markets. From an initial random sample of 1000 SMEs, only 164 responded, of which 70 were engaged in a co-operative alliance. The following tables describe the most important attributes of the analyzed companies.

Table 7.1   Attributes of companies

Industry sector		Number of employees		Management	
Commerce	35.7%	1–9	2.85%	Run by owners	72%
Trade	31.4%	10–99	54.3%	Run by professionals	28%
Manufacturing	20.0%	100–500	42.9%		
Services	12.9%				

Source: Hoffmann and Schlosser 2001: 366

Table 7.2   Field of co-operation, objectives and configuration types

Field of co-operation (more than one field of co-operation could be stated)		Objectives (more than one objective could be stated)		Configuration type	
Sales and logistics	74.3%	Market entry	76.8%	Contractual alliances	44.3%
Production	42.9%	Cost reduction	72.5%	Joint ventures	32.9%
Procurement	35.7%	Access to new technologies	46.4%	Minority shareholding	12.9%
Administration	28.6%	Risk diversification	21.7%	Other	9.9%
R&D	21.4%				

Source: Hoffmann and Schlosser 2001: 367

Even though the authors did not use the definitions of SMEs as proposed by the European Commission, a clear size-pattern emerges. Only 2.85 per cent of microenterprises were involved in strategic alliances, while for small and medium-sized enterprises the percentage was about 50 per cent. Moreover, the attributes identified, for example, cost reduction, R&D, access to new knowledge, and so on, are in line with the three theories outlined earlier for the reasons an SME could enter into a co-operative alliance.

As explained earlier, governments in the majority of the European Union member states are developing policy schemes, training and funding programmes to induce SMEs to establish alliances in order to overcome their resource shortages and increase their viability in these difficult and competitive times. Inter-firm collaborations, such as strategic alliances and joint ventures, have become important management instruments that SMEs adopt, or should adopt, to improve their competitiveness and innovative capabilities by providing access to external resources, providing synergies and fostering knowledge sharing, learning and creative change, the prerequisites to innovation. Alliances bridge the gap, according to Hoffmann and Schlosser (2001), between the firm's present resources and its expected future requirements.

The Open Innovation Paradigm

> *Companies that don't innovate die. This is not news. In the current environment, however, to innovate effectively, you increasingly must innovate openly. (Chesbrough 2006: xiii)*

Since the seminal work of Henry Chesbrough in 2003, *open innovation* has been proposed as a new paradigm for the management of innovation and has emerged as one of the most debated topics in innovation and management research and literature (Chesbrough 2003; Christensen et al. 2005; Gassmann 2006). It is defined as the use of, 'purposive inflows and outflows of knowledge to accelerate innovation and to expand the markets for external use of innovation, respectively' (Chesbrough et al. 2006: 1). According to Chesbrough and Growther (2006), open innovation has two dimensions:

1. *Inbound open innovation* refers to the acquisition and transfer of external technologies, ideas and knowledge into the firm through, for example, R&D contracts, university collaborations, in-licensing, mergers and acquisitions, and so on.

2. *Outbound open innovation* refers to the transfer of technology, ideas and knowledge to external firms and their commercial exploitation through, for example, out-licensing, joint ventures, venture spin-outs, and so on.

In 2003, Henry Chesbrough coined the term *'open innovation'* to describe an emerging shift in innovation paradigms from closed/secret, in-house/ internal R&D of new products and services to open innovation models that combine internal and external ideas, knowledge and technologies to create and commercialize new products and services. For most of the twentieth century, a strong, internal R&D capability was associated with successful innovativeness. Companies assumed that the right way to innovate was to generate your own ideas, develop, produce and market the product and finance and support the whole process from A to Z. This process, which has been extremely successful for the majority of the companies (e.g., Xerox PARC, IBM, Bell Laboratories, General Electric, etc.) to sustain their competitive advantages, was labelled by Cherbrough (2003) as *closed innovation*.

However, the business and innovation environment has changed rapidly in the past few decades, as we have discussed throughout Part 2 of this book. Ideas and knowledge are widely disseminated and distributed around the world (in large part due to the development of information and communication technologies), while highly experienced and skilled individuals are more mobile than ever before. Thus, the logic of closed innovation, the traditional vertical integration model, is largely challenged. The comfortable and dominant monopoly positions of large Goliath-type multinational companies are threatened by the smallest David-type start-up or spin-off companies. According to Chesbrough et al. (2006: 1), 'open innovation is a paradigm that assumes that firms can and should use external ideas as well as internal ideas, and internal and external paths to market, as they look to advance their technology. It is a model that seeks to make the most of organizational networks, such as suppliers, customers, public and private research centres, institutions, universities even competitors in order to enhance the innovation capabilities of the firm.' In other words, the firm should constantly seek to form partnerships with a diverse variety of players/actors in the market and business environments rather than rely on its own internal four walls and its R&D department as in the closed innovation paradigm.

Van de Vrande et al. (2009) draw on a sample of 605 innovative Dutch SMEs to find out that mainly medium-sized companies are increasingly adopting open innovation practices during the last seven years, but smaller companies are also trying to catch up. The authors argue that open innovation practices in SMEs focus mainly on market-related targets, that is, to open up new markets, serve customers more effectively and efficiently, maintain growth and commercialize their innovations (SMEs are using twice as much inbound than outbound innovation practices). Bianchi et al. (2010) focus on one Italian SME in the packaging sector to develop a methodology to assist SMEs to put outbound, open innovation into practice. The authors illustrate a quick and friendly-to-use approach to identify opportunities for out-licensing an SME's technologies to other firms.

INNOVATION THROUGH PARTNERSHIPS, COLLABORATIONS AND ALLIANCES

To gain access and utilize these external sources of ideas and knowledge, firms need to develop certain abilities. Cohen and Levinthal (1990: 128) were the first scholars to define these abilities as a firm's *absorptive capacity*, 'the ability of a firm to recognise the value of new, external information, assimilate it, and apply it to commercial ends'. Companies use their R&D facilities and capabilities to identify, monitor and exploit external knowledge and technologies. Zahra and George (2002) extended the theory by specifying four distinct dimensions to absorptive capacity: acquisition, assimilation, transformation and exploitation. An innovative firm needs to engage in continuous learning and flow of information, knowledge and ideas with its environment, hence, its R&D cannot rely on conducting internal developments based on knowledge they already possess, rather they have to look outside to incorporate externally generated knowledge.

Eric von Hippel (1988) was the first scholar to note the idea that users and consumers are the real creators of innovations instead of the suppliers of these innovations. He identified four external sources of knowledge and innovation: (a) suppliers and customers; (b) university, government and private laboratories; (c) competitors; and (d) other nations. Powell (1990, 1996), Gerlach (1992) and Gomes-Casseres (1997) argue that firms increasingly use (or at least should use) alliances, networking, licensing agreements and joint-ventures (as well as informal, arms-length relationships) as a fruitful means of seeking out and incorporating external expertise and knowledge into the innovative processes of the firm.

Stuart (2000) suggests that partnerships, collaborations and alliances provide the necessary innovative capacities for the firms (especially SMEs) to sustain the fierce competition and attract customers and corporate partners. In complex and turbulent environments where firms become more and more widely dispersed around the globe, collaborations with suppliers, customers, universities, research institutes or even competitors have become important management instruments for companies to improve their competitiveness and innovativeness by providing access to external resources, providing synergies and creating, accessing, transferring and integrating new knowledge to the firm (Muller and Zenker 2001). In fact, Koschatzky (2001: 6) found that, 'firms which do not cooperate and which do not exchange knowledge reduce their knowledge base on a long-term basis and lose the ability to enter into exchange relations with other firms and organizations'.

8

Tacit Knowledge and Emotional Intelligence; the Intangible Values of SMEs

The Creative and Innovative Power of the Human Mind[1]

In today's highly competitive era and especially with the present economic downturn, SMEs should be pursuing strategies towards creativity and innovation (as we have been discussing throughout this book) that could provide them with sustainable competitive advantages and create value for the firm. The importance of innovation for an organization of any kind, even for a country as a whole, is undisputed in the management literature and the business world of the twenty-first century, as we have already examined. What innovative enterprises need are innovative people (Kanter 1997). According to Goyal and Akhilesh (2007: 209), innovation is the successful implementation of creative ideas within an organization. Creativity is defined as putting innovative ideas into practice, producing novel and useful ideas that could lead to a competitive advantage for the enterprise (Amabile 1988, Cook 1998, Gurteen 1998, Zhou and George 2003). Harnessing employees' creative potential and innovative ideas can thus become the cornerstone for an SME's survival and growth in the present economic turbulences and ultimately produce value for the enterprise. As Kanter (1997) argues, cultivating innovative people is one of the most important elements that distinguish companies that lead from companies that lag:

---

1 This chapter is based on my article: Piperopoulos, P. 2010. Tacit Knowledge and Emotional Intelligence: the 'Intangible' Values of SMEs. *Strategic Change: Briefings in Entrepreneurial Finance*, 19(3–4), 125–139.

> *Ideas are now the DNA of organizations and therefore learning and development of people become crucial to economic survival. Indeed people, and the way they are managed and deployed, are the single most sustainable source of competitive advantage as … the current drive for differentiation is to generate ideas and innovation through the organization's human resources. (Appleby and Mavin 2000: 555)*

In the search for competitive advantages, knowledge has emerged as one of the most important, although intangible, assets for any organization. Knowledge and intellectual capital are increasingly becoming the core competencies and the cornerstones for sustainable superior performance. It is not the products or services that the company is producing and selling that will differentiate it from its competitors, but rather the knowledge, skills, norms, management processes and routines that are acquired over time and experience, which are very difficult to imitate, that provide organizations with long-term capabilities and increased performance (Trott et al. 2009). Human experience and practical expertise are the foundations of tacit knowledge (Polanyi 1966, Nonaka and Takeuchi 1995, Koskinen and Vanharanta 2002). The capacity to manage and harness the creative power of the human mind and convert it to innovative products and services should be the critical core competence of any organization. Quinn (1992: 439) says, 'increasingly, developing and managing human intellect and skills, more than managing and deploying physical and capital assets, will be the dominant concerns for managers in successful companies'.

From a slightly different perspective, Fenwick (2003) suggested that emotions play an important role in people's readiness to be creative and innovative, while Park (2005) argued that the quality of the emotional environment of an organization could enhance productivity and creativity. Emotional intelligence (EI) is a relatively new and growing field of research among scholars and practitioners of business, management and psychology (Lam and Kirby 2002, Rozell et al. 2002, Jamali et al. 2008). Stimulated by the work of Salovey and Mayer (1990) and the popular book by Goleman (1995), emotional intelligence has been identified as a crucial element in sustaining higher job performance, organizational productivity and profits (Lam and Kirby 2002, Wong and Law 2002, Diggins 2004, Sy et al. 2006). Emotionally intelligent managers can enhance employees' willingness to act entrepreneurially (Brundin et al. 2008). In contrast to general intelligence, emotional intelligence can be enhanced through training and development (Goleman, 1998, Prati 2005, Chrusciel 2006).

In the present economic downturn, in which the balance sheets and the financial assets may include collaterals and derivatives that have been heavily devalued, the real value of the firm might come in the form of strategies for unleashing the creative and innovative power of the human mind, that is, the development of an emotionally intelligent workforce. In this highly competitive and financially volatile era, SMEs, which as we discussed earlier in this part of the book are usually sculptured around the personality and the competencies of the owner/manager/entrepreneur, should be properly utilizing employees' creative potential and innovative ideas that could become the cornerstone for their survival and growth. The main argument in this chapter is that what is missing in entrepreneurship research and literature and management practice is the role emotional intelligence can dramatize in affecting employees' creativity, innovation and tacit knowledge, as well as the manager's/entrepreneur's personality in leading their employees and the SME towards increased performance and competitiveness and thus augmenting a firm's value. Attempting a creative synthesis of the above, a conceptual model is developed in this chapter, based on eight propositions, attempting to link and organize entrepreneurial characteristics, emotional intelligence, tacit knowledge and innovation, creativity and firm performance/competitiveness.

Entrepreneurs, Innovation and SMEs

The analysis and connection of innovation and entrepreneurship in a free enterprise system was long framed by the work of Joseph Schumpeter (Martin and Scott 2000, McDaniel 2000, Casson 2005). An entrepreneur, according to Schumpeter (1942), is everyone who 'carries out new combinations'. The fundamental impulse that sets and keeps the capitalist engine in motion comes from the introduction of so-called new combinations (i.e., new consumers' goods, new methods of production or transportation, new markets, new forms of industrial organization) that capitalist enterprise creates (Schumpeter 1942).

The link between entrepreneurship and innovation further emerges from the writings of Drucker (1985). He argues that innovation is the specific function of entrepreneurship. It is the means by which entrepreneurs either create new wealth-creating resources or endow existing resources with enhanced potential for generating wealth. Entrepreneurs, whether individuals starting their own businesses or entrepreneurial organizations that want to continue to thrive, regard innovation as a strategy, as an ongoing process that will bring profits and a competitive advantage to their business (Drucker 1985). The author suggests that above all innovation is work rather than genius. It requires knowledge and hard, focused and purposeful work. According to Drucker (1985), entrepreneurship and innovation require talent and creativity as well as hard and focused efforts, diligence, persistence and commitment to the work. This leads us to the first proposition:

> *Proposition 1*: The entrepreneur's commitment to the organization (hard and focused work, rather than genius) will positively affect the competitive advantages of an enterprise.

The Role and Personality of the Entrepreneur

Several researchers in their studies give special emphasis to the influential role of entrepreneurs in affecting the performance, survival and growth of firms, particularly when these firms are small. The basic role played by the owner/manager/entrepreneur is one of the major determinants of an SME's competitiveness and performance; this turns out to be so because the concentration of decision-making power in the owner/manager in an SME environment consequently affects the firm's overall strategy. In SMEs there may be different layers of managers, supervisors, job descriptions, and so on, but the distinguishable characteristic of entrepreneurs is that they retain almost total control and remain at the centre of the decision-making web, in a unique and powerful position within the firm (Goffee and Scase 1995, Aaboen et al. 2006). Such enterprises are sculptured around the personalities of their owner-managers and their growth potential and financial viability is highly dependent upon the proprietors' preferences, energies, talents and plans.

Hoffman et al. (1998) in their work identified several similar characteristics of SMEs across different industrial sectors that tend to engage in innovative activities. Among the most important sources of innovative efforts in SMEs are the levels of qualified scientists and engineers among the employees and the leadership provided by a charismatic owner/founder or manager of the company. According to recent research results in 305 small tourism firms in Israel, the entrepreneurial human capital, and particularly the managerial skill, was the strongest contributor to both short-term and long-term business performance and growth (Haber and Reichel 2007).

The role and personality of the entrepreneur/manager/owner of the small firm and their strategic decisions are in direct relationship with the competitiveness and innovative performance of the SME (Hausman 2005, Hoffman et al. 1998). Further research focusing on the concept of competitiveness and the competency approach by Man et al (2002) develops a conceptual model to link the characteristics of an SME's owner-manager and their firm's performance. Competitive scope, organizational capabilities, entrepreneurial competencies and performance are the four components of the model. According to the authors, the focal point of the model concentrates on the entrepreneurial tasks that link the different competency areas with the constructs of competitiveness. The entrepreneur's managerial skills and technical know-how and their demographic, psychological and behavioural characteristics are often cited as the most influential factors related to the performance of an SME; particularly since quite often small firms or even medium-sized companies have a dominating entrepreneur, who is most likely to be the founder of the business.

The authors in their study concluded that the organizing, relationship and conceptual competencies of the entrepreneur are positively related to the organizational capabilities of an SME. They focused upon the competencies of the entrepreneur and found a positive relationship between the firm's long-term performance and the strategic and commitment competencies. The authors suggest that in order for the entrepreneur to ensure the competitiveness and survival of the firm, they must set the direction for the company since it is often the owner-manager of SME that leads the strategic planning process. The entrepreneur also needs to be persistent and committed to the task in order to enhance the performance of the firm and motivate employees through inspiration. The above leads us to the following two propositions:

> *Proposition 2*: The personality of the owner/manager/entrepreneur of the SME is in direct relationship with the company's performance.

> *Proposition 3*: The entrepreneur's competencies are positively related to the competitive performance of an SME.

Tacit Knowledge

Michael Polanyi (1958, 1961 and 1966) was one of the first scholars to identify and classify two different types of knowledge: explicit (or codified) knowledge and tacit knowledge. Explicit knowledge concerns the expertise that can be transmitted using formal language and can be codified via artifacts, in contrast to tacit knowledge that involves direct experience that cannot be communicated in any codified way (Howells 2002). Hall and Andriani (2003: 145) argue that, 'tacit knowledge is acquired by experience; it is knowledge of what works and it is characterized by causal ambiguity while explicit knowledge is knowledge that has been captured in a code, or a language that facilitates communication.'

Tacit knowledge is primarily acquired through experiential and accumulated learning and is manifested in employees' and managers' understanding of an organization's norms, processes and procedures (Levitas et al. 1997). Polanyi (1966) encapsulates the real meaning of tacit knowledge in the phrase, 'we know more than we can tell' and provides examples such as our ability to recognize faces, ride a bicycle or swim without even the slightest idea of how these things are done. Rosenberg (1982: 143) defines tacit knowledge as, 'the knowledge of techniques, methods and designs that work in certain ways and with certain consequences, even when one cannot explain exactly why.'. Consistent with Polanyi (1966) and Rosenberg (1982), Wagner and Sternberg (1985) define tacit knowledge as the unspoken knowledge gained from experience.

Tacit knowledge is derived from a lifetime of experience, practice, perception and learning by doing, learning by using and learning to learn (Mascitelli 2000, Howells 2002). Polanyi (1966) argues that tacit knowledge is personal, context specific, based on an individual's subjective intuitions, ideals, values and emotions and is very difficult to be shared unless it is converted into words, numbers, pictures or any other form that can be communicated to and understood by others. In the same line of reasoning, Popper (1972) suggests that tacit knowledge is deeply embedded in personal beliefs, attitudes, values and experiences. Moreover, Sternberg and Wagner (1992: 6–7) argue that this informally acquired learning, tacit knowledge, can have three main forms:

1.   Tacit knowledge about managing oneself, which refers to knowledge about how to motivate, organize and evaluate oneself in on-the-job performance.

2.   Tacit knowledge about managing others, which refers to knowledge about dealing with one's subordinates, and to some extent, one's peers and superiors.

3.   Tacit knowledge about managing tasks, which refers to knowledge about how to get tasks accomplished expeditiously and well.

TACIT KNOWLEDGE, INNOVATION AND COMPETITIVE ADVANTAGES

Michael Porter (1985) is one of the first scholars to recognize the competitive advantage that innovations bring to the company and to a nation, and how they should be mastered. Porter (1990) argues that firms will not ultimately succeed unless they base their strategies on improvement and innovation, an eagerness to compete and a thorough understanding of their national environment and ways to improve it. According to the author, firms create and sustain a competitive advantage by perceiving or discovering new and better ways to compete in an industry and bringing them to market, which is ultimately an act of innovation. Innovation, according to Porter (1990), requires investment in developing skills and knowledge. The author focuses on the significant role of information and knowledge in the innovation process. Sometimes it can be the result of sheer R&D investment or market research, but quite often it is just unconventional wisdom, simply looking in the right place at the right time. Innovation for Porter is, with few exceptions, the result of unusual effort. Companies that innovate are frequently not large or established companies, but rather new, early movers or small companies. Innovative processes and methods are increasingly seen as inherent to the firm's strategy and an important source of competitive advantage (Foulds and West 2006, McDonough III et al. 2006). Therefore, I make the following proposition:

> *Proposition 4*: Business strategies based on innovation will positively influence the performance and competitiveness of an SME.

In the past few decades there has been a growing and intense interest in harnessing the intellectual capital of the firm (employees' and managers' tacit knowledge) in order to develop sustainable competitive advantages. The tacitness of tacit knowledge (if we can define it in such a way), in other words, the knowledge that is difficult to be imitated and copied from the competitors, makes it an important organizational resource (Grant 1996). In 1993 Drucker argued that in the twenty-first century, economies and organizations would not base their strategies on capital, labour or natural resource but on knowledge. In addition, Nonaka and Takeuchi (1995) argue in their work that tacit knowledge is the main element in creating new knowledge and innovation.

According to Kakabadse et al. (2001), effectively managing people, creating organizational environments that allow individuals to be creative and allowing a free flow of knowledge and information between the members of the organization will ultimately lead to the creation of new knowledge and innovations. Consistent with this view, Lubit (2001) argues that since competitive advantage is all about knowing how to do things and not so much relying on access and plethora of resources (capital, labour, natural, etc.), knowledge and intellectual capital are the cornerstones of superior performance. In a survey of American and Canadian executives, Joyce and Stivers (2000) conclude that the vast majority of the respondents believed that in 2005, as compared to 1995, the key to successfully managing and operating their companies would be the management of knowledge resources. Quinn et al. (1996: 8) argue that once a firm obtains a knowledge-based competitive edge, it becomes even harder for competitors to catch up.

The fundamental difficulty of expressing, codifying and disseminating tacit knowledge makes it easier for the company to protect it. Hence, this kind of knowledge can become the cornerstone of a rather inimitable competitive advantage. While managers should redesign their enterprises to allow tacit knowledge to be spread amongst all employees and departments (e.g., apply different motivation techniques, challenge old structures and beliefs and train their subordinates and employees to knowledge management) that would ultimately lead to continuous innovation, increased performance and a much more motivated labour force, this tacit knowledge will be very difficult, if not impossible, for other firms to copy. According to Lubit (2001), tacit knowledge may only be efficient and effective when entrenched in a particular firm's culture, norms and set of processes and routines. Hence, competitors should be delayed in understanding and imitating the innovations of a particular firm since there will be some 'invisible' ambiguous resources and knowledge (Winter 1987, Hart 1995). These invisible assets (tacit knowledge) are often the only source of competitive advantage that can be sustained over long periods.

Emotional Intelligence

Emotional intelligence (EI) is a relatively new and growing field of research among scholars and practitioners of business, management and psychology (Lam and Kirby 2002, Rozell et al. 2002, Jamali et al. 2008). Peter Salovey and John Mayer (1990) were the first scholars to introduce the concept of emotional intelligence, but it was not popularized until a book by Daniel Goleman in 1995 which stimulated researchers' and the public's interest in the concept. Dulewicz and Higgs (2004) argue that EI, in the last decade, has become a very important topic in occupational psychology and human resource management, exhibiting potential value for managers, educationalists, professionals and psychologists. The basic idea behind emotional intelligence is that intelligence quotient (IQ) alone should no longer be considered as the principal predictor of job performance and success (Dulewicz and Higgs 2000, Suliman and Al-Shaikh, Jamali et al. 2008).

The history behind the emotional intelligence theory dates back to the work done by psychometric researchers like E.L. Thorndike (1920), who used the term *social intelligence* to describe the skill of managing and understanding others and explain parts of success that could not be attributed to IQ. Similarly to Thorndike (1920), Moss and Hunt (1927), Hunt (1928) and Vernon (1933) described defined and assessed social intelligence and socially competent behaviour. Howard Gardner (1983) introduced the concept of *multiple intelligences* that included both *interpersonal intelligence* (the capacity to understand the intentions, motivations and desires of other people) and *intrapersonal intelligence* (the capacity to understand oneself, to appreciate one's feelings, fears and motivations). The author argued that traditional types of intelligence (typically measured by IQ and similar tests) fail to fully explain individual performance and cognitive ability.

Similar to most concepts in organizational and management theory, a variety of definitions have emerged in the relevant literature for the concept of emotional intelligence. Salovey and Mayer (1990: 189) defined EI as, 'the subset of social intelligence that involves the ability to monitor one's own and other's feelings and emotions, to discriminate among them and to use this information to guide one's thinking and actions'. Bar-On (1997: 1) defined EI as, 'an array of personal, emotional, and social abilities and skills that determine how well the individual functions in his or her given environment'. Weisinger (1998: xvi) defined EI as, 'the intelligent use of emotions: you intentionally make your emotions work for you by using them to help guide your behaviour and thinking in ways that enhance your results'. Van Rooy and Viswesvaran (2004: 72) defined EI as, 'the set of abilities (verbal and non-verbal) that enable a person to generate, recognize, express, understand, and evaluate their own, and others, emotions in order to guide thinking and action that successfully cope with environmental demands and pressures'.

Koman and Wolff (2008) in their research argue that despite the different definitions of EI, there is an agreement that emotional intelligence will affect not only individual performance but also team and organizational performance.

EMOTIONAL INTELLIGENCE, CREATIVITY AND PERFORMANCE

EI has been identified as a crucial element in sustaining higher job performance, organizational productivity and profits (Lam and Kirby 2002, Wong and Law 2002, Diggins 2004, Sy et al. 2006). According to a literature review by Dimitriades (2007: 223–224), people with higher EI lead more effectively, feel satisfied with their job, are committed to their organization, feel less job insecurity and withdrawal intentions and in general experience more career success. As I argued in the introductory part of this chapter, taking advantage of employees' creative potential and innovative ideas can become the cornerstone of an SME's survival and growth.

Emotionally intelligent managers can enhance employees' willingness to act entrepreneurially (Brundin et al. 2008). Evidence exists to suggest that executives and managers that can control and understand their emotions as well as the emotions of others (usually their subordinates) are more likely to achieve their goals, effectively lead their employees and keep the company ahead of the pack (Diggins 2004, Rosete and Ciarrochi 2005, Suliman and Al-Shaikh 2007). Fenwick (2003) suggested that emotions play an important role in people's readiness to be creative and innovative, while Park (2005) argued that the quality of the emotional environment of an organization could enhance productivity and creativity. Sosik and Megerian (1999) suggested that EI influences self-motivation positively, while leaders with high EI provide the momentum for their employees to collectively perform. Zhou and George (2003) proposed and provided evidence that leaders with high emotional intelligence excelled in stimulating their personnel to identify and seize upon opportunities for creativity. This leads to the following propositions:

Proposition 5: Entrepreneurs/managers with high emotional intelligence will stimulate their subordinates and personnel to act entrepreneurially and creatively.

Proposition 6: High emotional intelligence is positively related to improved creativity.

Goleman (1998), in his research of 121 companies around the world, found that EI abilities are doubly important in organizational performance excellence than are technical and cognitive abilities. Further research suggests that employees with high EI tend to display superior job performance profiles in organizations (Jordan and Troth 2004, Morehouse 2007). Diggins (2004: 34) suggests, 'in organizations, the inclusion of emotional intelligence in training programs has helped employees to cooperate better and be more motivated, thereby increasing productivity and profits.'

Emotional intelligence develops throughout one's life and it can be enhanced through appropriate training and development (Goleman 1998, Rozell et al. 2001, Pratt 2005). Slaski and Cartwright (2003) in their research found that after six months of training on emotional intelligence, participants showed an increase in their EI which was subsequently revealed in higher morale, quality of work and performance among others. Prati's (2005) research validated the results of Slaski and Cartwright (2003). Organizations that have implemented EI training and development programs to enhance the EI of their human capital have witnessed quicker and sustainable changes in employees' job satisfaction and performance (Wong and Law 2002, Carmeli 2003, Park 2005, Carmeli and Josman 2006).

Chrusciel (2006) argues that in a highly competitive business environment, managers are looking for elements of competitive advantage and EI, and specific techniques for improving individual and organizational EI can assist them in their search. Recent research suggests that organizations are emotional areas and as long as managers can control and regulate their emotions as well as the emotions of their employees, they can facilitate a competitive advantage for the company (Bolton 2005, Brundin et al. 2008, Akgün et al. 2009). The above leads us to two final propositions:

> *Proposition 7*: Emotional intelligence can be improved through appropriate training and development programs.

> *Proposition 8*: Higher emotional intelligence is positively related to increased competitive advantages for an organization.

A Model Towards Augmenting an SME's Value

In the discussion above, I organized existing theories and empirical researches (conducted by a plethora of academicians) into relationships between entrepreneurial characteristics, emotional intelligence, tacit knowledge, innovation, creativity and firm performance/competitiveness. Eight propositions, based on existing theoretical and empirical data, were constructed and brought together in this section, aiming to create a hypothetical model for enhancing the competitiveness and performance of the SME and hence augment the real value of the firm as presented in the figure below.

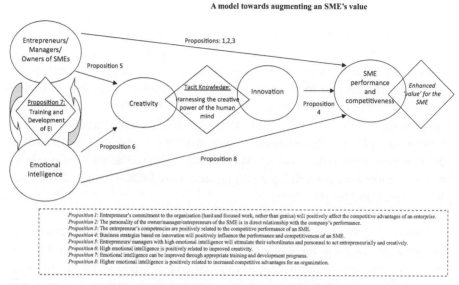

Figure 8.1   A model towards augmenting an SME's value

This chapter argues that in a highly competitive and financially volatile era, SMEs should be pursuing business strategies that would provide to them sustainable competitive advantages and augment their value. The underlying principle behind the model I propose is that owners/managers/entrepreneurs can enhance their emotional intelligence as well as their employees' emotional intelligence through training and development programs and seminars (Proposition 7). As we explained in this chapter (and in fact throughout this part of the book), the personality and the competencies of the owner/manager/entrepreneur, along with their commitment (hard and focused work rather than mere genius) to their enterprise and personnel, are in direct relationship with the company's performance (Propositions: 1, 2 and 3). Furthermore, business strategies based on innovation can positively influence the performance and competitiveness of an SME (Proposition 4). These propositions are combined with the emotional intelligence theory, which states that entrepreneurs/ managers with high emotional intelligence will stimulate their subordinates and personnel to act entrepreneurially and creatively (Proposition 5). Moreover, the theoretical framework of EI presented earlier suggests that high EI is positively related to improved creativity for personnel as well as increased productivity/ performance and competitiveness for the organization. Furthermore, people, as a resource, are important not only as participants in the labour force but as creative minds and producers of intangible assets. These invisible assets (tacit knowledge) can be a source of sustainable creativity and competitive advantages. To be able to innovate requires a process of using existing knowledge, acquiring new knowledge and finally developing new knowledge. Hence, taking advantage of employees' creative potential and innovative ideas (putting creative ideas into action) can become the cornerstone in augmenting an SME's value.

The major contribution of this model is the organization of the existing theories and findings in a model around emotional intelligence, tacit knowledge, entrepreneurs and SME performance/competitiveness. For instance, in terms of theoretical considerations, as it focuses on the central and dominating role that the entrepreneur has on a small business, it highlights the importance of the development of EI of the entrepreneur. The more the entrepreneur improves their emotional intelligence, the more they can excel in stimulating their personnel to identify and seize upon opportunities for creativity and innovation. A policy implication is that developing competent, highly emotionally intelligent entrepreneurs/managers/owners in SMEs could prove to be more important in forming successful business strategies than providing them with more resources, run of the mill lifelong learning programs and further formal education.

This model is probably less applicable to large enterprises or companies that do not have a dominating entrepreneur/owner/manager who will set the business strategy of the enterprise. In SMEs an atmosphere is said to reign which is more favourable to creative work (Acs and Audretsch 1991). Nurturing a creative and innovative open communication culture in a small business, developing knowledge-sharing groups and teams can diffuse and simultaneously synthesize the tacit knowledge of individuals and, as a result, it could unleash the creative powers of the human minds and lead to innovations and increased performance (Mascitelli 2000).

The more complicated the enterprises, with formal structures, various departments, board of directors and shareholders, the less applicable will this model be. Nevertheless, even in this type of enterprise, middle and upper level managers should recognize the possible competitive advantages that their enhancement of emotional intelligent levels, the parallel improvement of EI of their employees and the harnessing of the creative power of tacit knowledge could bring to their companies.

Part 2: References/Bibliography

Aaboen, L., Lindelöf, P., von Koch, C. and Löfsten, H. 2006. Corporate governance and performance of small high-tech firms in Sweden. *Technovation*, 26(8), 955–968.

Acs, Z.J. and Audretsch, D.B. 1991. *Innovation and Small Firms*. Hong Kong: Palatino.

Akgün, A.E., Keskin, H. and Byrne, J. 2009. Organizational emotional capability, product and process innovation, and firm performance: An empirical analysis. *Journal of Engineering and Technology Management*, 26(3), 103–130.

Aldrich, H.E. 1989. Networking among women entrepreneurs, in *Women-Owned Businesses*, edited by O. Hagan, C. Rivchun and D.L. Sexton, New York: Praeger, 103–132.

Aldrich, H. and Waldinger, R. 1990. Ethnicity and Entrepreneurship. *Annual Review of Sociology*, 16, 111–135.

Amabile, T.M. 1988. A model of creativity and innovation in organizations, in *Research in Organizational Behaviour*, edited by Staw, B.M. and L.L. Cummings, Greenwich, CT: JAI Press, 10, 123–167.

Appleby, A. and Mavin, S. 2000. Innovation not imitation: human resource strategy and the impact on world-class status. *Total Quality Management*, 11(4/6), 554–561.

Asquith, D. and Weston, F. 1994. Small business, growth patterns and jobs. *Business Economics,* 29(3): 31–34.

Bar-On, R. 1997. The Bar-On *Emotional Quotient Inventory (EQ-i): Technical Manual*. Toronto: Multi-Health Systems.

Barrett, G.A., Jones, T.P. and McEvoy, D. 1996. Ethnic minority business: Theoretical discourse in Britain and North America. *Urban Studies*, 33, 783–809.

Barrett, G.A., Jones, T.P. and McEvoy, D. 2001. Socio-economic and policy dimensions of the mixed embeddedness of ethnic minority business in Britain. *Journal of Ethnic and Migration Studies*, 27(2), 241–258.

Basu, A. 2004. Entrepreneurial aspirations among family business owners: An analysis of ethnic business owners in the UK. *International Journal of Entrepreneurial Behaviour & Research*, 10(1/2), 12–33.

Basu, A. and Altinay, E. 2002. The interaction between culture and entrepreneurship in London's immigrant businesses. *International Small Business Journal*, 20(4), 371–393.

Basu, A. and Goswami, A. 1999. South Asian entrepreneurship in Great Britain: Factors influencing growth. *International Journal of Entrepreneurial Behavior & Research*, 5(5), 251–275.

Benschop, Y. and Essers, C. 2007. Enterprising identities: Female entrepreneurs of Moroccan or Turkish origin in the Netherlands. *Organisation Studies*, 28(1), 49–69.

Bianchi, M., Cavaliere, A., Chiaroni, D., Frattini, F. and Chiesa, V. 2011. Organisational modes for open innovation in the bio-pharmaceutical industry: an exploratory analysis. *Technovation*, 31, 22–33.

Birch, D.L. 1979. *The Job Generation Process*. Cambridge, MA: MIT.

Boden, Jr. R.J. 1999. Gender inequality in wage earnings and female self-employment selection. *Journal of Socio-Economics*, 28(3), 351–364.

Bolton, J.E. 1971. *Report of the Committee of Inquiry on Small Firms*. London: Cmnd.4811, HMSO.

Bolton, S. 2005. *Emotion Management in the Workplace*. New York: Palgrave Macmillan.

Boyd, R.L. 1998. The storefront church ministry in African American communities of the urban north during the great migration: The making of an ethnic niche. *The Social Science Journal*, 35(3), 319–332.

Brundin, E., Patzelt, H., Shepherd, D.A. 2008. Managers' emotion displays and employees' willingness to act entrepreneurially. *Journal of Business Venturing*, 23(2), 221–243.

Brush, C. 1992. Research on women business owners: Past trends, a new perspective and future directions. *Entrepreneurship Theory and Practice*, 16(4), 5–30.

Burns, P. 1996. The significance of small firms, in *Small Business and Entrepreneurship*, edited by P. Burns and J. Dewhurst, 2nd Edition, Basingstoke: Macmillan Press Ltd.

Burns, P. and Dewhurst, J. 1996. *Small Business and Entrepreneurship*. 2nd Edition, Basingstoke: Macmillan Press Ltd.

Burns, P. and Harrison, J. 1996. Growth, in *Small Business and Entrepreneurship*, edited by P. Burns and J. Dewhurst, 2nd Edition, Basingstoke: Macmillan Press Ltd.

Buttner, E.H. and Rosen, B. 1988. Bank loan officers' perceptions of characteristics of men, women and successful entrepreneurs. *Journal of Business Venturing*, 3(3), 249–258.

Carmeli, A. 2003. The relationship between emotional intelligence and work attitudes, behavior and outcomes: An examination among senior managers. *Journal of Managerial Psychology*, 18(8), 788–813.

Carmeli, A. and Josman, Z.E. 2006. The relationship among emotional intelligence, task performance, and organizational citizenship behaviours. *Human Performance*, 19(4), 403–419.

Carter, S., Anderson, S. and Shaw, E. 2001. Women's business ownership: A review of the academic, popular and internet literature. London: Department of Trade and Industry, Small Business Service Industry Report: RR002/01.

Casson, M. 2005. Entrepreneurship and the theory of the firm. *Journal of Economic Behavior & Organization*, 58(2), 327–348.

Castro, E.A., Rodrigues, C. Esteves, C. and Pires, A.R. 2000. The triple helix model as a motor for the creative use of telematics. *Research Policy*, 29, 193–203.

Chan, S.Y. and Foster, M.J. 2001. Strategy formulation in small business: The Hong Kong experience. *International Small Business Journal*, 19(3), 56–71.

Chaudhry, S. and Crick, D. 2004. Understanding practices at the 'ethnic' marketing/entrepreneurship interface: A case study of Kirit Pathak. *Qualitative Market Research: An International Journal*, 7(3), 183–193.

Chesbrough, H. 2003. *Open Innovation: The New Imperative for Creating and Profiting from Technology*. Boston: Harvard Business School Press.

Chesbrough, H. 2006. *Open Business Models: How to Thrive in the New Innovation Landscape*. Boston, MA: Harvard Business School Press.

Chesbrough, H., Crowther, A.K. 2006. Beyond high tech: Early adopters of open innovation in other industries. *R&D Management*, 36, 229–236.

Chesbrough, H., Vanhaverbeke, W., and West, J. 2006. *Open Innovation: Researching a New Paradigm*. London: Oxford University Press.

Christensen, J.F., Olesen, M.H. and Kjaer, J.S. 2005. The industrial dynamics of open innovation: Evidence from the transformation of consumer electronics. *Research Policy*, 34, 1533–1549.

Chrusciel, D. 2006. Considerations of emotional intelligence (EI) in dealing with change decision management. *Management Decision*, 44(5), 644–657.

Cohen, W.M. and Levinthal, D.A. 1990. Absorptive capacity: A new perspective on learning and innovation. *Administrative Science Quarterly*, 35(1), 128–152.

Coleman, S. 2000. Access to capital and terms of credit: A comparison of men- and women owned small businesses. *Journal of Small Business Management*, 38(3), 37–52.

Constant, A. and Shachmurove, Y. 2006. Entrepreneurial ventures and wages differentials between Germans and immigrants. *International Journal of Manpower*, 27(3), 208–229.

Cook, P. 1998. The creative advantage – is your organization the leader or the pack? *Industrial and Commercial Training*, 30(5), 179–184.

Corsino, L. and Soto, M. 2005. Socializing the ethnic market: A frame analysis. *Research in the Sociology of Work*, 15, 233–256.

Cromie, S. and Birley, S. 1992. Networking by female business owners in Northern Ireland. *Journal of Business Venturing*, 7(3), 237–251.

Deakins, D. 1996. *Entrepreneurs and Small Firms*. London: McGraw-Hill.

Deakins, D., Mohammed, I., Smallbone, D., Whittam, G. and Wyper, J. 2007. Ethnic minority businesses in Scotland and the role of social capital. *International Small Business Journal*, 25(3), 307–326.

Devine, T.J. 1994. Characteristics of self-employed women in the United States. *Monthly Labor Review*, 117(3), 20–34.

Dierckx, M.A.F. and Stroeken, J.H.M. 1999. Information technology and innovation in small and medium-sized enterprises. *Technological Forecasting and Social Change*, 60, 149–166.

Diggins, C. 2004. Emotional intelligence: the key to effective performance … and to staying ahead of the pack at times of organizational change. *Human Resource Management International Digest*, 12(1), 33–35.

Dimitriades, Z. 2007. Managing emotionally intelligent service workers. Personal and positional effects in the Greek context. *Journal of European Industrial Training*, 31(3), 223–240.

Drucker, P.F. 1985. *Innovation and Entrepreneurship*. USA: Harper Business.

Drucker, P.F. 1993. *Post-Capitalist Society*. Oxford: Butterworth/Heinemann.

Dulewicz, V. and Higgs, M. 2004. Can emotional intelligence be developed? *The International Journal of Human Resource Management*, 15(1), 95–111.

Engelen, E. 2001. Breaking in and breaking out: A Weberian approach to entrepreneurial opportunities. *Journal of Ethnic and Migration Studies*, 27(2), 203–223.

European Commission, 2002. Observatory of European SMEs: Highlights from the 2001 Survey, No. 1. Available at: http://ec.europa.eu/enterprise/policies/sme/files/analysis/doc/smes_observatory_2002_report1_en.pdf [accessed 09 May 2011].

European Commission, 2003. Proceedings of the European Forum on Female Entrepreneurship 28 March, Available at: http://ec.europa.eu/enterprise/entrepreneurship/craft/craft-women/documents/proceedings-en.pdf [accessed 01 July 2009].

European Commission, 2005. The New SME Definition: User Guide and Model Declaration. Available at: http://ec.europa.eu/enterprise/policies/sme/files/sme_definition/sme_user_guide_en.pdf [accessed 09 May 2011].

Fenwick, T. 2003. Examining workplace learning in new enterprises. *The Journal of Workplace Learning*, 15(3), 123–132.

Fielden, L.S., Davidson, J.M., Dawe, J.A. and Makin, J.P. 2003. Factors inhibiting the economic growth of female owned small businesses in North West England. *Journal of Small Business and Enterprise Development*, 10(2), 152–166.

Fong, E., Luk, C. and Ooka, E. 2005. Spatial distribution of suburban ethnic businesses. *Social Science Research*, 43, 215–235.

Foulds, L.R. and West, M. 2006. Innovation of e-procurement: A case study. *International Journal of Business Innovation and Research*, 1(1/2), 51–72.

Galbraith, C.S. 2004. Are ethnic enclaves really tiebout clubs? Ethnic entrepreneurship and the economic theory of clubs, in *Ethnic Entrepreneurship: Structure and Process*, edited by C. Stiles and C.S. Galbraith, Amsterdam: Elsevier Ltd, Amsterdam, 45–58.

Gallup Organisation, 2007. Flash EB No196 – Observatory of European SMEs: analytical report. Available at: http://ec.europa.eu/enterprise/policies/sme/files/analysis/doc/2007/03_analytical_report_en.pdf [accessed 10 May 2011].

Gardner, H. 1983. *Frames of Mind: The Theory of Multiple Intelligences*. New York, NY: Basic Books.

Gassmann, O. 2006. Opening up the innovation process: Towards an agenda. *R&D Management*, 36(3), 223–228.

Gerlach, M.L. 1992. *Alliance Capitalism: The Social Organization of Japanese Business*. Berkeley: University of California Press.

Goffee, R. and Scase, R. 1995. *Corporate Realities: The Dynamics of Large & Small Organisations*. UK: International Thomson Business Press.

Goleman, D. 1995. *Emotional Intelligence: Why it Can Matter More Than IQ*. New York, NY: Bantam Books.

Goleman, D. 1998. *Working with Emotional Intelligence*. New York, NY: Bantam Books.

Gomes-Casseres, B. 1997. Alliance strategies of small firms. *Small Business Economics* 9, 33–44.

Goyal, A. and Akhilesh, K.B. 2007. Interplay among innovativeness, cognitive intelligence, emotional intelligence and social capital of work teams. *Team Performance Management*. 13(7/8), 206–226.

Grant R. 1996. Towards a knowledge based theory of the firm. *Strategic Management Journal*, 17(1), 109–122.

Greene, P. G., Hart, M.M., Gatewood, E.J., Brush, C.G. and Carter, N.M. 2003. Women entrepreneurs moving front and center: An overview of research and theory, Coleman Foundation White Paper Series. Available at: http://usasbe.org/knowledge/whitepapers/greene2003.pdf. [accessed 20/07/2009].

Greiner, L.E. 1972. Evolution and Revolution as Organisations Growth. *Harvard Business Review*, 4, July/August.

Greve, A. 1995. Networks and entrepreneurship – an analysis of social relations, occupational background, and use of contacts during the establishment process. *Scandinavian Journal of Management*, 11(1), 1–24.

Gurteen, D. 1998. Knowledge, creativity and innovation. *Journal of Knowledge Management*, 2(1), 5–13.

Haber, S. and Reichel, A. 2007. The cumulative nature of entrepreneurial process: The contribution of human capital, planning and environment resources to small venture performance. *Journal of Business Venturing*, 22(1), 119–145.

Haines, Jr. G.H., Orser, G.H. and Riding, A.L. 1999. Myths and realities: An empirical study of banks and the gender of small business clients. *Canadian Journal of Administrative Studies*, 16(4), 291–307.

Hall, R. and Andriani, P. 2003. Managing knowledge associated with innovation. *Journal of Business Venturing*, 56, 145–152.

Hammarstedt, M. 2001. Immigrant self-employment in Sweden – its variation and some possible determinants. *Entrepreneurship & Regional Development*, 13(2), 147–161.

Hart, S.L. 1995. A natural resource-based view of the firm. *Academy of Management Review*, 20(4), 986–1014.

Hausman, A. 2005. Innovativeness among small businesses: Theory and propositions for future research. *Industrial Marketing Management*, 34(8), 773–782.

Heilman, M.E. and Chen, J.I. 2003. Entrepreneurship as a solution: The allure of self-employment for women and minorities. *Human Resource Management Review*, 13(2), 347–364.

Hiebert, D. 2002. Economic associations of immigrant self-employment in Canada. *International Journal of Entrepreneurial Behavior & Research*, 8(1/2), 93–112.

Hisrich, R.D. and Brush, C.G. 1983. The woman entrepreneur: Implications of family, educational and occupational experience, in *Frontiers in Entrepreneurship Research: Proceedings of the 1983 Conference on Entrepreneurship*, edited by J.A. Hornaday, J.A. Timmons and K.H. Vesper, Wellesley, MA: Babson College, Wellesley, 255–270.

Hisrich, R.D. and Brush, C.G. 1984. The woman entrepreneur: Management skills and business problems. *Journal of Small Business Management*, 22(1), 30–37.

Hisrich, R.D. and Drnovsek, M. 2002. Entrepreneurship and small business research – a European perspective. *Journal of Small Business and Enterprise Development*, 9(2), 172–222.

Hisrich, R.D. and O'Brien, M. 1981. The women entrepreneur from a business and sociological perspective, in *Frontiers of Entrepreneurship Research*, edited by K. Vesper, Wellesley, MA: Babson College.

Hoffman, K., Pajero, M., Bessant, J., and Perren, L. 1998. Small firms, R&D, technology and innovation in the UK: A literature review. *Technovation*, 18(1), 39–55.

Hoffmann, W.H. and Schlosser, R. 2001. Success factors of strategic alliances in small and medium-sized enterprises: An empirical survey. *Long Range Planning*, 34, 357–381.

Howells, J.R.L. 2002. Tacit knowledge, innovation and economic geography. *Urban Studies*, 39(4/5), 871–884.

Hunt T. 1928. The measurement of social intelligence. *Journal of Applied Psychology*. 12(3), 317–334.

Hussain, J. and Matlay, H. 2007. Financing preferences of ethnic minority owner/managers in the UK. *Journal of Small Business and Enterprise Development*, 14(3), 487–500.

Inkpen, A.C. and Tsang, E.W.K. 2005. Social capital, networks, and knowledge transfer. *Academy of Management Review*, 30(1), 146–165.

Iyer, G.R. and Shapiro, J.M. 1999. Ethnic entrepreneurial and marketing systems: Implications for the global economy. *Journal of International Marketing*, 7(4), 83–110.

Jalbert, S.E. 2000. *Women Entrepreneurs in the Global Economy*. Washington, DC: Centre for International Private Enterprise.

Jamal, A. 2005. Playing to win: an explorative study of marketing strategies of small ethnic retail entrepreneurs in the UK. *Journal of Retailing and Consumer Services*, 12, 1–13.

Jamali, D, Sidani, Y, Abu-Zaki, D. 2008. Emotional intelligence and management development implications. Insights from the Lebanese context. *Journal of Management Development*, 27(3), 348–360.

Jan Nederveen, P. 2003. Social capital and migration. *Ethnicities*, 3(1), 29–58.

Jordan, P.J. and Troth, A.C. 2004. Managing emotions during team problem solving: emotional intelligence and conflict resolution. *Human Performance*, 17(2), 195–218.

Joyce, T. and Stivers, B.P. 2000. Leveraging knowledge in small firms. *Journal of Cost Management*, May/June, 6–10.

Kakabadse, N.K., Kouzmin, A. and Kakabadse, A. 2001. From tacit knowledge to tacit management: Leveraging intangible assets. *Knowledge and Process Management*, 8(3), 137–154.

Kanter, R.M. 1997. *Rosabeth Moss Kanter on the Frontiers of Management*. Boston, MA: Harvard Business Press.

Kloosterman, R.C. 2003. Creating opportunities. Policies at increasing openings for immigrant entrepreneurs in the Netherlands. *Entrepreneurship & Regional Development*, 15(2), 167–181.

Kloosterman, R.C. and Rath, J. 2001. Immigrant entrepreneurs in advanced economies: Mixed embeddedness further explored. *Journal of Ethnic and Migration Studies*, 27(2), 189–201.

Koman, E.S. and Wolff, S.B. 2008. Emotional intelligence competencies in the team and team leader. A multi-level examination of the impact of emotional intelligence on team performance. *Journal of Management Development*, 27(1), 55–75.

Kontos, M. 2003. Self-employment policies and migrants' entrepreneurship in Germany. *Entrepreneurship & Regional Development*, 15(2), 119–135.

Koschatzky, K. 2001. Networks in innovation research and innovation policy – an introduction, in *Innovation Networks: Concepts and Challenges in the European perspective*, edited by K. Koschatzky, M. Kulicke and A. Zenker, Heidelberg: Physica Verlag.

Koskinen, K.U. and Vanharanta, H. 2002. The role of tacit knowledge in innovation processes of small technology companies. *International Journal of Production Economics*, 80(1), 57–62.

Lam, L.T. and Kirby, S.L. 2002. Is emotional intelligence an advantage? An exploration of the impact of emotional and general intelligence on individual performance. *The Journal of Social Psychology*, 142(1), 133–143.

Laudon, K.C. and Laudon, J.P. 2001. *Essentials of Management Information Systems, Organisation and Technology in the Networked Enterprise*. 4th Edition, USA: Prentice Hall.

Levent, T.B., Masurel, E. and Kijkamp, P. 2003. Diversity in entrepreneurship: Ethnic and female roles in urban economic life. *International Journal of Social Economics*, 30(11), 1131–1161.

Levitas, E., Hitt, M.A. and Dacin, M.T. 1997. Competitive intelligence and tacit knowledge development in strategic alliances. *Competitive Intelligence Review*, 8(2), 20–27.

Light, I. 1972. *Ethnic Enterprise in America: Business and Welfare among Chinese, Japanese, and Blacks*. Berkeley: University of California Press.

Light, I. 1984. Immigrant and ethnic enterprise in North America. *Ethnic and Racial Studies*, 7(2), 195–216.

Light, I. 1985. Immigrant entrepreneurs in America: Koreans in Los Angeles, in *Clamor at the Gates*, edited by N. Glazer, San Francisco: Institute for Contemporary Studies, 161–180.

Light, I. and Bonacich, E. 1988. *Immigrant Entrepreneurs: Koreans in Los Angeles 1965–1982*. Berkeley: University of California Press.

Light, I. and Karageorgis, S. 1994. The Ethnic Economy, in *The Handbook of Economic Sociology*, edited by N.J. Smelser and R. Swedberg, Princeton, NJ: Princeton University Press, 647–671.

Ljunggren, E. and Kolvereid, L. 1996. New business formation: Does gender make a difference? *Women in Management Review*, 11(4), 3–12.

Lubit, R. 2001. Tacit knowledge and knowledge management: The keys to sustainable competitive advantage. *Organizational Dynamics*, 29(4), 164–178.

Man, T.W.Y., Lau, T. and Chan, K.F. 2002. The competitiveness of small and medium enterprises: A conceptualization with focus on entrepreneurial competencies. *Journal of Business Venturing*, 17,123–142.

Marger, M.N. 2001. Social and human capital in immigrant adaptation: The case of Canadian business immigrants. *Journal of Socio-Economics*, 30(2), 169–170.

Martin, J. 1996. *Cybercorp, the New Business Revolution*. USA: American Management Association, USA.

Martin, L.M. and Wright, L.T. 2005. No gender in cyberspace? Empowering entrepreneurship and innovation in female-run ICT small firms. *International Journal of Entrepreneurial Behaviour & Research*, 11(2), 162–178.

Martin, S. and Scott, J.T. 2000. The nature of innovation market failure and the design of public support for private innovation. *Research Policy*, 29(4), 437–447.

Mascitelli, R. 2000. From experience: Harnessing tacit knowledge to achieve breakthrough innovation. *Journal of Product Innovation Management*, 17(3), 179–193.

McDaniel, B.A. 2000. A survey of entrepreneurship and innovation. *The Social Science Journal*, 37(2), 277–284.

McDonough, III E.F., Athanassiou, N. and Barczak, G. 2006. Networking for global new product innovation. *International Journal of Business Innovation and Research*, 1(1/2), 9–26.

McManus, P.A. 2001. Women's participation in self-employment in Western industrialised nations. *International Journal of Sociology*, 31(2), 70–97.

Morawska, E. 2004. Immigrant transnational entrepreneurs in New York: Three varieties and their correlates. *International Journal of Entrepreneurial Behavior & Research*, 10(5), 325–348.

Morehouse, M.M. 2007. An exploration of emotional intelligence across career arenas. *Leadership & Organization Development Journal*, 28(4), 296–307.

Morrison, A. 2000. Entrepreneurship: what triggers it? *International Journal of Entrepreneurial Behaviour and Research*, 6(2), 59–71.

Moss, F.A. and Hunt, T. 1927. Are you socially intelligent. *Scientific American*, 137, 108–110.

Muller, E. and Zenker, A. 2001. Business services as actors of knowledge transformation: The role of KIBS in regional and national innovation systems. *Research Policy*, 30(9), 1501–1516.

Narula, R. and Hagedoorn, J. 1999. Innovating through strategic alliances: Moving towards international partnerships and contractual agreements. *Technovation*, 19, 283–294.

Nonaka. I. and Takeuchi, H. 1995. *The Knowledge Creating Company: How Japanese Companies Create the Dynamics of Innovation.* Oxford: Oxford University Press.

OECD, 2000. *Small and Medium Enterprise Outlook.* Paris: OECD.

Orhan, M. and Scott, D. 2001. Why women enter into entrepreneurship: An explanatory model. *Women in Management Review*, 16(5), 232–247.

Park, J. 2005. Fostering creativity and productivity through emotional literacy: The organizational context. *Development and Learning in Organizations*, 19(4), 5–7.

Park, K. 1997. *The Korean American Dream.* Ithaca N.Y.: Cornell University Press.

Pavitt, K., Robson, M. and Townsend, J. 1989. Technological accumulation, diversification and organisation in UK companies: 1945–1983. *Management Science*, 35(1), 81–99.

Perrow, C. 1992. Small-Firm Networks, in *Networks and Organizations: Structure, Form and Action*, edited by N. Nohria, and R.G. Eccles, Boston: Harvard Business School.

Petridou, E., Sarri, A. and Kyrgidou, L.P. 2009. Entrepreneurship education in higher educational institutions: The gender dimension. *Gender in Management: An International Journal*, 24(4), 286–309.

Phizacklea, A. and Ram, M. 1995. Ethnic Entrepreneurship in comparative perspective. *International Journal of Entrepreneurial Behaviour & Research*, 1(1), 48–58.

Piperopoulos, P. 2007. Barriers to innovation for SMEs: Empirical evidence from Greece. *International Journal of Business Innovation and Research*, 1(4), 365–386.

Piperopoulos, P. and Scase, R. 2009. Competitiveness of small and medium enterprises: Towards a two-dimensional model of innovation and business clusters. *International Journal of Business Innovation and Research*, 3(5), 479–499.

Piperopoulos, P. 2010. Ethnic minority businesses and immigrant entrepreneurship in Greece. *Journal of Small Business and Enterprise Development*, 17(1), 139–158.

Pissarides, F. 1999. Is luck of funds the main obstacle to growth: EBRD's experience with small and medium-sized businesses in Central and Eastern Europe. *Journal of Business Venturing*, 14, 519–539.

Polanyi, M. 1958. *Personal Knowledge: Towards a Post-critical Philosophy*. London: Routledge & Kegan Paul.

Polanyi, M. 1961. Knowing and being. *Mind*, 70(280), 458–470.

Polanyi, M. 1962. Tacit Knowing-its bearing in some problems of philosophy. *Reviews of Modern Physics*, 34(4), 601–616.

Polanyi, M. 1966. *The Tacit Dimension*. London: Routledge and Kegan Paul.

Popper, K. 1972. *Objective Knowledge: An Evolutionary Approach*. Oxford: Clarendon Press.

Porter, M.E. 1985. *Competitive Advantage, Creating and Sustaining Superior Performance*. USA: The Free Press.

Porter, M.E. 1990. *The Competitive Advantage of Nations*. USA: The Free Press.

Portes, A. and Sensenbrenner, J. 1993. Embeddedness and immigration: Notes on the social determinants of economic action. *American Journal of Sociology*, 98, 1320–1350.

Portes, A. and Shafer, S. 2007. Revisiting the enclave hypothesis: Miami twenty-five years later. *Research in the Sociology of Organisations*, 25, 157–190.

Powell, W.W. 1990. Neither market nor hierarchy: Network forms of organization. *Research in Organizational Behavior*, 12, 295–336.

Powell, W.W. 1996. Inter-organizational collaboration in the biotechnology industry. *Journal of Institutional and Theoretical Economics*, 120(1), 197–215.

Prabhu, G.N. 1999. Implementing university-industry joint product innovation projects. *Technovation*, 19(8), 495–505.

Prati, M. 2005. Emotional intelligence as a facilitator of the emotional labour process. *Dissertation Abstracts International*, 66(1), 251–461.

Quinn, J.B. 1992. *Intelligent Enterprise*. New York: The Free Press.

Quinn, J.B., Anderson, P. and Finkelstein, S. 1996. Leveraging intellect. *Academy of Management Executives*, 10(3), 7–27.

Raghuram, P. and Hardill, I. 1998. Negotiating a market: A case study of an Asian woman in business. *Women's Studies International Forum*, 21(5), 475–483.

Raghuram, P. and Strange, A. 2001. Studying economic institutions, placing cultural politics: Methodological musings from a study of ethnic minority enterprise. *Geoforum*, 32(3), 377–388.

Raijman, R. and Tienda, M. 2003. Ethnic foundations of economic transactions: Mexican and Korean immigrant entrepreneurs in Chicago. *Ethnic and Racial Studies*, 26(5), 783–801.

Ram, M. 1997. Ethnic minority enterprise: An overview and research agenda. *International Journal of Entrepreneurial Behavior & Research*, 3(4), 149–156.

Ram, M. and Carter, S. 2003. Paving professional futures: Ethnic minority accountants in the United Kingdom. *International Small Business Journal*, 21(1), 55–71.

Ram, M. and Smallbone, D. 2003. Special issues. *Entrepreneurship & Regional Development*, 15(2), 99–102.

Ram, M. and Smallbone, D. 2003a. Policies to support ethnic minority enterprise: The English experience. *Entrepreneurship & Regional Development*, 15(2), 151–166.

Ram, M., Smallbone, D., Deakins, D. and Jones, T. 2003. Banking on 'break-out': Finance and the development of ethnic minority businesses. *Journal of Ethnic and Migration Studies*, 29(4), 663–681.

Rath, J. 2002. A quintessential immigrant niche? The non-case of immigrants in the Dutch construction industry. *Entrepreneurship & Regional Development*, 14(4), 355–372.

Razin, E. 2002. Conclusion the economic context, embeddedness and immigrant entrepreneurs. *International Journal of Entrepreneurial Behavior & Research*, 8(1/2), 162–167.

Rosenberg, N. 1982. *Inside the Black Box: Technology and Economics*. Cambridge: Cambridge University Press.

Rosenfeld, S.A. 1996. Does cooperation enhance competitiveness: Assessing the impacts of inter-firm collaboration. *Research Policy*, 25(2), 247–263.

Rosete, D. and Ciarrochi, J. 2005. Emotional intelligence and its relationship to workplace performance. *Leadership & Organization Development Journal*, 26(5), 388–399.

Rozell, E.J., Pettijohn, C.E and Parker, R.S. 2002. An empirical evaluation of emotional intelligence; the impact of management development. *Journal of Management Development*, 21(4), 272–289.

Salovey, P. and Mayer, J.D. 1990. Emotional intelligence. *Imagination, Cognition, and Personality*, 9(3), 185–211.

Samitas, A.G. and Kenourgios, D.F. 2005. Entrepreneurship, small and medium sized business markets and European economic integration. *Journal of Policy Modelling*, 27(3), 363–374.

Sanders, J.M. and Nee, V. 1996. Immigrant self-employment: The family as social capital and the value of human capital. *American Sociological Review*, 61, 231–249.

Sarri, K. and Trihopoulou, A. 2005. Female entrepreneurs' personal characteristics and motivation: A review of the Greek situation. *Women in Management Review*, 20(1), 24–36.

SBS, 2004. *A Government Action Plan for Small Business*, London: Small Business Service.

Schmiemann, M. 2008. *Enterprises by Size Class – Overview of SMEs in the EU: Industry, Trade and Services*. Available at: http://epp.eurostat.ec.europa. eu/portal/page/portal/product_details/publication?p_product_code=KS-SF-08-031 [accessed 24 January 2011]

Schumpeter, J.A. 1942. *Capitalism, Socialism and Democracy*. London: George Allen & Unwin.

Schwartz, E. 1976. Entrepreneurship: A new female frontier. *Journal of Contemporary Business*, 5(1), 47–76.

Scott, C.E. 1986. Why more women are becoming entrepreneurs. *Journal of Small Business Management*, 27(4), 37–44.

Shabbir, A. and Di Gregorio, S. 1996. An examination of the relationship between women's personal goals and structural factors influencing their decisions to start a business: The case of Pakistan. *Journal of Business Venturing*, 11(6), 507–529.

Singh, G. and DeNoble, A. 2004. Psychological acculturation of ethnic minorities and entrepreneurship. *International Research in the Business Disciplines*, 4, 279–289.

Slaski, M. and Cartwright, S. 2003. Emotional intelligence training and its implications for stress, health and performance. *Stress and Health*, 19(4), 233–239.

Smallbone, D., Ram, M., Deakins, D. and Baldock, R. 2003. Access to finance by ethnic minority businesses in the UK. *International Small Business Journal*, 21(3), 291–314.

Sosik, J.J. and Megerian, L.E. 1999. Understanding leader emotional intelligence and performance: The role of self-other agreement on transformational leadership perceptions. *Group and Organization Management*, 24(3), 340–366.

Sriram, V., Mersha, T. and Herron, L. 2007. Drivers of urban entrepreneurship: An integrative model. *International Journal of Entrepreneurial Behavior & Research*, 13(4), 235–251.

Stefansson, G. 2002. Business-to-business data sharing: A source for integration of supply chains. *International Journal of Production Economics*, 75, 135–146.

Sternberg, R.J. and Wagner, R.K. 1992. Tacit knowledge: An unspoken key to managerial success. *Creativity and Innovation Management*, 1(1), 5–13.

Storey, D.J. 2000. *Understanding the Small Business Sector*. London: Thomson Learning.

Stuart, T.E. 2000. Interorganisational alliances and the performance of firms: A study of growth an innovation rates in a high-technology industry. *Strategic Management Journal*, 21(8), 791–811.

Suliman, A.M. and Al-Shaikh, F.N. 2007. Emotional Intelligence at work: Links to conflict and innovation. *Employee Relations*, 29(2), 208–220.

Swedberg, R. 1998, Max Weber's Vision of Economic Sociology. *Journal of Socio-Economics*, 27(4), 535–555.

Sy. T., Tram, S. and O' Hara, L.A. 2006. Relation of employee and manager emotional intelligence to job satisfaction and performance. *Journal of Vocational Behavior*, 68(3), 461–473.

Teixeira, C. 2001. Community resources and opportunities in ethnic economies: A case study of a Portuguese and black entrepreneurs in Toronto. *Urban Studies*, 38(11), 2055–2078.

Tether, B.S. 2000. Small firms, innovation and employment creation in Britain and Europe: A question of expectations. *Technovation*, 20(2), 109–113.

Thorndike, E.L. 1920. A constant error in psychological ratings. *Journal of Applied Psychology*, 4(1), 25–29.

Thwaites, A.T. and Wynarczyk, P. 1996. The economic performance of innovative small firms in the south east and elsewhere in the UK. *Regional Studies*, 32(2), 135–149.

Trott, P. Maddocks, T. and Wheeler, C. 2009. Core competencies for diversifying: Case study of a small business. *Strategic Change*, 18(1/2), 27–43.

U.S. Small Business Administration, 1999. *The Facts About Small Business 1999*. Washington, DC: Government Printing Office.

Van De Vrande, V., De Jong, J.J., Vanhaverbeke, W. and De Rochemont, M. 2009. Open innovation in SMEs: Trends, motives and management challenges. *Technovation*, 29, 423–437.

Van Rooy, D.L and Viswesvaran, C. 2004. Emotional intelligence: A meta-analytic investigation of predictive validity and nomological net. *Journal of Vocational Behavior*, 65(1), 71–95.

Verheul, I. and Thurik, R. 2001. Start-up capital: Does gender matter? *Small Business Economics*, 16(4), 329–345.

Vernon, P.E. 1933. Some characteristics of the good judge of personality. *Journal of Social Psychology*, 4, 42–57.

Von Hippel, E. 1988. *The Sources of Innovation*. New York: Oxford University Press.

Wagner, R.K and Sternberg, R.J. 1985. Practical intelligence in real world pursuits: The role of tacit knowledge. *Journal of Personality and Social Psychology*, 49, 436–458.

Waldinger, R. 1986. *Through the Eye of the Needle: Immigrants and Enterprise in New York's Garment Trades*. New York: New York University Press.

Waldinger, R. 1996. *Still the Promised City? African-Americans and New Immigrants in Post-Industrial New York*. Cambridge: Harvard University Press.

Waldinger, R. 1999. Network, bureaucracy, exclusion: Recruitment and selection in an immigrant metropolis, in *Immigration and Opportunity: Race, Ethnicity, and Employment in the United States*, edited by F. Bean and S. Bell-Rose, New York: Russell Sage Foundation.

Wauters, B. and Lambrecht, J. 2008. Refugee entrepreneurship: The case of Belgium, in: *Entrepreneurship, Competitiveness and Local Development: Frontiers in European Entrepreneurship Research*, edited by L. Iandoli, H. Lanström H. and M. Raffa, Cheltenham: Edward Elgar, 200–222.

Weeks, J.R. 2001. The face of women entrepreneurs: What we know today, in *Women Entrepreneurs in SMEs: Realising the Benefits of Globalisation and the Knowledge-Based Economy*, edited by OECD, France, Paris: OECD Publications, 127–143.

Weisinger, H. 1998. *Emotional Intelligence at Work*. San Francisco: Jossey-Bass.

Wilson, F.D. 2003. Ethnic niching and metropolitan labour markets. *Social Science Research*, 32, 429–466.

Winter, S. 1987. Knowledge and competence as strategic assets, in *The Competitive Challenge – Strategies for Industrial Innovation and Renewal*, edited by, D. Teece, Cambridge, MA: Ballinger.

Wong, C. and Law, K.S. 2002. The effects of leader and follower emotional intelligence on performance and attitude: An exploratory study. *Leadership Quarterly*, 13(3), 243–274.

Wynarczyk, P. 2010. Key Ingredients of innovation: The case of science and technology-based SMEs in the UK, presented at *Triple Helix 8th International Conference*, October, 19–21, Madrid, Spain.

Zhara, S.A. and George, G. 2002. Absorptive capacity: A review, reconceptualization, and extension. *Academy of Management Review*, 27(2), 185–203.

Zhou, M. 1992. *Chinatown: The Socioeconomic Potential of an Urban Enclave*. Philadelphia, PA: Temple University Press.

Zhou,. J. and George, J.M. 2003. Awakening employee creativity: The role of leader emotional intelligence. *Leadership Quarterly*, 14(4/5), 545–568.

PART 3

Business Clusters, Small and Medium-Sized Enterprises and Innovation

Prolegomena of Part 3

As we explained in the Part 2, SMEs can play a key role in triggering and sustaining economic growth in developed and developing countries. We illustrated that in the EU there are currently over 23 million enterprises, employing one or more persons, representing 99 per cent of all EU companies and providing jobs for some 75 million people. However, we also argued that the enormous potential of the role of SMEs is often not fulfilled because of particular sets of problems which characterize them, for example, their size or the manager's/owner's lack of competence. Furthermore, individual SMEs are often unable to capture market opportunities, which require large production capacities, homogenous standards and regular supply.

By the same account, small size constitutes a significant hindrance to the internationalization of functions, such as training, market intelligence and innovation, all of which are at the very core of firm dynamism according to management literature. We have also examined the importance and the central role of entrepreneurs for SMEs, and attempted to understand how business networks and strategic alliances affect the competitiveness and innovative performance of SMEs. Parts 1 and 2 of the book provided the conceptual framework and springboard for the presentation and analysis of the main themes of this third part, Part 3; the concepts of business clusters and networks, investigation of the innovative potential of SMEs within clusters, the university-industry-government relations and examination of regional economies like the *Third Italy* and *Silicon Valley*.

The aim of Part 3 is to provide an understanding of business clusters. In this part of the book we discuss the literature thus providing a review for clusters and networks, we examine how and why clusters can affect SMEs' innovative capabilities and competitiveness, as well as the importance and central role of entrepreneurship and innovation. Furthermore, we attempt to answer how important is the role of institutions, agents, authorities and the government in promoting and supporting business clusters and university-business relations. The attempt will be to clarify the characteristics of clusters and networks by providing examples of well-known cases. Operating within this conceptual framework, we will examine Silicon Valley since it is the most documented cluster in management literature. Hence, having investigated, analyzed and presented the concepts of entrepreneurship and innovation in Parts 1 and 2, and business clustering in the following two chapters (namely Chapter 9 and Chapter 10), in the last chapter we set up, describe and analyze a two-dimensional model of SMEs that aims to link the concepts and their relations and to provide a descriptive framework for understanding the dynamics of SMEs' growth.

According to Enright and Ffowcs-Williams (2000), clusters, which are properly defined in Chapter 9 immediately following, could for the time being be delineated as a sectoral and geographical concentration of interrelated and interconnected enterprises which produce and sell a range of related or complementary products. They are thus faced with common challenges and opportunities and these can help SMEs realize the opportunities and meet the challenges associated with internationalization and intense competition. The authors argue that membership of clusters can enhance the productivity, rate of innovation and competitive performance of firms. Moreover, according to the European Commission (2002), clusters are widely recognized by scholars and policy makers around the world as important settings in stimulating the productivity and innovativeness of companies and the formation of new businesses:

> Competition is increasingly seen to occur between clusters, value chains or network of firms rather than just between individual firms. It is also argued that regional clusters are the best environment for stimulating innovation and competitiveness of firms. (European Commission 2002b: 13)

The influential writings of Porter (1998) also underline the importance of clustering in affecting competitiveness within countries and across national borders. Porter introduces a way of thinking where companies reconfigure themselves, institutions such as universities contribute to competitive success and governments promote economic development and prosperity.

As we present and examine with supportive data throughout Part 3 of the book, clusters, or as otherwise stated, industrial districts of firms, were first observed in Italy in the 1960s, mainly consisting of SMEs which proved to be not only equal, but also more dynamic than large-scale, private or government run industries, often establishing a strong presence on world markets. Italy's industrial districts became a reference point in the discussion of regional clustering in management literature. Another important reference point at the other side of the Atlantic has been Silicon Valley in California which is also described as a cluster, or rather an agglomeration, consisting of several interrelated clusters (Meyer-Stamer 2001). As Porter (1998: 77) quotes, 'paradoxically the enduring competitive advantages in a global economy lie increasingly in local things – knowledge, relationships and motivation that distant rivals cannot match.'

The examples of prosperous and well-performing regional and industrial clusters established in the 1970s and 1980s in Northern Italy and in the Silicon Valley increased the focus of interest of academics and policy makers in the phenomenon of clustering. In the course of the 1990s, clusters became a target for regional and national initiatives and policies to promote competitiveness and innovation, stimulate productivity, growth and the formation of new businesses:

> *The increased focus on regional clusters and innovation systems reflects a (re) discovery by many academics of the importance of the regional level, and the importance of specific local and regional resources in stimulating the innovation capability and competitiveness of firms. Specific regional resources such as a stock of 'sticky' knowledge, learning ability, entrepreneurial attitudes etc. are seen to be of great importance in firms' efforts to be at global competitive level. Building regional clusters is even perceived by some as the way to compete globally, as economic 'specialization is (seen as) the only way to overcome 'the globalisation trap', that is, outrunning the risk of being out competed across the board. (European Commission 2002b: 9)*

In this section we explore the emerging concept of business clustering as a means for regional and national initiatives and policies to promote competitiveness and innovation, stimulate entrepreneurship, productivity, growth and the formation of new businesses. Delving into these issues obliges us to explore clusters through a historical perspective and address a series of questions, such as where and when they first appeared, in which economic sectors, how and why they emerged, how they are defined and what their characteristics are.

9

The Concept of Business Clusters and their Life Cycle

Geographical Proximity

In an increasing internationalization of the global marketplace with efficient and effective transportation and communication means, the significance of regions and location should have been eliminated (DeWitt et al. 2006, Smedlund and Toivonen 2007). In contrast though, networking, developing strong regional clusters, capitalizing on spatial proximity and tacit knowledge and achieving synergies through competition alongside co-operation in geographical proximity, has never been more crucial for the economic development and competitiveness of regions and SMEs (DeWitt et al. 2006, Jackson 2006; Smedlund and Toivonen 2007). The success of some regional clusters such as, for example, the Silicon Valley and Prato region in Italy have triggered attention to the role of knowledge and local environment in stimulating the competitiveness of networks of firms. With the advent of information and communication technologies, information and knowledge flow is scarcely affected by distance and nowadays even oceans and mountains are considered as relatively small barriers. Physical transportation is no longer as important or as difficult as it used to be. The ever declining cost of transporting goods and people by air and the improved surface and shipping transportation has led to physical boundaries becoming less important.

The broad pattern that seems to be emerging is that of markets being big and based on global regions, whereas producing units is smaller and based on subnational regions (Padmore and Gibson 1998):

> *Economic geography in an era of global competition, then, poses a paradox. In a global economy -which boasts rapid transportation, high-speed communication, and accessible markets – one would*

expect location to diminish in importance. But the opposite is true. The enduring competitive advantages in a global economy are often heavily local, arising from concentrations of heavily specialised skills and knowledge, institutions, rivals, related business, and sophisticated customers. Geographical, cultural, and institutional proximity leads to special access, closer relationships, better information, powerful incentives, and other advantages in productivity and innovation that are difficult to tap from a distance. The more the world economy becomes complex, knowledge based and dynamic, the more this is true. (Porter 1998: 90)

Industrial districts capture the attention of a substantial body of researchers and policy makers across a wide range of countries and organizations. According to several influential scholars and researchers, industrial districts do constitute a potentially attractive model of regional development. Nassimbeni (2003: 153) provides a broad list of the main features of 'industrial districts' that summarizes the views and works of many scholars on the subject:

1. High proportion of small and very small firms.

2. Clustering of firms in a geographical location.

3. Firms engaged at various stages of production-intense specialization.

4. Dense networks of a social and economic nature.

5. Blend of competition and co-operation between firms.

6. Rapid and mainly informal diffusion of information, new ideas, experiences and know-how.

7. Adaptability and flexibility.

The Genesis of Industrial Districts

A proper understanding of the concept of clustering obliges us to begin our analysis with the British economist, Alfred Marshall, who carried out the first and most important work in the field of industrial agglomeration at the end of the nineteenth century. His seminal work sparked a series of studies on districts. In his work, *Principles of Economics*, first published in 1890, Marshall (1922) describes districts as a territorial concentration of numerous (small) enterprises characterized by high vertical and horizontal specialization, a dense network of social and economic, competitive and co-operative relations. The exchange of commercial and technical information including any innovations is prompt but informal:

> *The mysteries of the trade become no mysteries, but are as it were in the air, and children learn many of them unconsciously. Good work is rightly appreciated, inventions and improvements in machinery, in processes and the general organization of the business have their merits promptly discussed: if one man starts a new idea, it is taken up by others and combined with suggestions of their own, and thus it becomes the source of further new ideas. (Marshall 1922: 271)*

Marshall, in his early writings on Sheffield cutlery, Lancashire cottons and other British regions, ascribes their competitive advantage to the presence of external economies, as the 'commons', the infrastructure and other services from which each individual firm in an industrial district might draw. These include faster dissemination of new ideas, experience and know-how thanks to geographic proximity, cultural homogeneity, common manufacturing traditions, reduced cost of transport (and of transactions in general) and the easier access to complementary services or capabilities.

Furthermore, examples include improved job search and job matching, more favourable access to capital finance and inter-firm labour migration. According to Marshall (1922), the availability of such common resources to a number of firms then enhances their size and diversity as both capital and labour are attracted to such areas to exploit the larger markets for their services. This, in turn, leads to reductions in factor prices and/or increases in factor productivities. The external benefit to firms of a location in the industrial district manifests itself in these ways. Unit production costs will be lower within the industrial district than out of it. As Zeitlin (1992: 80) argues, the external economies in Marshall's analysis assume three main forms:

1.   Economies of specialization arising from an extended division of labour between firms in complementary activities and processes.

2.   Economies of information and communication arising from the joint production of non-standardized commodities. (similar to modern notions of transaction costs)

3.   Economies of labour supply arising from the availability of a large pool of trained workers.

In addition, the author argues that Marshall also noted the more dynamic but less narrowly economic in character; advantages that the industrial districts seemed to gain from a distinctive industrial atmosphere which facilitated the acquisition of specialized skills and the diffusion of knowledge and innovations through socialization and interchange between local actors. According Zeitlin (1992) it was much later in the course of time, during the 1970s, that a number of influential writers sought to elaborate Marshall's notion of industrial atmosphere by including a set of more explicitly social features drawn mainly from the 'Third Italy'. Beccatini (1990) developed one of the most influential works on industrial districts as a *socio-economic notion*. Among the new elements introduced into the Marshallian ID (industrial district) was a non-metropolitan, small town environment, a set of shared values such as hard work, co-operation and collective identity, and a social structure based on the prevalence of entrepreneurs and industrial workers. According to Beccatini (1990: 39), an industrial district is defined as, 'a socio-economic entity, which is characterised by the active presence of both a community of people and a population of firms in one naturally and historically bounded area.'

THE SMALL FIRMS ECONOMY AND THE FLEXIBLE SPECIALIZATION

An influential work on business clusters and especially on when, how and why they emerged is presented in Piore and Sabel's text, *The Second Industrial Divide* (1984), that draws together a meta-historical analysis of the late nineteenth and early twentieth century capitalistic mode of production. In their text the authors argue that the epoch of mass production is fading away, giving way to the small firm economy:

> *Our claim is that the present deterioration in economic performance results from the limits of the model of industrial development that is founded on mass production: the use of special-purpose (product-specific) machines and of semiskilled workers to produce standardised goods. (Piore and Sabel 1984: 4)*

The authors argue that throughout the nineteenth century, two forms of technological development were in collision. One was craft production, based on the idea that machines and processes could augment the craftsman's skill, allowing the worker to embody his knowledge in even more varied products, while the other form of technological development was mass production. Its foundation was the idea that the cost of making any particular good could be significantly reduced if only machinery could be substituted for the human skill needed to produce it.

According to the authors, a strong inter-firm division of labour among clusters of small firms, connected by horizontal and vertical competitive and co-operative relationships, can lead to greater collective efficiency than that of large-scale Fordist enterprises. They cite industrial districts in central and northern Italy where co-operation and innovation is promoted by establishing an ethos of interdependence among producers in the same market, while competition is encouraged but controlled by mechanisms of social cohesion within the local community. Piore and Sabel (1984: 17) call this *flexible specialization:*

> *It is seen in the networks of technologically sophisticated, highly flexible manufacturing firms in central and northwest Italy. Flexible specialisation is a strategy of permanent innovation: accommodation to ceaseless change, rather than an effort to control it. This strategy is based on flexible – multi-use – equipment; skilled workers; and the creation, through politics, of an industrial community that restricts the forms of competition to those favouring innovation. For these reasons, the spread of flexible specialisation amounts to a revival of craft forms of production that were emarginated at the first industrial divide.*

The following table illustrates the practical and conceptual differences between *mass production* and *flexible specialization*. The table facilitates the identification of the concepts central to the flexible specialization system, namely innovation, inter-firm co-operation, joint problem solving, inter-organizational relations, local and regional infrastructure, the role of institutions and competition based on innovation. Furthermore, both the analysis of the Marshallian theory of industrial districts, and the theory of Piore and Sabel's flexible specialization bring forth the central role of small firms in business clusters.

Table 9.1   Two industrial systems compared mass production and flexible specialization

Dimension	Mass Production	Flexible Specialization
1. Market conditions	Market stability with supplying equal demand.	Market instability, innovation and product development are key to securing market share.
2. Production technology	Purpose built machinery, dedicated to a particular task.	Flexible and multi-use machinery.
3. Products	Low variety, standardized range of products.	Semi-customized and mass variety goods, niche markets.
4. Productive organization	Managerial hierarchies, span of control, large and centralized factories.	Flatter organization structures, centralized planning and control system, dispersed production across the network, sub-contracting and franchising.
5. Work processes, operative skills	Rigid divisions between metal and manual labour, semi-skilled workers, predominantly unskilled labour.	Core and periphery of workers, multi-skilled artisans and semi-skilled operatives linked by a chain of sub-contractors.
6. Inter-organizational relations	Adversarial, little communication or inter-company projects.	Co-operative, collaborative, based on trust and dependence.
7. Supplier relationship	Arm's length and adversarial, negotiation on price norm.	Obligational contracting relations, joint problem solving.
8. Regional infrastructure	Importance placed on wider macroeconomic policies to ensure supply equals demand.	Local and regional infrastructure central to industrial district development, co-operation between many non-industrial institutions.
9. Competitive strategy	Competition on price, economies of scale; overproduction compensated by stock-piling or markdowns.	Competition based on innovative products and processes, responds to falling market by diversification, innovation or contracting to core business.

Source: Day 2000: 6

A BLEND OF TRUST AND CO-OPERATION

Piore and Sabel (1984) list a number of famous industrial districts of the nineteenth century: silks in Lyon; ribbons, hardware and specialty steel in neighbouring Saint-Etienne; edge tools, cutlery and specialty steel in Solingen, Remscheid and Sheffield; calicoes in Alsace; woollen and cotton textiles in

Roubaix; and cotton goods in Philadelphia and Pawtucket, the history of which challenges the classical view of economic progress. According to the authors, small firms in those industrial districts often developed or exploited new technologies without becoming larger, suggesting a craft alternative to mass production as a model of technological advance. Day et al. (2000: 7), quoting from the work of Hirst and Zeitlin, illuminate the physiology of an industrial district as proposed by Piore and Sabel (1984):

> *Geographically-localised networks of small firms that sub-contract between one another and share a range of common services beyond the economic or productive capacity of the single firm ... within the district there may be differing roles played by the firms, from productive units though to trade associations, trade unions and local government agencies.*

According to Day et al (2000), trust and co-operation between firms in the industrial district are central to its existence. In order for the firms to live in a creative and innovative environment, they must share their expertise and proprietary information with others. This mix of trust and dependence creates an atmosphere where competitors are also collaborators. This type of exchange allows the specialist firm to provide its expertise to build products that benefit from a pool of expert knowledge.

Piore and Sabel (1984) argue that industrial districts are also dependent upon the creation and operation of regional institutions that balance the co-operation and competition among firms, to encourage permanent innovation. Institutions create an environment in which skills and capital equipment could be constantly recombined in order to produce rapidly shifting assortments of goods. The institutions discourage firms from competition in the form of wage and price reduction, as opposed to competition through innovation of products and processes. In addition, Day et al. (2000) suggest that the role of the state is to act as a facilitator for the industrial district to thrive within a geographically defined region. The type of support offered could be in form of economic regeneration zones, financial assistance for research and development, provision for training staff and funding for research agencies. The main aim according to the author is to provide the infrastructure support that would foster the industrial district to flourish.

The Californian School

The importance of the role of institutions in promoting business clustering is further supported in the Californian School of External Economies, which argues that the disintegration of productive systems leads to an increase in firms' transaction costs (Scott and Storper 1986, Scott 1988, Storper, 1989). Changes in market and technological conditions have led to increased uncertainty and greater risks of over-capacity (of labour and capital) and of being locked into redundant technologies. The response of deepening the organizational division of labour leads to an increase in the number of formal market transactions external to the firm. There may also be an increase in the unpredictability and complexity of transactions. The costs of carrying out certain types of transaction, especially those where tacit knowledge is important or trust is required and thus complete contracting is impossible, varies systematically with distance. Thus, according to the authors, agglomeration is the result of the minimization of these types of transaction costs in a situation where such minimization outweighs other production cost differentials.

The Californian school analyzed the growth of new industrial spaces, emphasizing vertical disintegration of production chains in a new era of flexible accumulation, which leads to agglomeration of firms to reduce inter-firm transaction costs and the formation of specialized local labour markets (Scott 1988). Being at the start of a mainly structural approach referring to universal causal mechanisms and circumstances, the attention soon shifted to examining the role of culture, institutions and governance in the creation of new industrial spaces (Storper and Salais 1997). The approach considers the agglomeration itself as a source of industrial dynamics and, in particular, sees the region as the locus of what Storper (1997) denotes as untraded interdependencies, which are conventions, informal rules, practices and institutional norms that co-ordinate economic players under the conditions of uncertainty.

Underpinning this concept is the principle that economic forms are embedded in particular institutional frameworks. Thus, according to Storper and Salais (1997), the construction of any production system is the creation of behavioural-institutional sources of learning. These interdependencies, as delineated above, help the firm to define strategies in an environment characterized by market and technological uncertainty. The most crucial point according to Stroper (1997) is that these interdependencies often take place outside of conventional traded market mechanisms. Furthermore, since this knowledge is often tacit and localized, it is argued that it helps to create territorialized forms of production.

Business Clusters: Competition and Co-operation

The influential writings of Porter first on industrial clusters in his work, *The Competitive Advantage of Nations* (1990) and then on regional clusters in his work, *Clusters and the New Economics of Competition* (1998), describe the tight relationships between participation of firms and industries in clusters and enhanced competitiveness. For Porter (1990), a nation's competitive industries are not evenly spread throughout the economy but are connected and geographically concentrated in what he terms as 'clusters', consisting of industries usually linked through vertical (buyer/supplier) and/or horizontal (customers, technology, channels, etc.) relationships. Porter (1998: 78) explicitly defines a cluster as, 'critical masses – in one place – of unusual competitive success in particular fields ... clusters are geographic concentrations of interconnected companies and institutions in a particular field.'

Porter (1998) defines clusters as concentrations that include a range of related industries and other entities important to competition. They could include suppliers of specialized inputs, for example on one hand, machinery and components and on the other hand, services and providers of specialized infrastructure. The author argues that clusters often extend downstream to several channels and customers, as well as manufacturers of complementary products and to companies in industries related by skills, technology or common inputs. He also suggests that clusters encompass governments and institutions such as universities, research centres, trade associations and so on that provide education, information and knowledge, research activities, training and technical support.

Consider, for example, the Italian leather fashion cluster (as shown in Figure 9.1) which contains well-known footwear companies, such as Gucci and Ferragamo, as well as a number of specialized suppliers of footwear components, design services, injection-moulding machinery, lasts and tanned leather as shown in the Figure 9.1. It also includes several chains of related industries, such as those producing leather handbags, belts and so on and those producing different types of footwear, for example, hiking boots and ski boots. The former industries are linked by common inputs and technologies while the latter industries by overlapping channels and technologies. All these industries employ common marketing media and compete in related customer segments. Another Italian cluster, the textile fashion, encompassing clothing, scarves, accessories, and so on, often employs common channels with the leather fashion cluster. The multiple linkages and synergies of the businesses participating in the Italian leather fashion cluster can to a great degree explain the astonishing strength of the cluster.

According to Porter (1998) clusters can and should promote both competition and co-operation since they occur on different dimensions and among different players. The author recognizes that clusters are formed by independent and informally linked companies and institutions, usually in arm's-length relationships, thus representing a robust, effective, efficient and flexible organizational form without the inflexibility of vertical integration and the management challenges imposed by formal strategic alliances, networks and partnerships.

Several other scholars define clusters in a somewhat similar manner to that of Porter (1998). Padmore and Gibson (1998: 627) argue, 'a cluster is a concentration of firms that prosper because of their interaction, whether that is through competition and cooperation, or by serving as suppliers or customers in the value chain.' According to Steinle and Schiele (2002: 850–851), 'clusters are localised sectoral agglomerations of symbiotic organisations

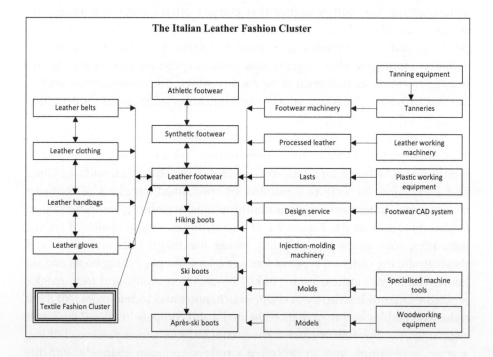

Figure 9.1   The Italian leather fashion cluster
Source: Porter 1998: 80

that can achieve superior business performance because of their club like interaction … moreover … innovative clusters display at an inter-industrial level, underlying networks of interrelated co-operating businesses…such an environment is characterised by intensive knowledge sharing.' Furthermore, Lyon and Atherton (2000: 4) consider a cluster as, 'a group of organisations in related industries that have economic links, and, concentrations of competing, collaborating and interdependent companies and institutions, which are connected by a system of market and non-market links.'

Synthesizing the aforementioned positions, we could surmise then that industrial or regional clusters are groups of competing, collaborating and interdependent businesses working in common or similar industries and concentrated in a geographic region. Furthermore, institutions, governments, universities and other agents and entities appear to hold a decisive role in the promotion and success of a business cluster. Businesses draw on shared infrastructures and a pool of skilled workers. This form of co-operation between enterprises is a fundamental strategy for SMEs; capable to reach goals which would not be obtained by the single enterprise. Co-operation could optimize costs, favour the exchange of knowledge, make easier the access to strategic information, support learning dynamics and enhance innovation.

Regional Innovation System

The European Commission (2002b), as presented in the following table, attempts to differentiate three distinct concepts, namely those of regional clusters, regional innovation networks and regional innovation systems.

Table 9.2   A hierarchy of three concepts

Concepts	Definitions and differences
Regional cluster	A concentration of 'interdependent' firms within the same or adjacent industrial sectors in a small geographical area.
Regional innovation network	More organized co-operation (agreement) between firms, stimulated by trust, norms and conventions, which encourages firms' innovation activity.
Regional innovation system	Co-operation also between firms and different organizations for knowledge development and diffusion.

Source: European Commission 2003b: 14

Regional clusters are seen mainly as a spontaneous phenomenon, a concentration of interdependent firms in a geographic location often because of spin-offs and entrepreneurial activity. On the other hand, regional innovation systems are more planned and systemic in character according to the European Commission. The regional innovation system denotes regional clusters plus supporting institutions. To create a regional innovation system, regional clusters must first establish regional innovative networks with more formal and organized co-operation towards innovative projects. Finally, the complete regional innovation system according to the table above will involve co-operation in innovation activity between firms, different institutions, such as research centres, universities, training associations, knowledge creating and diffusion organizations, business associations and finance institutions and other related institutions.

It should be noted that the European Commission (2002b) simply ramifies in three distinct entities the concept of clusters that Alfred Marshall, Michael Porter and other scholars defined earlier. It does not offer an alternative or different definition but rather defines clusters as a regional innovation system and adds emphasis on the innovative orientation of clusters.

The Life Cycle of Clusters

The final part of this chapter explores the 'life cycle' of clusters. As we discussed above, clusters, or as otherwise stated, industrial districts have been developing internationally since the nineteenth century. High profile examples of such clusters include the motion picture industry around Hollywood, the high technology Silicon Valley cluster in California and the Massachusetts' Route 128 in Boston. Moreover, clustering can been seen in the industrial districts of north and central Italy or Spain, Baden-Wuerttemberg and Bavaria in Southern Germany, the Toyota City and the company tows of Ludwigshafen, the fashion capitals of Paris and Milan and the metropolitan business service centres of London, Hong Kong and New York and several others around the world. According to Enright and Ffowcs-Williams (2000), it has been estimated that around 380 clusters of firms operate in the United States, which together employ some 57 per cent of the workforce and account for 61 per cent of the country's output. Furthermore, the majority of European government agencies encourage the development of business networks and clusters as a key factor in promoting regional economic growth, innovation and SMEs' success:

In 2003, Belgium for example had 23, France had 100 existing and 80 developing clusters and the UK was, with its 154 clusters, the country with the most projects. However, it must be mentioned that most of these countries have not yet developed a cluster policy. In Italy, clusters are widely spread and are part of the traditional economic process with no legislation in place. The Netherlands and Austria have years of experience with cluster policies, but they need to identify the gaps between the policy measures and the needs for clusters. (Novelli et al. 2006: 1143)

Although the cluster development process in individual clusters could be different, the history of development of several well-known and prosperous clusters reveals a set of similar characteristics or steps in their evolution process. Since it appears that clusters often go through a life cycle of emergence, growth and decline, we will examine, briefly, each one of these phases below. At this point, it is important to note that exploring the cluster life cycle adds to the identification of the concept and nature of clusters while it also attempts to answer the key questions we addressed in the opening of Part 3 that are explored in the content of this book. The analysis that follows and the examples of clusters that are presented explore the central role of entrepreneurship and innovation in the emergence and growth of the cluster: the university-business relations; the important role of institutions, agents, associations and the government in fostering the development of clusters; the competitive advantages that these regions gain; the inter-firm collaborations and networking between small enterprises and the various institutions and agents that compose the cluster; and the socio-economic environment appropriate for new business start-ups.

THE EMERGENCE/GENESIS OF A CLUSTER

The emergence of a cluster can often be traced to numerous reasons such as:

- the availability and uniqueness of natural, raw materials

- specific knowledge or traditional know-how

- local demand

- the specific needs of a group of customers or firms

- the location of firms and entrepreneurs performing some important innovation that stimulates the growth and accumulation of others

- proximity to markets

- reduced transaction costs

- shared infrastructure, and the presence of local input or equipment suppliers

- economies of scale and localized externalities

- labour pooling.

An example of a cluster is the following:

> *The industrial milieu of Mirandola and surrounding area (Emilia Romagna Region) which is characterised by a well defined and specialised device/bio-medical sector placing the area at the second place in the world for concentration of companies and production. The industrial history of the cluster is connected to the history of a single entrepreneur, who was the first to introduce the disposable medical idea in Italy in the 60s. Since then, this entrepreneur started a number of specialised medium companies, which have been later on acquired by big multinationals. Further, over the years, a number of spin-offs took place. Nowadays, around 100 companies and a total of 2,300 employees compose the industrial milieu. The composition and features of firms comprises: (a) multinational companies, (b) local independent companies, (c) a group of original equipment manufacturers, and (d) a large number of very small assembly companies. Recently, an interesting sub-cluster appears consisting of a Consortium of companies working together on a well defined common-project. Besides that, some training and service centres support the cluster. (European Commission 2002a: 58)*

Unique natural resources and traditional know-how provide the most straightforward rationale for the emergence of a cluster. According to Porter (1998), for example, the Dutch transportation cluster owes its success to Holland's maritime history and accumulated skills and knowledge, also to the extensive waterway networks and the efficiency of the port of Rotterdam. The development of specific knowledge that may be turned into new productive use is another reason for the emergence of a cluster. The author argues that the research conducted at Harvard and MIT universities resulted in many clusters and spin-off enterprises in the area of Massachusetts. Moreover, Herbig and Golden (1993) claim that Stanford and California-Berkeley Universities have a reputation for fostering research and facilitating ties between faculty and the business world was one of the major contributing factors for the emergence and growth of the Silicon Valley cluster (as we shall examine in more detail in Chapter 10). The authors quote the words of the late Professor Terman of Stanford University, who emphasizes that universities are more than places for learning:

> *They are major economic influences in the nation's industrial life, affecting the nation's industrial life, the location of industry, population groups and the character of communities. Universities are a natural resource. (Herbig and Golden 1993: 77)*

Clusters could also arise due to local demand conditions. Enright and Ffowcs-Williams (2000) argue that local demand led to the establishment of the factory automation industry around Turin and the textile machinery industry of Eastern Switzerland. Porter (1998) also notes that local demand could lead to the emergence of a cluster and sets as an example the environmental cluster in Finland, which simply emerged due to the pollution problems created by local heavy industry, such as metal, forestry, energy and chemicals.

Sometimes a group of customers or firms with specific needs fosters cluster development, although this is rarely the case. As the author argues, the outstanding telecommunications capabilities and infrastructure developed in Omaha, Nebraska, owe much to the decision of the United States Air Force to establish the Strategic Air Force Command (SAC) in the area. SAC was the site of the first installation of fibre-optic telecommunication cables in the United States and many more innovations in the telecommunication industry. Furthermore, the author argues that new clusters may also occur from one or two innovative and entrepreneurial companies that foster the growth of others. America Online and MCI have been hubs for encouraging the development of new businesses in the telecommunication cluster in Washington, D.C., metropolitan area. Route 128 of Massachusetts and Silicon Valley had an initial leading entrepreneur firm, Shockley/Fairchild and Ken Olsen/Digital Equipment in the Silicon Valley, and Wang/Wang in Massachusetts Route 128 that provide success stories for other entrepreneurs and spin-off companies (Herbig and Golden 1993).

In a world of efficient transportation and the globalization of economies and markets, proximity to markets and reduced transaction costs can still be a major reason for the creation of clusters. According to Enright and Ffowcs-Williams (2000), proximity of markets, for example of the stock exchanges and financial markets, helped establish the financial and insurance business services of London, Hong Kong and New York. Localization can reduce the cost of transaction, information communication, negotiating and monitoring:

> *In a May 1998 article, for example, Ben Edwards assessed London's enduring power as a financial centre ... Developing financial markets requires a wide range of talents, and clusters make it easier to co-ordinate them. Lawyers must ensure ... Accountants must check. ... As long as these people prefer to meet in person to co-ordinate their work, there will be a need for financial centres. (Edwards, 1998: 8)*

The presence and existence of already established local input and supplier industries and related industries could be another seed for the creation of new clusters. The presence of local suppliers can allow quicker and more efficient access to local companies. The golf equipment cluster near San Diego took advantage of suppliers of castings and advanced materials as well as engineers with experience and knowledge in those technologies from the southern California's aerospace industry cluster (Porter, 1998).

The shared infrastructure is yet another reason for the development of a cluster. The physical infrastructure in terms of highways, water, sewage, airports and ports, hospital and medical facilities, and so on, helped in the creation of the cargo service industries in Singapore and Hong Kong, the flower and food industry of the Netherlands and of the numerous tourist centres as Enright and Ffowcs-Williams (2000) suggest. Universities have also been recorded as hubs generating regional clusters, as we present in the Silicon Valley model the next chapter. The European Commission (2002a) provides an example of a regional cluster developing around the Cambridge University:

> *The Cambridge region has experienced rapid growth since the 1960s. The cluster contains both high technology manufacturing and service sectors, the latter representing the dominant growth component in the region during the 1990s. The cluster contains around 800 high tech*

firms with more than 27,000 employees in 1998, and has developed around the University of Cambridge with its collaborative research activity, academic spin-offs and graduate researcher recruitment. A process of regional collective learning occurs in the Cambridge region. In the 1990s, the Cambridge region was 'characterized by active processes of entrepreneur and firm spin-off, (...) of inter-firm and organization networking and linkages, and of research and management staff recruitment from the local labour market' (Keeble et al. 1999: 331). At the same time, local high technology firms take part in global and national innovation networks, research collaboration and labour market processes, which complement regional collective learning by bringing into the region supplementary technological and managerial expertise. Finally, new collective initiatives, venture capital funds and active intervention by development agencies create more institutional thickness, which are seen to be beneficial to further growth of the high technology cluster in the region. (European Commission 2002a: 40)

THE PERIOD OF GROWTH FOR A CLUSTER

Once an agglomeration of firms becomes established, progressively a self-reinforcing cycle and several other forces promote its growth. As the cluster develops and expands, so will its influence with public and private institutions, governments and local associations. A successfully growing cluster will signal opportunities for entrepreneurs, institutions such as universities, research and training centres, talented people and government initiatives. It should be noted that a cluster requires a decade or more to develop its potential to create a competitive advantage and prosper.

According to the European Commission (2002b), as a cluster develops, progressively more external economies of scale are created, thus leading to a cumulative process. Numerous specialized suppliers and service firms emerge to cover the needs of the cluster, lowering the cost of shared inputs for the client firms. In addition, labour pooling allows a higher degree of efficiency and specialization of the labour market around the cluster. For example, the labour pools associated with the motion picture industry around the Los Angeles area allows for the Hollywood cluster to bring together a unique workforce for each film (Enright and Ffowcs-Williams 2000).

Knowledge organizations, specialized education establishments, such as universities and technical institutes, public and private research centres and business associations are established in the region of the cluster. These organizations and institutions advance local collaboration, information flow, enhance the learning process and knowledge creation and result in technological and other forms of spin-off and entrepreneurial companies. According to the European Commission (2002b), these centres hold specialized competence and industry-specific knowledge that could be diffused in the marketplace and are able to supply the businesses with professional competence and a skilled workforce, which SMEs seldom acquire themselves but are often necessary in order to develop innovations. Thus, information, skills and knowledge accumulation spark new businesses and innovations.

The prosperity of the cluster, the development of external economies, the emergence of an innovative infrastructure and the formation of new businesses increases the visibility, attractiveness and prestige of the cluster (European Commission 2002b). These could result in more skilled employees being attracted to the region; they could also lead to a high rate of enterprise start-ups and in general create a fertile and prosperous regional economic environment.

Government initiatives could also foster the development of a cluster and provide strong incentives and a fertile ground for the cluster. Government financed research centres, public universities and government funding could be valuable to the financing and assistance of start-up businesses and other SMEs. For example, both the Silicon Valley and the Massachusetts Route 128 had heavy support from the US military and space programs while firms located near the Research Triangle and in Austin, Texas were recipients of substantial government funds (Herbig and Golden 1993):

> Bizkaia in the Basque Countries refers to a well defined industrial milieu specialised in the automotive component sector. The cluster includes different productive activities: foundry, melting, tooling, mechanising, assembly, plastic injection and rubber treatment. In 1991, the cluster was formed by 156 enterprises including in this classification enterprises with more than 20% of their sales aimed at the automobile sector. The auxiliary automobile industry in the Basque Country was historically very open to the participation of foreign investment. Since 1992, the Basque Government has being trying to promote an integrated approach supporting the regional clusters and among these the automotive cluster. Its main tool is the setting up of thematic working groups. These groups are participated by representatives from firms and their association, technological centres and Universities,

experts and consultants. Besides that, the Association of the Cluster of Industries and Automobile Components (ACICAE) was established in 1991 for the revitalisation of the sector and the improvement of its competitiveness, but it is scarcely representative of local SMEs. A Basque Country Technological Centres Network (EITE) operates for the cluster. (European Commission 2002a: 60)

THE PERIOD OF DECLINE FOR A CLUSTER

Clusters continually evolve as new businesses emerge and others decline, as institutions develop and change, as the competition becomes more vigorous and technological and as global economic conditions change. Although successful clusters are regions of dynamic economic growth and innovation that can prosper for decades and sustain their competitive advantages, they can and often do lose their competitiveness for a number of forces external and internal to the cluster. Eventually, a cluster could find itself in a period of decline, reflecting a situation of technological, institutional, social and cultural 'lock-in' in business behaviour as the Observatory of European SMEs (2002) observes:

> *Upper Styria in Austria is a well defined industrial milieu characterised by a centuries-old industrial tradition based on rich deposits of iron-ore and coal. It has been dominated by nationalised industry, guaranteeing a stable employment situation till 1986. Decreasing competitiveness led to far-reaching structural changes like the subdivision into companies and a shift towards concentration on manufacturing. In 1986, 22,700 people were employed in 19 companies, and in 1994 the number of employees was only 9,350, in 38 companies. Still large companies in iron and steel industries are dominating the scene. As low-tech production is facing severe competition, an upgrading of the cluster is essential. That is why technology transfers between manufacturing companies and research institutions is so important. (European Commission 2002a: 58)*

Porter (1998) argues that technological discontinuities are a significant external threat to the cluster as they can potentially neutralize many of the cluster's competitive advantages simultaneously. The author sets as an example the decline of New England's market share in golf equipment, based on steel shafts, steel irons and wooden-headed woods. When California based industries started making golf equipment with advanced materials, the New

England producers had difficulty in competing and many went out of business. As the author (1998: 85) argues, 'a cluster's assets – market information, employee skills, scientific and technical expertise and supplier bases – may all become irrelevant.'

Another external threat is a change in the buyers' needs due to a divergence between local needs and customer needs. According to Porter, the US companies traditionally enjoyed the relatively low energy prices. When energy efficiency grew in importance around the world, the US companies were lacking the insight into customer needs and were slow to innovate and catch up with European and Japanese competitors, resulting in tremendous losses for many firms.

As the European Commission (2002b: 15) states, clusters can be locked in by the same socio-economic reasons that once gave the region the competitive advantage to prosper and succeed:

> *The initial strength of a regional cluster in the past – be it a well educated or experienced workforce holding unique know-how and skill; a highly developed and specialised infrastructure of firms, knowledge organisations, and education and training institutions; close inter-firm linkages; or strong political support by regional institutions – may turn into an inflexible obstacle to innovation.*

Finally, Porter (1998) draws attention to companies being too inward looking or persisting in behaviours and relationships that no longer contribute to enhancing competitiveness, stagnation of the quality of universities and institutions, cartels, over-consolidation and increased government protection and regulatory inflexibility. These internal forces make it hard for the cluster to perceive the need for continual innovation and renewal of competitive advantages, resulting in a decline of the cluster's productivity.

10

Business Clusters, SMEs, Innovation and Competitiveness

The Importance and the Role of SMEs Within Clusters

The need to develop competitive SMEs has become crucial for achieving socio-economic stability and prosperity both in industrialized and in developing countries in the context of global competition. As we discussed in previous chapters, SMEs collectively represent, or at least potentially could represent, the dynamic engine of economic growth, and their aggregate actions are inherently transferable into aggregate economic benefits. SMEs could both take advantage within clusters and facilitate the widespread diffusion of know-how, innovations, knowledge sharing and learning processes.

The aim of this chapter is to explore the role of SMEs within clusters and the relative benefits that SMEs could gain from participating in a cluster. The essential assumption made here is that SMEs can co-operate in clusters that provide for specialization, creativity and innovation while at the same time they can reap the benefit of being part of a larger entity. In other words, SMEs can maintain the small company strengths and at the same time compete with the larger companies or, as Porter (1998: 81) argues, 'a cluster allows each member to benefit as if it had greater scale or as if it had joined with others without sacrificing its flexibility.'

The author claims that many new companies grow up in existing clusters rather than in isolated locations. He identifies several reasons that make clusters conducive to new business formations. First of all, individuals working within the cluster can more easily perceive market opportunities and unsatisfied customer needs around which they can build a business: a skilled workforce, needed skills, know-how, inputs and assets are already available in the region and can easily be assembled into new business forms. Financial institutions and investors are already familiar with the working and nature of the cluster and may require, according to Porter, lower risk premium on capital. Furthermore, an entrepreneur may exploit the networks, relationships and collaborations with other enterprises and research centres that are already established. The new business creation within a cluster can be very much affected by a positive feedback loop. As the cluster develops and prospers, more opportunities and competitive resources will emerge which will ultimately benefit all members of the cluster. Clusters can be seen as an extended enterprise, where competing and co-operating companies engage in a dense network of inter-firm and social relationships based on face-to-face contact, ease and speed of information and knowledge flow that will impact their viability and competitiveness collectively (Adebanjo et al. 2006, Carbonara 2005).

According to Bouwman and Hulsink (2002), within the network of a successful cluster such entities as information, creativity and entrepreneurial talent are available for reinvestment. Workforce mobility, talent recruitment and spin-offs are an inherent part of the process. Entrepreneurs often leave a larger company or a university to start their own company (what is termed as a spin-off company) by exploiting market opportunities, new technologies and innovations which usually originate in private or public R&D laboratories and universities. According to the authors, the majority of start-ups in the Silicon Valley are spin-offs of this kind.

The European Commission (2002b) conducted an extensive survey to characterize the nature, working, performance as well as important development tendencies in 34 regional clusters in 17 European countries. A starting point for the research was to identify the dominating firm size category within the cluster, the role of SMEs and the role of MNEs (multinational enterprises). According to this survey, more than half of the clusters are dominated by SMEs in the sectors that define the cluster, as shown in the following table. Regional clusters seem to develop mainly from local networks of SMEs, or at least of a mixture of SMEs and large enterprises. The high number of SMEs in clusters can be explained both by the already underlined high level of entrepreneurship and spin-offs and by the increased vertical disintegration by cluster firms, which gives small companies the opportunity to exploit market niches and specialize in particular fields.

Table 10.1   Dominating firm size categories in clusters

	Number of clusters
Dominated by SMEs	19
Mix of sizes	12
Dominated by LSEs	3

Source: European Commission 2002b: 30

More important though is the fact that SMEs have increased their importance in 12 of the surveyed clusters in Europe. This could signify the increased importance of SMEs for the competitiveness and economic growth of a country as we mentioned in Part 2.

As the European Commission (2002b) argues, the increasing importance of SMEs clearly implies that small firms are highly dependent upon the local socio-economic environment since they seldom possess the necessary resources to hold a wide-reaching network and collaborations. The skills, knowledge, connections and relationships of the entrepreneur and business leader are usually concentrated on the places where they live and work. Moreover, the increased importance of SMEs implies that regional resources and know-how are significant for the workings of a regional cluster.

Another significant characteristic of clusters is the increased importance of multinational enterprises (MNEs). According to the European Commission (2002b), MNEs spread different activities, know-how, knowledge and technologies around the world. The existence of MNEs in local clusters may stimulate learning, diffusion of knowledge and innovations processes among the firms of a cluster and thus even affect the future development of the cluster. The figure below illustrates that the importance of MNEs has increased in most of the surveyed clusters in the last ten years.

Principles and Characteristics of Business Clusters

According to Pyke and Sengenberger (1992), a small firm in an industrial district does not stand alone; a condition of its success is the success of the whole network of firms of which it is a part, while they define an industrial district accordingly:

Strong networks of (mainly) small firms which, through specialisation and subcontracting, divide amongst themselves the labour required for the manufacture of particular goods: specialisation induces efficiency, both individually and at the level of the district; specialisation combined with subcontracting promotes collective capability. Economies of both scale and scope are the result. It is the firm as part of, and depending on, a collective network which perhaps more than anything else encapsulates the essence of the district's character. (Pyke and Sengenberger 1992: 4)

The authors argue that success for the SMEs and all organizations and institutions in an industrial district depends on certain key principles that would make the whole community of the firms a success. The industrial district is not simply a conglomeration of individually competing firms that happened to be geographically located together. The firms of a district are engaged in related activities according to definite principles. These principles and characteristics of the industrial districts account for the SMEs' enhanced competitiveness and innovation performance:

a) *Same industrial sector. In the sense of containing all the upstream and downstream processes and services needed for the manufacturing of a family of products. Geographical proximity between firms, and between individuals, firms and local institutions, improves effectiveness: for the spread of ideas and technical innovation; for various kinds of collaboration, between firms and of a broader political kind; for social cohesion, collective consciousness; ease and speed of inter-firm transactions.*

b) *Readiness for co-operation. There can be readiness to share information, such as ideas about new technologies or products, which can help all the firms in the district to become more efficient through improved productivity, quality, design, etc. This co-operation might be carried out informally at a personal level or more formally through especially established institutions and alliances. The collective provision of services and information makes affordable something, which small firms could not hope to manage as isolated individual units.*

c) *Entrepreneurial dynamism. This is a product of numerous conditions such as, ease of formation of new firms (access* to capital and premises), protection from domination and dependency upon large firms, access to the networks, ideas and services mentioned above, knowledgeable individuals capable and confident to establish new firms.

d)   Competing on a range of dimensions. At their best, they compete through differentiated high quality products, flexibility of adjustment, and the ability of innovation. The ability to offer quality, design flair, choice, flexibility, speed and innovation is itself a product of the particular mix or co-operation and competition intrinsic to an industrial district.

e)   Role of the workforce. Flexible response is one of the competitive strategies of a successful district. A crucial component for this kind of strategy is the availability of a trained, adaptable workforce that goes hand in hand with an innovative atmosphere, speed of reaction, and a co-operative attitude. Adaptability is aided by the breaking down of rigid divisions between managers and workforce and the pervasiveness of a trust.

f)   Trust and co-operation. An attitude that seeks competitive success not by aggressive cutting of direct labour costs but by general organisational competence, standards and productivity. The maintenance of high-labour standards, good wages, good basic conditions of work, safeguarding workers' rights and providing social protection, established in co-operation with trade unions and the government, increases the performance of labour and subsequently the performance of the district. (Pyke and Sengenberger 1992: 4–6)

Competitive Advantages for SMEs

'Modern competition depends on productivity, not on access to inputs or the scale of individual enterprises. Productivity rests on *how* companies compete, not on the particular fields they compete in' (Porter 1998: 80). As the author argues, clusters are instruments that can stimulate and contribute to the competitiveness and productivity of SMEs and of the other companies operating in the same geographic region. It should be mentioned that most of the perceived benefits a cluster has on its member companies affect as much the SMEs as they do the larger companies. Several elements that generate and enhance the competitiveness of SMEs within a cluster, as they emerge from a careful examination of existing bibliographical sources on this subject, are abstracted and presented below: the examples of the industrial district of Prato and the Silicon Valley high-tech clusters that are presented later in this chapter provide further evidence for the arguments noted here. In sum, we could establish that SMEs working in clusters are competitive because:

- They are focused in terms of business, competencies and resource destination.

- They develop capabilities and relationships for quick and appropriate problem solving.

- They are aided in an advantageous manner by collective resources, otherwise inaccessible to them.

- They work in a stimulating environment, enriched by competitive pressure and rivalry, information and examples.

- They work on a context of trust in which even smaller producers feel protected and respected by the community.

An element generating competitiveness is the low cost of information and of product differentiation, due to the presence of a wide number of subcontractors, component producers, and to the possibility to efficiently manage the production process by pieces.

SMEs in clusters can focus their limited resources on just one objective – one product/service, a single part of the production cycle or of the value chain. This is possible because they can easily find complementarities and specialized resources around themselves and in this way entering the market is less expensive and less risky. At the same time, they can accentuate their specific competencies on the product, process technology and practice and clients' needs in their unique business. This is at the base of their capacity for problem solving and the improvement of quality, continual incremental innovations.

When the cluster reaches a certain level of development, SMEs can exploit collective advantages due to their local concentration. The region in which they are located becomes a point of attraction for clients, providers of raw materials, technology providers, professionals and so on. Companies in prosperous clusters can tap into the pool of a specialized and experienced workforce that is provided by universities operating in the area and by employees working in relative industries. In addition, when a cluster becomes very relevant in a region, the local government and the private business associations concentrate much more of their attention on specific sector problems and needs of public support to firms. The whole community seems to become involved towards the success of the cluster. This leads to the consolidation of sector external economies (specific infrastructure, image and sector oriented services) for SMEs.

A cluster also provides companies with a deep and specialized supplier and input base with the advantage of being locally based thus lowering the transaction costs. SMEs can thus exploit the collective advantages due to their local concentration. It minimizes the need for inventory and delays as well as offering better communication between the parties and provision of specialized auxiliary services and inputs involving embedded technology. When suppliers and buyers operate in close proximity, negotiations and monitoring are more efficient and could become less costly.

Porter (1998) suggests that the linkages between the cluster members result in a whole that is greater than the sum of its individual parts. As an example, the author sets the classical tourist cluster: in a tourist cluster the quality of the visitor's experience will depend on the quality and efficiency of several complementary businesses and institutions such as hotels, bars, restaurants, transportation means, hospital facilities, shopping outlets and others. Because the members of the cluster are mutually dependent on each other, the good performance of one will benefit the productivity and performance of the other and in total the competitiveness of the cluster. Moreover, Porter argues that private investment such as training programs, infrastructure development, quality centres, R&D laboratories and others are often made collectively because the cluster members recognize the potential for collective benefits that contribute to enhance productivity and competitiveness that cannot be individually achieved.

The way clusters are formed and operate clearly suggests a new agenda of collective actions in the private sector. Whilst in the past, private collective action was mainly targeted on seeking government subsidies and investments, Porter (1998) suggests that trade and business associations in successful clusters provide forums for the exchange of ideas and knowledge, and a central point for collective action to overcome impediments to productivity and growth. In the Netherlands the author argues that the Dutch flower cluster's greatest competitive advantages arise from growers' co-operatives building specialized auction and handling facilities. Moreover, the Dutch Flower Council and the Association of Dutch Flower Growers Research Group (in which most growers participate) have assumed joint marketing and applied research activities. SMEs can increase their competitiveness and productivity through the participation and networking with these kinds of associations; as Porter (1998: 88–89) observes, 'associations can lead in such activities as establishing university-based testing facilities and training or research programs, collecting cluster related information, offering forums on common managerial problems, investigating solutions to environmental issues, organising trade fairs and delegations, and managing purchasing consortia.'

Enhancing Innovation Through Clusters

The increasing interest in regional clusters relates strongly to the view of clusters as instruments that can enhance competitiveness and productivity as well as innovation. So far, in Part 3 of the book, we have only abstractly linked the concept of innovation with clusters. In this chapter an effort will be made to explore how clusters promote innovation and thus enhance the competitiveness and productivity of SMEs. We begin by an examination of the innovation performance of the cluster, according to data selected by the European Commission (2002b) survey.

Competition by innovation is denoted as strong competition in contrast to competition via low cost strategy, which is considered as weak competition, according to the European Commission (2002b). Consecutively, the following table indicates that clusters often have a fairly strong and competitive position in the world markets. Eight of the clusters are competing head-on with world leaders, that is, the firms are as competitive as the strongest in the world, while four others are competing with leading Europeans. The eight world-leader clusters have some common characteristics; namely, seven of them have some major multinationals in the region, seven have an innovation capability equal to the best in the world or European level and five are performing strategic R&D.

Table 10.2   Number of clusters categorized according to the highest competitive position of the 'average' firms* in the cluster

	Number of Clusters
World Leaders	8
European Leaders	4
National Leaders	9
Fairly Strong Competitors	8
Weak Competitors	3

Source: European Commission 2002b: 38

*Note: End firm denoted a firm that sells on the final market for capital goods or consumer goods, i.e. not producing components that enter into the value chain.

For the purposes of the research conducted by the European Commission (2002b: 38), technological innovation was separated into radical and incremental innovations:

1.   *Radical innovation* processes lead to totally new products or ways of producing commodities

2.   *Incremental innovation* processes bring about more cautious 'step-by-step' improvements with a lower economic risk.

Table 10.3   Regional clusters according to level of innovation activity

	Number of clusters	Number of science-based clusters	Number of traditional clusters
Technology generators	8	8	0
Incremental innovators	10	2	8
Technology adapters	6	2	4
Technology users	10	3	7
Total	34	15	19

Source: European Commission 2002b: 39

Additionally, the clusters were examined according to the importance of the different types of innovation activities in the clusters. As illustrated in the following figure, product development is seen to be the most important type of innovation in the clusters.

Organizational marketing and distribution, as well as innovations in the production processes, are generally of high importance for more than 50 per cent of the clusters, according to the figure. In contrast, the development of new machinery and capital equipment production is of little importance for the majority of the clusters. Furthermore, the European Commission (2002b: 40) illustrates the importance of innovation processes for the competitiveness of a cluster, setting as an example the successful shipbuilding cluster in Sunnmøre, Norway:

> *Sunnmøre constitutes the largest ship building area in Norway, showing job growth and good performance since 1970. The ship building industry in Sunnmøre covered 4200 jobs in 1997. The competitiveness of the local ship building industry is to a large degree based on the innovation capability in the cluster. Local user-producer interaction has been a main driving force behind continual incremental improvements of products to satisfy new demands and needs by customers and users. Shipyards have long-term cooperation with some ship owners that often return to the yards to discuss new solutions and build new ships. Discussions with skippers, chief engineers and other crewmembers also give important feedback on how the firms' – and competitors' – products work, as well as suggestions for improvements.*

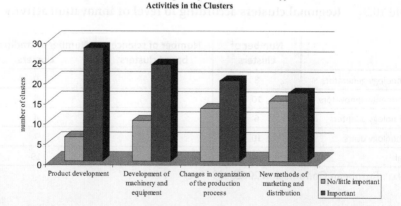

Number of Regional Clusters According to Importance of Different Types of Innovation Activities in the Clusters

Figure 10.1   Number of regional clusters according to importance of different types of innovation activities in the clusters

Source: European Commission 2002: 39

The 'Third Italy' and the Prato Cluster

A great impetus for the industrial district/cluster model has undoubtedly come out of Italy. At this point, we examine the well-known district of Prato and the concept of the *'Third Italy'* that presents an example of how clustering enhances innovation and creativity for SMEs and the importance of institutions, government and authorities in promoting business clustering and fostering their success.

Textiles are considered widely as the most mature of industries. From the early nineteenth century to the present, the construction of a textile industry has provided industrialized regions everywhere with an apprenticeship in mechanical production. Because the mass production of textiles can be done with large amounts of unskilled labour and small amounts of capital equipment, upstart manufacturers have regularly in the course of time displaced established ones. Some textile producers have withstood the competition and despite the high labour costs have also expanded. A relevant example of this process is the district of Prato, which we examine in detail in the next few paragraphs; a group of towns in the provinces of Florence and Pistoia in central Italy. Italy offered an impetus for the industrial district model, a novel and dynamic approach to regional economic development.

The Italian districts are concentrated in the north central and north east parts of the country, with the heartland being the province of *Emilia-Romagna* with its capital Bologna, the so-called *'Third Italy'* (Pyke and Sengenberger 1992, Trigilia 1992). According to the authors, the industrial districts in Italy tend to specialize in traditional sectors – textiles, clothing, footwear and furniture – but there has also been a significant development in modern sectors, especially in mechanical engineering. Industrial districts usually coincide with small urban areas and cover one or a handful of communes, while the population of an industrial district does not usually exceed 100,000:

> *Between 1966 and 1976, employment in Western European textile industry was generally declining – by about 25 per cent in France and W. Germany, and by more than 35 per cent in Great Britain. But employment in Pratese textiles remained steady (at about 45,000 workers, distributed in roughly 10,000 firms), and export boomed. By 1977, Pratese exports totalled about 820 million current dollars, roughly 60 per cent of output and in 1982 the value of exports had risen to about 1.5 billion dollars, equal to 75 per cent of total production.*

Prato's success rests on two factors: a long-term shift from standard to fashionable fabrics, and a corresponding reorganisation of production from large integrated mills to technologically sophisticated shops specialising in various phases of production ... In 1927 just under 80 per cent of the 11,560 persons employed in Prato's textile sector worked in large mills. The pattern changed in the 1930s depression when firms were forced to lay off workers and sold or rented to them equipment for subcontracting work; the firms did this to convert fixed costs to variable costs ... the firms reacted to the crisis of the 1950s in the same way. A vast network of small shops emerged in its place, employing one to twenty workers who possessed an intimate knowledge of materials and machines. While these small shops were springing up they needed to be formed into a network. To combine them into a flexible production system, and to reduce their dependence on the large firm, it was necessary to coordinate their separate skills in autonomous federations ... such coordination became, as of the late 1950s, the function of impannatore ... this person purchased raw materials, organised a network of small shops to produce cloth according to well-known specifications, and then brought the product to the market or sold it to a merchant ... as markets for standardised products became inaccessible, the impannatore ... urged the firms to experiment with materials and processes; and the firms' successes, in turn, fanned the creativity of the impannatore, making him or her still more demanding. In this way, small firms coalesced into a network, and this network expanded ... the local banks, trade unions, and artists' and industrialists' associations collaborated in a vast project ... to devise computer-based technologies to increase the flexibility of the links among firms, as well as the efficiency of each production unit ... a system that gave birth to a distinctive technology and a vital economy. (Piore and Sabel 1984: 213–216)

According to Piore and Sabel (1984), the Pratese district made a habit of rapidly adapting to the latest textile technology. In the early 1970s, automatic models, costing 100,000 dollars or more, at a rate of 1,000 per year, were replacing the area's 13,000 old looms. The Pratese small firms also prided themselves on their ability and creativity to modify new machines to perform unsuspected tricks. Their creative and innovative efforts led to the introduction of numerically controlled looms in small shops by the late 1970s. As the authors (1984: 215) suggest, 'technological innovation, constant subcontracting rearrangements, and the search for new products became the structuring elements of a resilient regional economy.'

As Trigilia (1992: 36–37) argues, three institutional factors appear to have been of crucial importance in the growth of industrial districts in the 'Third Italy', in general:

1.   A network of small and medium-sized urban centres with strong craft and trading traditions. These centres have acted as the principal pools from which entrepreneurial skills and resources could be drawn.

2.   The spread of family-based agricultural smallholdings (sharecropping, peasant firms), helping to create an original, flexible supply of an inexpensive workforce whose skills and motivations were well suited to the development of a small business.

3.   The presence of local political traditions and institutions linked in with a Catholic tradition and a socialist and communist movement. This influence should not be misconstrued. In contrast with what has happened, for example, in the south, politics have thus become more independent of family and private interests, and more strongly tied to the defence of collective interests. This has helped to institutionalize the market. It has promoted good industrial relations and locally based policies, and hence the generation of collective goods.

Innovative Capabilities Within Clusters

As we saw earlier, in the shipbuilding cluster in Sunnmøre, Norway and the Prato district, the user-producer interaction has, as a result, continuous incremental innovations which maintain high productivity and competitiveness in the cluster. The innovative capabilities created in a cluster allow it to compete successfully against dispersed competitors. According to Enright and Ffowcs-Williams (2000), the effectiveness of innovative activities is a function of the managers and employees, the skills and knowledge of researchers and professionals, the information and knowledge availability and the firm's ability to bring innovations into the marketplace. According to the authors, the innovative performance and the incentives to innovate will also be affected by the nature of the rivalry and the market structure found in the cluster.

Even in an era of rapid and technologically advanced communication and information systems, a geographic concentration provides unique advantages for certain types of communication. The authors suggest that the informal, unplanned, face-to-face personal and oral communications are critical components of the innovation processes. They argue that these types of communication between suppliers and buyers, producers and consumers and business-to-business provide feedback loops for creative and innovative ideas, particularly for incremental innovations and for industries in which suppliers and buyers are significant sources of new products and services. They also claim that sophisticated buyers from around the world will be attracted by the success of a cluster and offer new insights into advanced market demands:

> *Despite the fact that the cost of transmitting information has declined tremendously and has become largely invariant of distance, the importance of location to innovation and production remains. The primary reasons for this are the benefits that the proximity of others generates to the firms in the area, i.e. Marshallian externalities. Firms located in the area of a specialized cluster of firms may benefit from knowledge spillovers; information concerning new applications or other innovative practices may spread faster among the firms that are located geographically closer to each other. In addition, there are other factors fostering spatial agglomeration such as the availability of skilled labour, good infrastructure, and supporting institutions, e.g. specialized suppliers, universities, and research centres. In other words, there is a difference between knowledge and information. The costs of transmitting knowledge, particularly highly contextual and uncertain knowledge that is best transmitted via face-to-face interaction, still rise with distance. (Koski 2002: 147)*

BUSINESS NETWORKING AND GEOGRAPHICAL PROXIMITY

As we saw earlier, one of the advantages of clusters is that they tend to accumulate industry specific skills, capabilities, knowledge and information that are diffused widespread in the region, adding significantly to the innovation process. According to Baptista (2001), firm networking is an essential element in a region's knowledge infrastructure. Baptista suggests that numerous scholars have demonstrated that network effectiveness and cohesiveness are positively correlated to the degree of innovative success and on the diffusion of industrial innovations. According to the author (2001: 33):

If firms rely on each other to learn about new technology, the diffusion process is punctuated by externalities ... associated with the learning and transfer of new technological knowledge ... their intensity is likely to be stronger at the local level, since this kind of new, tacit knowledge flows more easily through interpersonal contacts. It should also depend positively on the proximity of early users and of technologically close firms, either acting as competitors, customers, suppliers, or service providers ... the accumulated experience and demand pressure of a technologically progressive user is also likely to influence incremental improvements and expansion of innovation into new areas. Close interaction and day-to-day contact between users and producers, where allowed by geographical proximity, should deepen (the user-producer) relationships.

Regional clusters are seen as a focal point of entrepreneurship, investments and new business activities as we have highlighted earlier. Some of the characteristics described as enhancing productivity have an even more profound effect on innovation and hence on productivity growth. Local universities, research centres, public and private investments on industry specific infrastructure allow a firm to leverage its own abilities and investments to innovate. This infrastructure, coupled with the accumulation and diffusion of knowledge and information, creates a fertile environment for innovative spin-offs and start-up companies. In fact, many clusters have emerged and developed through such innovative spin-offs and entrepreneurial activities. Virtually every semiconductor company in the Silicon Valley can be traced to an innovative spin-off company.

We thus have established a theoretical framework that supports and explains how business clusters affect innovation in an SME, the role of institutions, governments and authorities in promoting business clustering and the university-business relations that are fostered within a cluster.

The flexibility that SMEs sustain within a cluster together with the benefits they gain by communicating and co-operating with numerous companies and institutions within the cluster provides them with the capacity and flexibility to act rapidly to a new opportunity and implement innovations more quickly. Moreover, a company's close links and geographical proximity with its suppliers and customers can secure delivery, technical and service support and efficient and effective co-ordination of activities, thus enhancing the innovation processes. The competitive pressure, constant comparison and peer pressure that occur in a successful cluster forces executives to outdo one another. This creates a highly innovative environment that fosters productivity and competitiveness. Liyanage (1995) believes that innovative clusters draw together companies and industrial partners who understand that they can mutually benefit from collaborating in research and innovative activities undertaken within the region. Mutual dependency and collaborative efforts create the foundation for innovation and increased productivity.

The Central Role of Learning and Knowledge

The ongoing relationships and communication between the agents and entities within the cluster helps the companies learn about new technologies, service and marketing concepts and means they always have a better window in the market than isolated companies and competitors have. According to Carbonara (2004: 2–3):

> The 'learning process' is thought of as a managerial tool that allows organisations the possibility of coping (and adopt pro-active behaviour and practice) with change and the complexity of the environment in which they compete (Cohen and Levinthal, 1990). In particular, 'organisational learning' is interpreted as a process of development/ acquisition of new knowledge necessary for solving organisational, manufacturing, and marketing problems, and creating platforms for the development of new ideas.

This learning process is made more efficient and easy by the geographic proximity of institutions and firms within the cluster, and is stimulated through the co-operation and communication of the numerous agents and entities in the region. As Carbonara (2004) suggests, the development, acquisition and movement of new knowledge from one firm to another or from an institution to a firm enhances the innovative capabilities of the cluster and of the individual firms respectively.

Another line of enquiry is the learning economy, according to Lundvall and Johnson (1994), which highlights innovation as the basis for obtaining competitiveness for firms, regions and nations. The crucial role of knowledge figures in the related and highly influential concepts of the *learning economy* and the *learning region*, within both of which knowledge is the most important resource fostering competitive advantage and innovation. Innovation is conceptualized as a complex and interactive learning process, emphasizing the importance of co-operation and mutual trust that are further promoted by proximity. Learning is furthermore seen as mainly a localized process (Asheim and Isaksen 2000a). Diverging innovative capabilities between regions are the result of specific learning trajectories embedded in different institutional systems. Learning is seen as sticky due to the fact that some important types of knowledge are of an informal, tacit nature, and also the efficient use of formal, codified knowledge may demand some tacit knowledge. This kind of knowledge cannot easily be isolated from its individual, social and territorial context; it is a socially embedded knowledge, which is difficult to codify and transfer through formal channels of information. The fact is that while information is relatively globally mobile, some important kinds of knowledge are remarkably spatially rooted (Cooke 2000).

THE CONCEPT OF THE INNOVATIVE MILIEU

Another direction of research has been in pursuit of the notion of an *innovative milieu,* which is largely based on the work of the group of researchers called GREMI (Groupe de Recherché Europeen sur les Milieux Innovateurs), which emphasized the importance of social capital in promoting innovation (Aydalot and Keeble 1988, Camagni 1991, Camagni 1995 Maillat 1995). According to the authors in the innovative milieu, social networks are established between individuals within firms and between individuals in different firms. These networks are based on experience of working together in the past and therefore trust bonds within the network are created. This type of cluster tends to be located in urban areas where established relations between firms and individuals have existed for some time. As Capello (1999: 9) has noted, 'cumulative and collective learning processes enhance local creativity and innovative output, through the informal exchange of information and specialised knowledge.'

Learning takes place in a variety of ways with individuals in different firms exchanging information or individuals moving from one firm to another. Examples of innovative milieu clusters include Emilia-Romagna and parts of northeast Milan. Firms in these types of clusters are willing to jointly pursue common goals on innovative projects, which may involve risk.

The innovative milieu cluster is largely based on SMEs within urban areas that rely heavily on the skills and knowledge of a common workforce which, in turn, means the firms are deeply embedded in their locale. There are also important differences as well. These types of clusters actively seek to promote innovation rather than simply rapidly responding to it and actively work together to promote common, medium and long-term innovative goals. The firms in the innovative milieu respond to the threats posed by the innovative process, once again, by seeking to spread the risk through active and continuing syndication of their production arrangements (Aydalot and Keeble 1988, Camagni 1991, Camagni 1995, Maillat 1995).

The Silicon Valley Cluster

We have presented various schools of thought on the relationship between innovation and business clustering. One line of enquiry has focused on the conditions for the establishment and growth of such high technology complexes as the Silicon Valley and Route 128. While many factors have been identified, the most discussed is the role of local research-intensive universities; Stanford in the case of the Silicon Valley and MIT in the case of Route 128. A large literature on the relationship between research and development and regional development has been spawned. At this point we examine the well-known Silicon Valley region that presents an example of how clustering enhances innovation and creativity for SMEs and the importance of institutions, government and authorities in promoting business clustering and fostering their success.

As Bouwman and Hulsink (2002) argue, politicians, entrepreneurs, investors, government institutions and companies in every day practice understand the importance and are interested in the growth of potentially dynamic local and regional economies, that is, clusters. The most common example that stands out in people's minds is the Silicon Valley model. The authors argue that the inspiration and imitation of the Silicon Valley cluster is so profound that it even makes people around the world imitate its name, Silicon Alley (New York), Silicon Forest (Seattle), Silicon Hills (Austin, San Antonio), Silicon Dominion (Washington, DC), Silicon Valley (Fairfield, Iowa), Silicon Fen (Cambridge, GB), Shalom Valley, also called Silicon Wady (Israel), Silicon Plateau (Bangalore, India), Silicon Valley on Ice (Oulu, Finland), Amsterdam Alley and Dommel Valley (Eindhoven, the Netherlands).

THE GENESIS AND GROWTH OF THE CLUSTER

The emergence of the Silicon Valley, what is now being universally termed as a classic innovative *Hot Spot*, had its beginning in the early 1950s and grew to national distinction during the 1970s (Herbig and Golden 1993). Three interconnected factors and two key persons promoted its emergence and the consequent evolution and success, as Sternberg (1996) indicates:

1. A technologically and economically oriented university, Stanford University.

2. Electro-technical enterprises, such as Hewlett Packard.

3. The presence of military and aeronautics institutions and bases with a high demand for semiconductor products.

4. The vice president of Stanford University, Fred Terman, who persistently promoted the foundation of enterprises by university and the Nobel-prize-winning inventor of the transistor, Bill Shockley.

According to the author the reputation of Stanford University, under the vice presidency of Fred Terman, attracted numerous researchers and aided in acquiring state R&D funds. The immediate result was the creation of a highly qualified workforce. Moreover, the author claims increased governmental demand for technologically complicated semiconductor products boosted the life cycle of the Silicon Valley. Sternberg underlines that between 1955 and 1963 the share of public institutions was between 35 per cent and 40 per cent in the turnover of the cluster's semiconductor industry. On the other hand, a decisive role in the genesis of the cluster was the granting of R&D contracts to Stanford University and SMEs to develop high-tech electronic components and semiconductor products for military purposes. This had a decisive influence in the electronic industry to continually produce innovative products.

Gerstlberger (2004) argues that the long-time dynamic development and growth of the economy and population presented in the table below is a clear indicator of the success of the Silicon Valley region.

Table 10.4   Key figures on growth of population and companies in the Silicon Valley

	1980	1990	2000	2010 (projection)
Number of workplaces (absolute, 1000)	900	1174	1418	1601
Number of inhabitants (absolute, 1000)	1805	2105	2461	2684
Number of households (absolute, 1000)	646	741	806	875
Ratio of regional workplaces/working Inhabitants (%)	0.97	1.02	1.09	1.10
Number of children and youths at the age of education (5–19 years; absolute, 1000)	–	406	515	554

Source: Gerstlberger 2004: 756

SOURCES OF COMPETITIVE ADVANTAGE

Several scholars have examined the Silicon Valley model in an attempt to explain and understand the long-time sustainability of innovative performance and economic prosperity of the region. Several factors (some of which we have already mentioned) have been identified as having played a significant role in the competitiveness and productivity of the cluster, such as the role of the educational infrastructure, physical infrastructure, entrepreneurial activity, venture capitalists, government funds, resources and support, public and private research parks and incubators, networks, communication and the agglomeration effect (Piperopoulos and Scase 2009, Aoki and Takizawa 2002, Bouwman and Hulsink 2002, Herbig and Golden 1993).

The presence of top-class knowledge centres and universities is an important element in the promotion of regional development. Herbig and Golden (1993) argue that Stanford University, situated in the Silicon Valley region, collaborates with other private and public institutions providing entrepreneurial spirit and spin-off companies, creating and developing new technologies and applications for industries and businesses, and attracting talented scientists, engineers and students. Moreover, according to Bouwman and Hulsink (2002), these institutes allow for the flow of information and knowledge within the cluster, and create a highly fertile environment for entrepreneurs and established businesses to spot market opportunities and commercialize innovative ideas. Herbig and Golden (1993) state that Stanford University established a technology park in 1951, the Stanford Research Park, which is fully leased with 90 companies employing over 25,000 people. The purpose of the park according to the authors is to allow companies to take advantage of university and intellectual resources and research labs while providing a base for faculty contract work.

According to the authors, the physical infrastructure of the Silicon Valley region is yet another important reason behind its development and success. Airports, highways, water, sewage, hospital and medical facilities, as well as the presence of R&D facilities, technical and managerial supply and access to markets, because of the presence of military and the aeronautics industry, provided a well-established infrastructure.

Start-up firms and small ventures need a heavy infusion of capital to survive and develop in the highly competitive clusters. Aoki and Takizawa (2002) argue that there are more than 200 venture capital companies in the Silicon Valley and are said to receive over 1000 applications for funding per year. The ease and flow of venture funds to spin-off and start-up companies was critical to the growth and development of the Silicon Valley cluster.

Saxenian (1991) argues that the Silicon Valley is far more than just an agglomeration of firms. It consists of networks of interdependent yet sovereign producers and firms organized to grow and innovate reciprocally. These networks promote new product development by encouraging innovation and by spreading the costs and risks associated with a highly demanding new product. The author goes on to suggest that the networks in the Silicon Valley region allow for the diffusion of knowledge and information and new technologies, while at the same time engage in problem solving and co-operation between businesses or even industries. These networks create an environment that according to Saxenian (1991) encourages new firms to be more willing, experiment and develop innovative ideas and products.

SUCCESS CANNOT BE IMITATED

However, the Silicon Valley model cannot be simply transferred and/or imitated to other regions. It can serve as a reference and imitation point without guarantees for duplication of this type of regional cluster, since as Bouwman and Hulsink (2002: 300) explain:

> One cannot plan the rise of successful clusters. Particularly, in the early stages, chance and fortunate coincidences have produced, for example, in the case of Silicon Valley, a process of co-evolution of technology,

market dynamics and institutions, that was to develop further along a path of innovation, depending on the influence of specific local circumstances. While these circumstances serve as a more or less successful breeding ground for regional entrepreneurship and cluster activities and for the structuring of the techno-industrial processes along certain trajectories, it is the spark of local initiative that is needed to start the fire of high-tech region formation. An initial combination of local entrepreneurship, chance, 'lucky success' and a positive feedback on business within the region will lead to a self-reinforcing and cumulative process of the location of several high-tech start-ups, their growth into independent knowledge-intensive businesses and the clustering of these core businesses with new companies (such as spin-offs and specialised suppliers), educational institutions and R&D laboratories.

Finally, according to Saxenian (1996: 33), the efficiency of the industrial system of the Silicon Valley region is based largely on the effectiveness and efficiency of communication and exchange of information between firms:

By all accounts, these informal conversations were pervasive and served as an important source of up-to-date information about competitors, customers, markets, and technologies. Entrepreneurs came to see social relationships and even gossip as a crucial aspect of their business. In an industry characterized by rapid technological change and intense competition, such informal communication was often of more value than more conventional but less timely forums such as industrial journals.

Hard commitment and open-minded approaches to co-operation and communication between rivalry enterprises, customers and suppliers, of private and public businesses and institutions can be seen as the foundation of the development, innovation capabilities and competitiveness of the Silicon Valley cluster. Another important point that needs to be noted is that the birth of the region dates back to the 1950s, and its evolution required a time period of over two decades in order to flourish.

A Two-Dimensional Model of Innovation and Business Clustering

Entrepreneurship, Innovation and Business Clustering[1]

According to what we have presented, examined and argued throughout this book it appears that there are two fundamental interrelationships between entrepreneurship, innovation and business clustering. These suggest that:

1.   Innovation and entrepreneurship are intertwined concepts affecting SMEs' competitiveness.

2.   Business networks appear to be associated with the innovative capabilities of SMEs and their competitiveness.

As we discussed in Part 1 of this book, in the last few decades it has become universally accepted that innovations of any kind are important sources of productivity growth; one of the major goals of economic activity and one of the most important instruments through which not only organizations, but countries as well gain and sustain competitive advantages in globally competitive marketplaces. We explored and delineated the origins of entrepreneurship and innovation and focused our attention on understanding what is innovation and entrepreneurship and how the two concepts are linked to each other, as put forward in the writings of various scholars. In the next

---

1   The two-dimensional model presented in this chapter is based on my PhD research and thesis at the Kent Business School, University of Kent, UK. The model has been published in: Piperopoulos, P. and Scase, R. 2009. Competitiveness of small and medium enterprises: towards a two dimensional model of innovation and business clusters. *International Journal of Business Innovation and Research*, 3(5), 479-499.

few paragraphs we recollect some of the theories that identify the link between entrepreneurship and innovation and provide our own definitions for the two concepts.

DEFINING INNOVATION

Weber (Lehmann and Roth 1993) recognizes the entrepreneur as a main actor of capitalism and defines them as a 'moving spirit' oriented towards market opportunities. This is in line with Schumpeter's (1942) arguments that the entrepreneur is a dynamic person or organization seeking new combinations and market opportunities where others fail to see them. According to Dollinger (1999: 4), 'entrepreneurship is the creation of innovative economic organisation (or network of organisations) for the purpose of gain or growth under conditions of risk and uncertainty.'

Schumpeter focuses on the producer and it is here that the entrepreneur enters the stage. Schumpeter (1942) defines production as the combinations of materials and forces that are within our reach. The producer is not an inventor (Schumpeter, 1947). All components that they need for their product or service, whether physical or immaterial, already exist and are in most cases also readily available. The basic driving force behind structural economic growth is the introduction of new combinations of materials and forces, not the creation of new possibilities.

The link between entrepreneurship and innovation further emerges from the influential writings of Drucker (1985). He argues that innovation is the specific function of entrepreneurship. It is the means by which the entrepreneur either creates new wealth-producing resources or endows existing resources with enhanced potential for creating new wealth. The entrepreneur must purposefully and systematically search the sources of innovation, the changes and the indications that create opportunities for a successful innovation. What all the successful entrepreneurs have in common is not a certain kind of personality, rather a commitment to the systematic practice of innovation (Drucker 1985). Entrepreneurs, whether individuals starting their own businesses or entrepreneurial organizations that want to continue to thrive, see, or at least they should see, innovation as a strategy, an ongoing process that will bring profits and a competitive advantage to the company.

Michael Porter (1985) recognizes the competitive advantage that innovations bring to the company and to a nation, and recognizes that they should be mastered. For Porter (1990), firms create and sustain a competitive advantage by perceiving or discovering new and better ways to compete in an industry and bringing them to market, which is ultimately an act of innovation. Porter (1990: 579) sees innovation in very broad terms and as inherent to the firm's strategic and competitive context:

> *Innovation includes not only new technologies but also new methods or ways of doing things that sometimes appear quite mundane. Innovation can be manifested in a new product design, a new production process, a new approach to marketing or a new way of training and organising. It can involve virtually any activity in the values chain.*

While business organizations of any kind acknowledge that innovation is important to their growth and success, the term innovation is still without a consistent, broadly agreed with definition in the business world. So in addition to the definitions we have presented in Part 1 of this book, I define innovation as:

> *Innovation is creating value by implementing new ideas. It is the process of taking ideas, needs and opportunities to the market. Innovation is the conversion of knowledge, creative ideas and information, into a benefit, a competitive advantage for the organization; under risk and uncertainty for the outcome of the innovation. Innovation then concerns the purposeful, focused, strategic search for and the conception, development, adoption and implementation of significantly improved or new processes, organizational structures, methods of production and products/services in order to differentiate the company from its competitors by creating and sustaining superior performance, and increased productivity.*

DEFINING ENTREPRENEURSHIP

As we discussed in Part 2 of this book, several researchers in their studies give special emphasis to the influential role of the entrepreneur in affecting the performance, survival and growth of the firm, particularly when the firm is small. The idea we brought forward is that the basic role played by the owner/manager/entrepreneur is one of the major determinants of SME competitiveness and performance; this turns out to be so because the concentration of decision-making power of the owner/manager in an SME environment consequently affects the firm's overall strategy.

According to Goffee and Scase (1995), in SMEs there may be different layers of managers, supervisors, job descriptions and so on, but the distinguishable characteristic of the entrepreneur is that they will retain almost total control and remain the centre of the decision-making web. Such enterprises, according to the authors, are sculptured around the personalities of their owner-managers and their growth potential and financial viability is highly dependent upon the proprietors' preferences, energies, talents and plans.

Further research focusing on the concept of competitiveness and the competency approach by Man et al. (2002) develops a conceptual model (as presented in Chapter 5, Figure 5.1) to link the characteristics of SMEs' owner-managers and their firm's performance. Competitive scope, organizational capabilities, entrepreneurial competencies and performance are the four components of the model. According to the authors, the focal point of the model concentrates on the entrepreneurial tasks that link the different competency areas with the constructs of competitiveness. The entrepreneur's managerial skills and technical know-how, their demographic, psychological and behavioural characteristics are often cited as the most influential factors related to the performance of an SME; particularly since quite often small firms or even medium-sized companies have a dominating entrepreneur who is most likely to be the founder of the business. The relationship is also affected by many industrial, environmental and firm-specific characteristics and firm strategies.

Following our analysis in Part 2 of the book, we come to the realization that entrepreneurship is often viewed as a function, which involves the purposeful identification and exploitation of opportunities, knowledge and information that exist within a market. Such exploitation is commonly associated with the direction and/or combination of productive inputs. Entrepreneurs usually are considered to bear risk while pursuing opportunities, and often are associated with commitment to creativity and innovation. In addition, entrepreneurs undertake a managerial role in their activities, but routine management of an ongoing operation is not considered to be entrepreneurship. Thus, I define entrepreneurship as:

> *Entrepreneurship is a creative process in which opportunities are perceived and resources mobilised in order to bring about change in pursuit of financial benefits. Entrepreneurship involves a broad range of activities necessary to create organizations, carry out new processes, organizational structures, methods of production, products and*

> *services, identify opportunities within the economic system, and bring together factors of production, aiming at the accumulation of wealth, under conditions of risk and considerable uncertainty.*

Summing up the distinctive themes of the analysis on innovation and entrepreneurship (as presented throughout Part 1 and Part 2 of the book and presented briefly above), we can suggest the close relation between innovation and entrepreneurship, as mentioned at the opening of this section:

- Innovation and entrepreneurship are intertwined concepts affecting SMEs' competitiveness.

On the basis of the above analysis, we hypothesize that innovation can be measured on a scale. This is proposed in Figure 11.1.

Vertical axis of the 2-dimensional model: Innovation

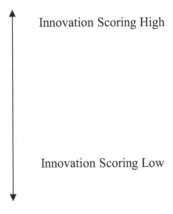

Figure 11.1   Vertical axis of the two-dimensional model: innovation

DEFINING CLUSTERS

As we discussed in Part 1 of the book, innovation systems can be national, regional or local. They are shaped by the specific and characteristic economic and social conditions and factors of a country. In understanding the competitiveness of a country and the competitive advantages of its businesses and its business sectors, we need to explore the concept of a system of innovation. Important factors such as institutions, authorities and governments at local, regional and national levels may affect the businesses' performance and innovative capabilities. Innovation processes are influenced by many factors; they occur in interaction between institutional and organizational elements, which together may be called systems of innovation. Thus, if we want to describe, understand, explain and even perhaps influence processes of innovation, we must take all important factors shaping and influencing innovations into account.

As we presented in Part 1, firms rarely innovate in isolation; rather in their pursuit of innovativeness they interact with other organizations such as other firms, but also universities, research institutes, investment banks, schools, government ministries and so on to exchange, develop and gain knowledge, information and other resources. Furthermore, Edquist (1997) argues that social patterns and social institutions, not necessarily economic in their nature, may operate positively or negatively, giving rise to constraints and/or incentives for innovation; these can be laws, health regulations, cultural norms, social rules and technical standards which also shape the behaviour of firms. Interaction and relations between the various agents, institutions and actors shape the system of innovation. The various actors and organizations that operate under certain institutional contexts are the elements of the system that create and use knowledge for economic purposes, while innovation emerges in such a system.

As examined and discussed thoroughly in Part 1 this book, one of the important elements that affects business competitiveness and innovative performance centers on the relations between universities and businesses and the role institutions, authorities, agents and governments play in triggering and sustaining such relations.

As we discussed in Part 2, one of the most rapidly emerging approaches to industrial competitiveness of small and medium sized enterprises (SMEs) is that it can be accelerated through inter-firm collaboration. When corporations share competencies and knowledge it becomes possible to tackle jobs that no single corporation could tackle alone. In the best cases the assembly of core competencies from different companies enables corporations to build a team of organizations and individuals who together have the highest level capabilities. This is increasingly essential for world-class competition and innovation. Today's networks, the Internet, video conferencing and computerized tools make possible flexible, but tightly coupled, linkages between corporations. Companies are increasingly using information systems and the Internet for strategic advantage by entering into strategic alliances with other companies in which both firms co-operate by sharing resources and/or services. Such alliances are often information partnerships in which two or more firms share data for mutual advantage. They can join forces without actually merging.

Some companies are extending their enterprise systems beyond the boundaries of the firm to share information and co-ordinate business processes with other firms in their industry. Industrial or business networks link together the enterprise system of firms in an entire industry. Internet technology has fuelled the growth of industrial and business networks because it provides a platform where systems from different companies can seamlessly exchange information.

As we presented in Part 2 of this book, in Europe several government agencies and private foundations are experimenting with and trying to support, stimulate and accelerate different forms of inter-firm collaboration, or as otherwise stated business networks. The assumption behind such efforts and programmes is that co-operative behaviour will help SME firms to first of all survive in their marketplace, innovate through collaborative research and development projects and shared knowledge, and then be able to successfully compete with larger enterprises. Alliances bridge the gap, according to Hoffmann and Schlosser (2001), between the firm's present resources and its expected future requirements. Hence, the second distinctive theme emerges from the theories on business networks and SMEs as follows:

- Business networks appear to be associated with the innovative capabilities of SMEs and their competitiveness.

According to the literature and research review in Chapters 8, 9 and 10 of this book, membership in clusters can enhance the productivity, rate of innovation and competitive performance of firms. Business clusters are widely recognized by scholars and policy makers around the world as important settings in stimulating the productivity and innovativeness of companies and the formation of new businesses.

As we extensively presented in Chapter 9, Marshall (1922), in his early writings on Sheffield cutlery, Lancashire cottons and other British regions, ascribes their competitive advantage to the presence of external economies, as the commons, the infrastructure and other services from which each individual firm in an industrial district might draw. These include faster dissemination of new ideas, experience and know-how thanks to geographic proximity, cultural homogeneity, common manufacturing traditions, reduced cost of transport (and of transactions in general), and the easier access to complementary services or capabilities. Furthermore, they include improved job search and job matching, more favourable access to capital finance and inter-firm labour migration.

The need to develop competitive SMEs has become crucial for achieving socio-economic stability and prosperity both in industrialized and in developing countries in the context of global competition. Usually SMEs are considered weak because of shortages of human and financial resources, scale inefficiency and low market power. On the other hand, as we discussed in Part 2, SMEs collectively represent, or at least potentially could represent, the dynamic engine of economic growth, and their aggregate actions are inherently transferable into aggregate economic benefits. We also brought forth and discussed in Chapter 10, using several case studies, researches and the Silicon Valley model, the benefits of a cluster for SMEs and its effect on business competitiveness and innovation. Operating within clusters, SMEs could both take advantage and facilitate the widespread diffusion of know-how, innovations, knowledge sharing and learning processes.

The essential assumption made here is that SMEs can co-operate in clusters that provide for specialization, creativity and innovation, while at the same time they can reap the benefit of being part of a larger entity. In other words, SMEs can maintain the small company strengths and at the same time compete with the larger companies or, as Porter (1998: 81) argues, 'a cluster allows each member to benefit as if it had greater scale or as if it had joined with others without sacrificing its flexibility.'

The author claims that many new companies grow up in existing clusters rather than at isolated locations. He identifies several reasons that make clusters conducive to new business formations. First of all individuals working within the cluster can more easily perceive market opportunities and unsatisfied customer needs around which they can build a business. A skilled workforce, needed skills, know-how, inputs and assets are already available in the region and can easily be assembled into new business forms. Financial institutions and investors are already familiar with the working and nature of the cluster and may require, according to Porter, lower risk premium on capital. Furthermore, an entrepreneur may exploit the networks, relationships and collaborations with other enterprises and research centres that are already established. The new business creation within a cluster can be very much affected by a positive feedback loop. As the cluster develops and prospers, more opportunities and competitive resources will emerge, which will ultimately benefit all members of the cluster. Clusters can be seen as an extended enterprise, where competing and co-operating companies engage in a dense network of inter-firm and social relationships based on face-to-face contact, ease and speed of information and knowledge flow that will impact their viability and competitiveness collectively (Adebanjo et al. 2006, Carbonara 2005).

According to Bouwman and Hulsink (2002), within the network of a successful cluster such entities as information, creativity and entrepreneurial talent are available for reinvestment. Workforce mobility, talent recruitment and spin-offs are an inherent part of the process. Entrepreneurs often leave a larger company or a university to start their own company (what is termed as a spin-off company) by exploiting market opportunities, new technologies and innovations, which usually originate in private or public R&D laboratories and universities. According to the authors the majority of start-ups in the Silicon Valley are spin-offs of this kind.

Liyanage (1995) believes that innovative clusters draw together companies and industrial partners who understand that they can mutually benefit from collaborating in research and innovative activities undertaken within the region: mutual dependency and collaborative efforts create the foundation for innovation and increased productivity.

Based on the analysis of clusters conducted thus far in Part 3 of the book, I define a cluster as:

> *Clusters are networks of competing, collaborating, complementary and interdependent businesses (including suppliers and service providers) associated agents and institutions, linked formally and informally, vertically and/or horizontally that work in common, similar and/or related industries and located in a geographically bounded space.*

On the basis of the above analysis we hypothesize that business clustering/ networking can be measured on a scale as seen in the following figure. The axis describes the classical and the emerging approaches to business competitiveness, internationalization, innovation and networking of small and medium-sized enterprises. At the right-hand side the new era of strategic management and competition follows the business clustering/networking approach, while on the left-hand side the go-it-alone strategy reflects the classical way of competing and formulating strategies. The higher the level the company is engaged in networking/clustering activities, the more to the right it will be positioned. On the other hand, the preference of the company for a go-it-alone strategy with no collaboration at all will position it at the left-hand side of the axis.

Horizontal axis of the 2-dimensional model: clustering/networking and go-it-alone strategies

Go-it-alone Strategy   Clustering/Networking

Figure 11.2   Horizontal axis of the two-dimensional model: clustering/ networking and go-it-alone strategies

The Two-Dimensional Model of Innovation and Business Clustering

If we explore the dynamics of SMEs, it is clear there is diversity in terms of: ownership (from sole proprietorships, partnerships and limited companies); structure (from highly formalized decision-making processes to informal work parties); and most importantly (for the purposes of the present discussion) *orientation towards innovation*. Thus, there are SMEs highly committed to developing innovative products and services while there are others content to start up by carving out market niches within which they are able to trade profitably but without the need to continuously update their product portfolios. In short, some will be highly innovative and others will 'tick along'.

Equally, SMEs may be classified in terms of the extent to which they are embedded in business networks in: (a) the development of their products and services; and (b) the roll out of these in the marketplace. Some SMEs will only develop their product portfolio through collaborations with others (as part of business networks) and deliver these to market through intermediaries or as integral members of business consortia. In other words, some SMEs will '*go it alone*' and others will '*collaborate*' in business networks.

Bringing together the two dimensions of innovation and business clustering/ collaboration (as we constructed them earlier in this chapter) we are able to hypothetically create a two-by-two model as shown in the following figure. The vertical axis shows the innovation performance of SMEs, scoring from very high to very low from the top to the bottom. The horizontal axis is the extent and the depth of networking and strategic alliances; scaling from the left, go-it-alone strategies with little or no collaboration to a high level of collaboration within dynamic clusters and strong business networks. The outcome is four analytical types of SMEs: *'classical entrepreneurs'*; *'path-breakers'*; *'survivors'* and *'collaborators'*.

The 2-Dimensional Model of Innovation and Business Clustering

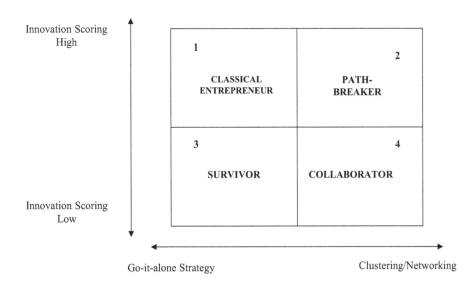

Figure 11.3   The two-dimensional model of innovation and business clustering

The model I present above is a schematic description encompassing the concepts of innovation and clustering and how these could affect SMEs' performance and competitiveness. The end result is the formation of four squares each representing a different type of SME based on the relations between the three concepts of innovation and business clustering and the relative scores of the companies in the two axes.

The aim of this hypothetical, descriptive two-dimensional model is to link the concepts of and relations between innovation and clusters/networks in an attempt to explain how the relations between these concepts affect the performance and competitiveness of an SME. The critical reader has to realize that this is a hypothetical model of how these concepts relate and affect the performance and competitiveness of an SME; it does not negate the possibility that other researchers might reach similar conclusions using different sets of relations that would have emerged from another heuristic point of view.

The following figure illustrates the output variables, namely the performance and growth of the SME that are driven by the two input variables, which are the innovation rate and the clustering/networking level.

The two-dimensional model attempts to provide answers to questions such as why some companies are more innovative and open to networking than other companies, and why some companies are more reluctant to collaborate than other companies. Further, how these characteristics affect the outcome, namely SMEs' growth and economic performance. It could also purport to add insights to a comparison and contrast between the different types of companies in order to answer questions, as those set above, that will act as guidelines to devise policies and measures to assist SMEs to improve their competitiveness

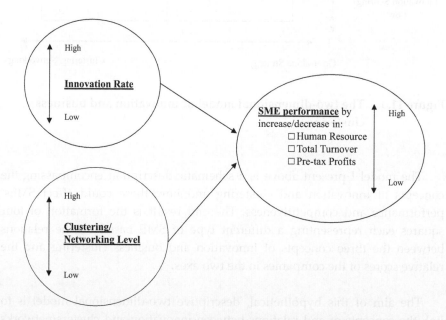

How the Innovation rate and the Clustering/network level affect the Performance of the SME

Figure 11.4   **How the innovation rate and the clustering/network level affect the performance of the SME**

and performance. The ultimate aim of the model is to add to the scientific knowledge concerning the concepts of entrepreneurship, innovation and business clustering by linking the concepts together and validating their relations and influence in businesses performance, competitiveness and viability.

CLASSICAL ENTREPRENEURS

In the upper left square of the two-dimensional model (as shown in Figure 11.5) belong SMEs characterized by high innovative performance but scoring very low on networking and strategic alliances, showing preference for the go-it-alone strategy; usually a strategy followed by the classical entrepreneur. We name this SME 'Classical entrepreneur', because the owner/manager of the company does not wish to engage in strategic alliances as they don't see the need for it or simply haven't got the knowledge and expertise and the adequate managerial abilities to pursue such a strategy. It is the type of SME where the entrepreneur is very reluctant to engage in inter-firm alliances and networks since they want to protect their innovations, believes in their own abilities and pursue a go-it-alone strategy in competing in the marketplace. Innovation is systematically pursued and is present in the enterprise's policy and it is one of its main components.

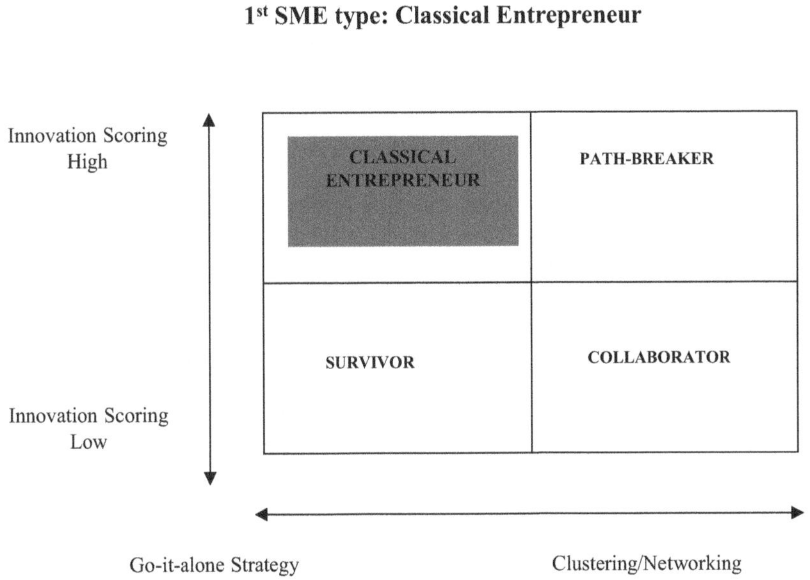

1st SME type: Classical Entrepreneur

Figure 11.5   1st SME type: classical entrepreneur

PATH-BREAKERS

In the upper right square of the two-dimensional model (as shown in the following figure) belong SMEs which exhibit high innovation performance and high clustering/networking performance, strong inter-firm alliances, networking with universities and research centres, other institutions and agents and are perhaps part of a cluster of firms in the same or adjacent industrial sectors. We name this SME '*Path-breaker*', because it is the optimal, ideal type of SME, the one that leads the way and from which we could draw conclusions on how to direct other SMEs to follow its example. This kind of an SME could be, for example, a high-tech organization operating within the Silicon Valley cluster in the United States. In this kind of SME there is a strong link between entrepreneurship and innovation. The entrepreneur exercises control over their business through directly imposed but mostly unwritten guidelines and instructions. The entrepreneur purposefully and systematically searches the sources of innovation, the changes and the indications that create opportunities for a successful innovation. Innovation is seen as a strategy, an ongoing process that will bring profits and a competitive advantage to the company. Furthermore, membership of business networks/clusters enhances the company's productivity, rate of innovation and competitive performance. In other words, the path-breaker can maintain the small company strengths and at the same time compete with the larger companies, on a regional, national and international basis.

2nd SME type: Path-Breaker

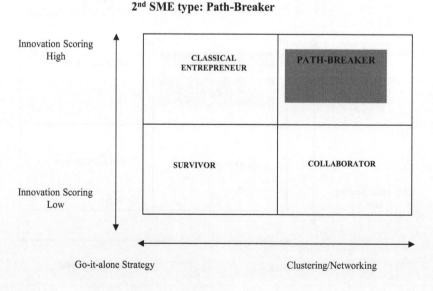

Figure 11.6   2nd SME type: path-breaker

SURVIVORS

In the lower left square of the two-dimensional model (as shown in Figure 11.7) belong those SMEs which score very low both on innovation rate and on networking/clustering levels, showing clearly characteristics of a business that simply aims to achieve an income for its owner, be it as it may one or more individuals or a family, and is not interested or cannot apply modern management and innovation techniques. We name this SME 'Survivor', since such an SME does not belong to any strategic alliance or co-operative networks of enterprises, does not have any co-operation with public and private research centres, universities and other agents and the innovative performance of the company is virtually nonexistent. This type of SME is the exact polar opposite of the one in the second SME type of model, the path-breaker, and is stuck in the old way of doing business. Innovation is something the nature of which the owner-manager may not even understand and is certainly out of the business strategy: the owner and/or manager of the company is not interested in changing anything in their company either because they lack the understanding and knowledge to do so or simply because they want to run the business in their own way.

3rd type of SME: Survivor

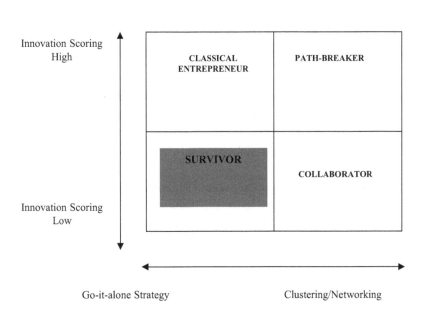

Figure 11.7   3rd SME type: survivor

If we could define the survivor type of SMEs we would place them on the typical family business, founded by the person that now is the manager and owner of the company. Unfortunately they describe a big majority of the companies in most of the developed and developing economies around the world that have only the one goal – to achieve a good income for the family. The survivor type of company does not necessarily fail to increase its sales or turnover but rather it is the lack of a modern approach to management and competitiveness that makes this type of company vulnerable to foreign and/or domestic competition by larger enterprises.

COLLABORATORS

In the lower right square of the two-dimensional model (as shown in the Figure 11.8) belong SMEs which score very low on innovation; in other words, for them innovation is not purposefully and systematically pursued, while on the other hand they do belong to networks of firms and/or have formed strategic alliances. We name this type of SME 'Collaborator', because the SME depends on and benefits by belonging to the network/cluster to survive and operate but fails to realize that it should be more innovative and create knowledge in order to build and sustain a competitive advantage for itself and for the network of the firms as well. The underlying difference with the second illustrative type of SMEs (path-breakers) arises from the fact that the innovation performance is very low, the company is not introducing any new products and/or services, nor is it collaborating with other companies and/or educational or research institutes in order to develop and launch new products. Business clustering/ networking activities are directed more towards the internationalization of the company's operations and increase in performance/growth, rather than on the enhancement of the innovative performance of the company. From this perspective alliances for the collaborator arise when the firm needs additional resources that cannot be purchased via market transaction and cannot be built internally with acceptable cost (risk) or within an acceptable amount of time.

The strategy of the collaborators would fit that of a benchmarking approach where the company just adapts to the business environment rather than trying to enact it. At the end of the day all the firms will mutually benefit from a high commitment to deposit knowledge and search for innovation rather than just wait till someone else does the job for them: or, as we explored previously in this part of the book, a firm in an industrial district does not stand alone; a condition of its success is the success of the whole network of firms.

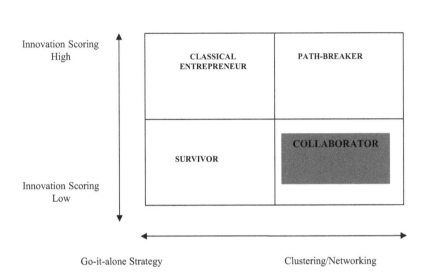

Figure 11.8   4th SME type: collaborator

Instead of an Epilogue

According to the analysis presented in this chapter (and as a matter of fact throughout this book), we trace two significant interrelationships between entrepreneurship, innovation and business clustering; that is, that innovation and entrepreneurship are intertwined concepts affecting SMEs' competitiveness and that business networks appear to be associated with the innovative capabilities of SMEs and their competitiveness. The two-dimensional model attempts to provide answers as to how the concepts of innovation and business networks/ clusters and their interrelationships affect SMEs' performance, competitiveness and growth. It also adds insights to a comparison and contrast between the four different types of SMEs (as defined earlier) and their relative scores on the areas of innovation and business networking/clustering activities, which are closely related to the chosen strategies followed by the owners/managers/ entrepreneurs of each type of SME. This model makes a small addition to the scientific knowledge concerning the concepts of entrepreneurship, innovation and business clustering by linking the concepts together and relating them to the SMEs' performance and growth.

Management theory scholars, in the past, have provided a variety of performance and growth models for businesses. For example, nearly four decades ago, as we presented in Part 2 of this book, Greiner (1972) developed a model of business growth based on evolution and revolution stages. It would be wrong to render this or other models as worthless but it will also be wrong to keep thinking that these models, as they stand, can apply usefully in today's economies. We should use these models as any other theory that tries to explain, forecast and predict the growth of a business, more for the creation of new models and less as explanatory paradigms. As we investigated in Part 2, classical models, such as Greiner's model (1972), seem to be inadequate in an economy that is based largely nowadays on the Internet and on information and communication technologies. The decreasing cost of accessing the Internet and its wide penetration both in home-users and businesses expands literally minute by minute, while more and more businesses see the advantages of being based locally and yet conduct their businesses in a global market.

As the Internet becomes more and more a means to conduct businesses, as it creates wider and more competitive marketplaces, what is needed is the development of theories that can explain how companies start up and grow, not only in the physically real but also in the virtual 'www' environment in which, for example, people work from their home in a small town in China for a company in Germany when they actually don't even know where the company is located. Furthermore, such operational management techniques as outsourcing, that is, putting some operations and services out to specialists which allow a company to concentrate on what directly wins its business in the marketplace, and subcontracting, for example, using people and/or other businesses on a contract basis for specific jobs/tasks, need to be included in the equation.

As the internationalization of businesses becomes more and more a reality even for the smallest of SMEs, which may be open to competition from anywhere in the world, nations need to focus on regional economies and to encourage the university-business-government relations towards the creation of regional clusters. As we described in the two-dimensional model and the case of the *path-breaker* type of SME, co-operation/networking amongst businesses in same or adjacent industrial sectors provides SMEs with the opportunity to reach markets that could not be reached individually, to collaborate with other companies in developing new products and services, to use research institutes and universities to conduct their R&D and to form dynamic global networks and alliances with other companies. Hence, within an increasingly challenging and demanding global business world, in order for SMEs to survive, grow, innovate and outperform their rivals, they should aim to become the *path-breakers*.

Part 3: References/Bibliography

Adebanjo, D., Kehoe, D., Galligan, P. and Mahoney, F. 2006. Overcoming the barriers to e-cluster development in a low product complexity business sector. *International Journal of Operations & Production Management*, 26(8), 924–939.

Aoki, M. and Takizawa, H. 2002. Information, incentives, and option value: The Silicon Valley Model. *Journal of Comparative Economics*, 30, 759–786.

Asheim, B.T. and Isaksen, A. 2000. Localised knowledge, interactive learning and innovation: Between regional networks and global corporations', in *The Networked Firm in a Global World: Small Firms in New Environments*, edited by E. Vatne and M. Taylor, Aldershot: Ashgate.

Aydalot, P. and Keeble, D. 1988. *High Technology Industry and Innovative Environments*. London: Routledge.

Baptista, R. 2001. Geographical clusters and innovation diffusion. *Technological Forecasting and Social Change*, Vol. 66, 31–46.

Beccatini, G. 1990. The Marshallian industrial district as a socio-economic notion, in *Industrial Districts and Local Economic Regeneration*, edited by F. Pyke, G. Beccatini, and W. Sengenberger, Switzerland: International Institute for Labour Studies.

Bouwman, H. and Hulsink, W. 2002. A dynamic model of Cyber-entrepreneurship and cluster formation: Applications in the United States and in Low Countries. *Telematics and Informatics*, 19, 291–313.

Camagni, R. 1991. *Innovation Networks: Spatial Perspectives*. New York: Belhaven Press.

Camagni, R. 1995. The concept of innovative milieu and its relevance for public policies in European lagging regions, *Papers in Regional Science*, 74, 317–340.

Capello, R. 1999. The Determinants of Innovation in Cities: Dynamic Urbanisation Economies vs. Milieu Economies in the Metropolitan Area of Milan, paper presented at: *Regional Studies Conference*, Bilbao, 18–21 September.

Carbonara, N. 2004. Innovation processes within geographical clusters: A cognitive approach. *Technovation*, 24(1), 17–28.

Carbonara, N. 2005. Information and communication technology and geographical clusters: opportunities and spread. *Technovation*, 25(3), 213–222.

Cooke, P., Boekholt, P. and Tödtling, F. 2000. *The Governance of Innovation in Europe, Regional perspectives on Global Competitiveness*, USA: Pinter Publishing.

Day, M., Burnett, J., Forrester, P.L. and Hassard, J. 2000. Britain's last industrial districts? A case study of ceramics production. *International Journal of Production Economics*, 65, 5–15.

DeWitt, T., Giunipero, L.C. and Melton, H.L. 2006. Clusters and supply chain management: The Amish experience. *International Journal of Physical Distribution & Logistics Management*, 36(4), 289–308.

Dollinger, M.J. 1999. *Entrepreneurship Strategy and Resources*. 2nd Edition, USA: Prentice Hall.

Drucker, P.F. 1985. *Innovation and Entrepreneurship*. USA: Harper Business.

Edwards, B. 1998. Capitals of capital: Financial centres survey. *The Economist*, 347 (8067), 8.

Edquist, C. 1997. *Systems of Innovation: Technologies, Institutions and Organisations*. London: Pinter.

Enright, M.J. and Ffowcs-Williams, I. 2000. Local partnership, clusters and SME globalisation, paper presented at: *Conference for Ministers responsible for SMEs and Industry Ministers*, Bologna, Italy, June.

European Commission, 2002a. *Developing Learning Organisation Models in SME Clusters (DELOS) Final Report*, UK: Instituto Guglielmo Tagliacarne.

European Commission, 2002b. *Observatory of European SMEs: Regional Clusters in Europe*, Available at: http://ec.europa.eu/regional_policy/innovation/pdf/library/regional_clusters.pdf [accessed 10 May August 2011].

Gerstlberger, W. 2004. Regional innovation systems and sustainability – selected examples of international discussion. *Technovation*, 24(9), 749–758.

Goffee, R. and Scase, R. 1995. *Corporate Realities: The Dynamics of Large & Small Organisations*. UK: International Thomson Business Press.

Greiner, L.E. 1972. Evolution and revolution as organisations growth. *Harvard Business Review*, 4, July/August.

Herbig, P. and Golden, J.E. 1993. How to keep that innovative spirit alive: An examination of evolving innovative hot spots. *Technological Forecasting and Social Change*, 43, 75–90.

Hoffmann, W.H. and Schlosser, R. 2001. Success factors of strategic alliances in small and medium-sized enterprises: An empirical survey. *Long Range Planning*, 34, 357–381.

Jackson, J. 2006. Developing regional tourism in China: The potential for activating business clusters in a socialist market economy. *Tourism Management*, 27(4), 695–706.

Keeble, D., Lawson, C., Moore, B. and Wilkinson, F. (1999) 'Collective learning processes, networking and institutional thickness in the Cambridge region', *Regional Studies*, Vol. 33, No. 4, pp.319–332.

Koski, H., Rouvinen, P. and Anttila, Y. 2002. ICT clusters in Europe: The great central banana and the small Nordic potato. *Information Economics and Policy*, 14, 145–165.

Lehmann, H. and Roth, G. 1993. *Weber's Protestant Ethic: Origins, Evidence, Contexts*. USA: Cambridge University Press.

Liyanage, S. 1995. Breeding innovation clusters through collaborative research networks. *Technovation*, 15(9), 553–567.

Lundvall, B.A. and Johnson, B. 1994. The learning economy. *Journal of Industry Studies*, 1, 23–42.

Lyon, F. and Atherton, A. 2000. *A Business View of Clustering: Lessons for Cluster Development Policies*. UK: University of Durham, Foundation for SME development.

Maillat, D. 1995. Territorial dynamic, innovative milieus, and regional policy. *Entrepreneurship and Regional Development*, 7, 157–165.

Man, T.W.Y., Lau, T. and Chan, K.F. 2002. The competitiveness of small and medium enterprises: A conceptualization with focus on entrepreneurial competencies. *Journal of Business Venturing*, 17,123–142.

Marshall, A. 1922. *Principles of Economics*. 8th Edition, London: MacMillan.

Meyer-Stamer, J. 2001. *Clustering and the Creation of an Innovation-Oriented Environment for Industrial Competitiveness: Experiences from a Comparative Perspective*. Germany: University of Duisburg.

Nassimbeni, G. 2003. Local manufacturing systems and global economy: Are they compatible; the case of Italian eyewear district. *Journal of Operations Management*, 21, 151–171.

Novelli, M., Schmitz, B. and Spencer, T. 2006. Networks, clusters and innovation in tourism: A UK experience. *Tourism Management*, 27(6), 1141–1152.

Padmore, T. and Gibson, H. 1998. Modelling systems of innovation: II. A framework for industrial clusters analysis in regions. *Research Policy*, 26, 625–641.

Piore, M.J. and Sabel, C.F. 1984. *The Second Industrial Divide, Possibilities for Prosperity*. USA: Basic Books Inc.

Piperopoulos, P. and Scase, R. 2009. Competitiveness of small and medium enterprises: towards a two dimensional model of innovation and business clusters. *International Journal of Business Innovation and Research*, 3(5), 479–499.

Porter, M.E. 1985. *Competitive Advantage: Creating and Sustaining Superior Performance*. USA: The Free Press.

Porter, M.E. 1990. *The Competitive Advantage of Nations*. USA: The Free Press.

Porter, M.E. 1998. Clusters and the new economics of competition. *Harvard Business Review*, November–December, 77–90.

Pyke, F. and Sengenberger, W. 1992. *Industrial Districts and Local Economic Regeneration*. Switzerland: International Institute for Labour Studies.

Saxenian, A. 1991. The origins and dynamics of production networks in Silicon Valley. *Research Policy*, 20, 423–437.

Schumpeter, J.A. 1942. *Capitalism, Socialism and Democracy*. London: George Allen & Unwin.

Schumpeter, J.A. 1947. The creative response in economic history, in *Essays: Joseph A. Schumpeter*, edited by R. Clemence, USA: Transaction Publishers.

Scott, A. and Storper, M. 1986. *Production, Work, Territory*. London: Unwin Hyman.

Scott, A. 1988. Flexible production systems and regional development: The rise of new industrial spaces in North America and Western Europe. *International Journal of Urban and Regional Research*, 12, 171–186.

Smedlund, A. and Toivonen, M. 2007. The role of KIBS in the IC development of regional clusters. *Journal of Intellectual Capital*, 8(1), 159–170.

Steinle, C. and Schiele, H. 2002. When do industries cluster: A proposal on how to assess an industry's propensity to concentrate at a single region or nation. *Research Policy*, 31, 849–858.

Sternberg, R. 1996. Reasons for the genesis of high-tech regions – theoretical explanation and empirical evidence. *Geoforum*, 27(2): 205–223.

Storper, M. 1989. The transition to flexible specialization in the US film industry: External economies, the division of labour, and the crossing of industrial divides. *Cambridge Journal of Economics*, 13, 273–305.

Storper, M. 1997. *The Regional World: Territorial Development in a Global Economy*. New York: Guilford Press.

Storper, M. and Salais, R. 1997. *Worlds of Production: The Action Frameworks of the Economy*. Cambridge MA: Harvard University Press.

Trigilia, C. 1992. Italian industrial districts: neither myth nor interlude, in *Industrial Districts and Local Economic Regeneration*, edited by, F. Pyke and W. Sengenberger, Switzerland: International Institute for Labour Studies.

Zeitlin, J. 1992. Industrial districts and local economic regeneration: overview and comment. *Industrial Districts and Local Economic Regeneration*, edited by, F. Pyke and W. Sengenberger, Switzerland: International Institute for Labour Studies.

Index